THE PASSIVE

SOLAR PRIMER:

THE PASSIVE SOLAR PRIMER:
SUSTAINABLE ARCHITECTURE

David Wright, AIA – Environmental Architect

Technical Advice: Jeffrey Cook, AIA
Illustrations: Dennis A. Andrejko and
Gregory J. Wolters

Schiffer Publishing Ltd

4880 Lower Valley Road, Atglen, Pennsylvania 19310

Designed by "Sue"
Type set in Exotc350 DmBd BT/Zurich BT

ISBN: 978-0-7643-3070-4
Printed in China

Schiffer Books are available at special discounts for bulk purchases for sales promotions or premiums. Special editions, including personalized covers, corporate imprints, and excerpts can be created in large quantities for special needs. For more information contact the publisher:

Published by Schiffer Publishing Ltd.
4880 Lower Valley Road
Atglen, PA 19310
Phone: (610) 593-1777; Fax: (610) 593-2002
E-mail: Info@schifferbooks.com

For the largest selection of fine reference books on this and related subjects, please visit our web site at **www.schifferbooks.com**
We are always looking for people to write books on new and related subjects. If you have an idea for a book please contact us at the above address.

This book may be purchased from the publisher.
Include $5.00 for shipping.
Please try your bookstore first.
You may write for a free catalog.

In Europe, Schiffer books are distributed by
Bushwood Books
6 Marksbury Ave.
Kew Gardens
Surrey TW9 4JF England
Phone: 44 (0) 20 8392-8585; Fax: 44 (0) 20 8392-9876
E-mail: info@bushwoodbooks.co.uk
Website: www.bushwoodbooks.co.uk
Free postage in the U.K., Europe; air mail at cost.

CONTENTS

ACKNOWLEDGMENTS

This book is dedicated to my daughters Megan and Heather; and the next generation of engineers and architects.

My Thanks and appreciation to the following for help with this book:

For making it possible
Peter Van Dresser
Ashley Rooney
Tina Skinner

For assistance
Jeffrey Cook
Benjamin Rogers
John Yellott
John Wingate

For inspiration
The Anasazi
Steve Baer
Ken Haggard & Polly Cooper
Harold Hay
Malcomb Wells

For their rules of thumb
Willian Church, AIA., Willian Davis, AIA., & Anthony Koach, AIA.
Jeffery Cook, AIA.
Raymond Darby, P.E.
Peter Dobrovolny, AIA.
Robert MacDonald Ford, AIA.
Edward Mazria, AIA. & Marc Schiff, AIA.
Tim Maloney & Peter Arsenault
Peter J. Pfister, AIA.
Travis Price, AIA.
R.H. Wantoch, P.E.
Donald Watson, FAIA.
Rodney Wright, FAIA.

PROLOGUE

The Past

The energy crisis blunders on. Nothing much has changed since 1978 when I first wrote *Natural Solar Architecture: A Passive Primer*. Thirty years later, yikes! Peak oil, green, sustainability, and global warming have entered the lexicon as buzz words for environmental activism. In recent years we have suffered from an administration which has acted not only irresponsibly with regard to energy depletion and environmental degradation due to the long term affects of burning fossil fuels – but in fact added to the problems thru corporate greed and personal arrogance (an unfortunate chapter in the life of our earth, the sun planet).

The first "solar age of enlightenment," not to be confused with the so called "age of enlightenment" and the "sun king," spanned from the late 1960s until the start of the 1980s and was enlightening because humanity suddenly faced the limitations of the fossil fuel era. I was fortunate to be a young hippie architect in Santa Fe, New Mexico, at the apex of the "back to the earth" movement in the late sixties. When I moved to Santa Fe in 1969, the first place I lived in was an experimental adobe solar home, (air collectors to rock bed). My friend from the Peace Corps, John March, was renting a 1930s home in the old part of Santa Fe that was retrofitted to use solar heating in 1958 by Peter Van Dresser, an early solar enthusiast, (Peter later introduced me to an editor who asked me to write this book). I soon met a group of idealistic "Adobe Heads" concerned about the environmental aspects of the built environment: "Bill" Lumpkins, Travis Price, Keith Haggard, Wayne & Susan Nichols, and I formed an alternative architectural/planning group called "Sun Mountain Design, Ltd." This was about 1972, prior to the Arab oil embargo, which began on October 17, 1973 with a decrease in oil production and doubling of the price of a barrel of oil by OPEC. They had us over a barrel, quickly leading to a petroleum crisis, gas lines at the pump, and eventually President Jimmy Carter's "War on Energy." A most exciting and disruptive time. The American dream was turning into a nightmare, facing potential economic hard times. The populace, for the first time, was made rudely aware of the fragility and finite realities of the fossil fuel age, which had been guzzling the earth's resources since the late nineteenth century. This first solar age came to a grinding halt when President Ronald Reagan's administration symbolically removed the solar collectors that President Carter had installed on the White House, and discontinued many alternative energy development programs.

The Sun Mountain Design Group, my partners, became interested in energy self sufficiency, (the term "sustainability" was not yet popular), as a part of the "back to the earth movement," which spawned many hippie communes and libertarian individualists. We were inspired by characters like the inventor/mathematician Steve Baer and his Zomeworks Company, the fanatic Robert Reines, who was inventing stand alone energy independent installations to market to the military, and we were influenced by the use of solar in the architecture of the Anasazi and Pueblo Indians. The Sun Mountain Design Group applied itself to creating environmentally responsive architecture. We started as an ad hoc brain trust toying with many self-sufficiency ideas. Solar energy provided a major non-polluting, free, and democratic way of heating water, keeping buildings warm and cool, and making electricity. We experimented with various systems: direct gain, thermal air and water collectors, rock beds, thermal storage, earth tubes, and green house designs. Most of our experiments were piecemeal and boot-strapped together, some worked, some worked well, and some didn't. I recall that the Carolyn Allen's cabin was one of our first successes. Carolyn wanted to disassemble an 1870s log cabin, relocate it, and reassemble it in Santa Fe. She was a free thinker and somehow we convinced her to solar heat it. This was the first solar thermal air collector, rock bed storage system we tried. It worked fairly well, if not an elegant design, at least it worked!

View of Mesa Verde

Encouraged, we stumbled on reinventing the wheel and learning by our mistakes. I also researched historical solar applications from the Persians, Egyptians, Chinese, and other civilizations that had made practical use of solar heat and environmental design. I began to understand that nearly every physical thing we have is, in a sense, solar powered.

There were a number of earlier American solar pioneers, from the late 1930s through the 1950s, who we copied, befriended, or otherwise emulated. Individuals like George Lof, Harold Hay, Farrington Daniels, John Yellot, Henry Mather, Felix Trombe, Maria Telkes, and even institutions like MIT and Harvard Universities had dabbled with solar experimentation and prototypes. These were the true pioneers who saw the light and power of the sun for more than growing vegetation, while most folks were simply working on their suntans.

My personal solar education came in a pragmatic way. I graduated from architecture school in the early 1960s. The Vietnam War was in full swing and the draft was sucking up my friends and spitting them out in Southeast Asia. I elected to honor John F. Kennedy's legacy by serving my country in the Peace Corps. I still remember the thought process: "Let's see, War Corps or Peace Corps? Exotic location with mines, bombs and bullets or exotic location helping friendly natives with improving their lives?" So, I wound up in Tunisia in North Africa with several other architects in training. We were to assist the Tunisian government with improving their built environment and infrastructure. I was an eager idealistic architect trainee, fresh out of university, who had received an excellent education in designing and building

beautiful and efficient structures. I had learned very little about climate design or alternative energy systems in school. Tunisia is an ancient Arabian culture, which evolved through the ages sandwiched between the Mediterranean Sea, Algeria, Libya, and the Sahara Desert. Waves of occupiers, including the Roman Empire, had left their marks both aesthetically and architecturally. I was exposed to earthen construction techniques, innovative water systems, architecture that responded to the sun, wind, and the seasons through design, ranging from the vaulted breeze-catching adobes in the north to the subsurface troglodyte dwellings of the northern Sahara Desert. All of these architectural solutions were practical, timeless, and self-sufficient. I quickly grasped the potential of integrating these time worn techniques with my own western technical knowledge of structure, mechanics, physics, and aesthetics.

One of my first projects in Tunisia was in the Arrondissement of Sousse about halfway down the eastern coast of Tunisia, a place affected by the Mediterranean climate yet quite hot in the summer and cold in the winter. The project was to design affordable housing for the ordinary people of modest means, officially called Maisons

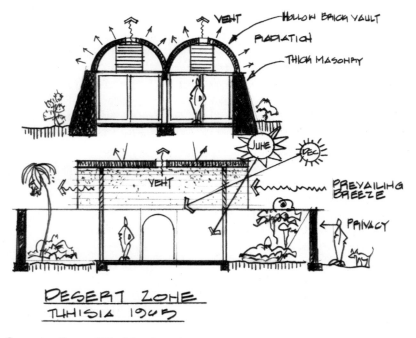
Cross sections of Tunisian housing

View of Tunisian housing

Populaire. Up to that point this type of housing consisted of concrete block walls and poured concrete roofs left over from the legacy of French Colonial architecture. These were laid out with a formal planning format; with little, if any, attention paid to the sun, wind, heat, cold, or local natural elements. To the government, personal comfort was not a top priority, just shelter. My designs were created to work with the sun's annual path, prevailing breezes, and indigenous earth construction techniques. I adapted the traditional interior private courtyard for Arabic family sensitivities, where women were guarded and kept at home. The walls were thick aglomere, a mixture of mud, rock, and some cement, which provided thermal time lag for insulation purposes. The roof system was borrowed from the ancient hollow-fired clay brick technique that allowed the construction of a continuous semi-circular vault structure that requires no support or centering to construct. These vaults helped to achieve maximum winter sun penetration for natural heating, and to channel summer sea breezes for cooling. I was proud of this simple, elegant, economical, and efficient solution.

I submitted my project to Monsieur Sassi, my French-educated Tunisian engineer boss for his approval. After a few days he commanded me for a formal review of my work. He was a bit of a dandy and quite intelligent. I was anxious to hear his critique and hopeful praise of my sensitivity and talent. He ushered me in, ordered tea, and then smiled. He said something like, "Congratulations Mr. Wright, you have designed a logical and affordable solution for our housing needs. However, our country needs engineers – not poets! We are a developing county anxious to become part of the 20th Century. We don't need things from the past. We want to be like America – we want things like television, Coca Cola, and Jackie Kennedy!"

Naturally my jaw dropped and I added this to my long list of life's great lessons. If only he had given me those words before I created the perfect indigenous solution for his Maisons Populaire! I almost immediately thought to myself, if I am going to use natural solar and time-proven techniques to solve architectural problems, I will have to come back to the U.S.A., my native habitat, and make it part of the American way. Then perhaps the rest of the world might accept advanced natural systems.

Mr. Sassi assigned me several more projects, which I dispatched with more of a technical western, energy consuming, and conventional approach. We grew to respect one another. So much, in fact, that I was selected to be sent to Guinea, West Africa, on special assignment to design a USAID Agricultural Junior College located deep in the jungle. This took a year and involved training teams of natives to make soil cement blocks to build a dozen various agricultural buildings. This effort was to be essentially self sufficient as power, fuel, and building materials were scarce. I designed the structures to resist pouring rain, insects, high humidity, and heat. No easy task, but the locals were quite resourceful and grateful for any means of comfort. My inspiration was drawn from an abundant pallet of indigenous native techniques for allowing air movement, waterproofing, and snake proofing.

After the Peace Corps, when I returned to California, I began to seriously apply natural solar design principals as I continued my architectural apprenticeship. My interest in natural organic architecture later led me to relocate to Santa Fe to pursue an education in adobe architecture under the tutorship of William Lumpkins, Architect. "Bill"

Sketch of Guinea agricultural school

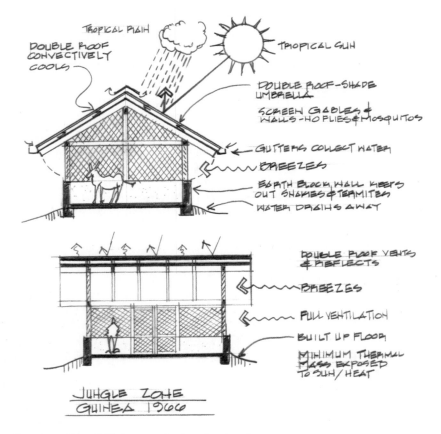

TROPICAL RAIN
DOUBLE ROOF CONVECTIVELY COOLS
TROPICAL SUN
DOUBLE ROOF-SHADE UMBRELLA
SCREEN GABLES & WALLS - NO FLIES & MOSQUITOS
GUTTERS COLLECT WATER
BREEZES
EARTH BLOCK WALL KEEPS OUT SNAKES & TERMITES
WATER DRAINS AWAY

DOUBLE FLOOR VENTS & REFLECTS
BREEZES
FULL VENTILATION
BUILT UP FLOOR
MINIMUM THERMAL MASS EXPOSED TO SUN/HEAT

JUNGLE ZONE
GUINEA 1966

Cross section of Guinea agricultural school

was a wonderful western gentleman, a Native New Mexican, who took adobe architecture to a very high level of sophistication. I learned many more practical lessons in life and adobe design from him.

The traditional adobe which evolved from the caves and stone structures of the Anasazi and later Pueblo cultures was refined and westernized by the Spanish settlers over centuries. The adobe home responds to searing heat and freezing snow. The thick clay and straw walls provide slow temperature change, and carefully placed doors and windows take advantage of the seasonal sun angles, prevailing winds, and forces of nature.

My peers in those exciting solar experimentation days were Hispanic contractors, hippie inventors, aspiring artists, and scientists – a social mix of inventiveness, optimism, resourcefulness, and independence.

By 1971 I received my architectural license and decided, a year later, to strike out on my own. I purchased a piece of land in the historic district of Santa Fe and launched into the design of "the perfect solar adobe." It took me a year or so to design and build "Sunscoop," a "D" shaped two-story adobe with a large glass south façade and thick insulated adobe walls on the other sides, in essence, a large solar collector. Herman Barkman and Benjamin T. Rogers, both mechanical engineers with Los Alamos Labs, helped me with the solar performance modeling. In those days they had large computers at the labs, but they elected to do a manual seasonal thermal performance model to determine how this new structure would perform and if, in fact, humans could live in it! We calculated the overhang shading, thermal mass absorption and release, and added rigid insulation beneath the floors, exterior walls, and roof and even installed high temperature tubing in the sand beneath the brick floor "just in case." We never hooked the tubing up to thermo siphon fluid collectors because the house worked fine. I developed some "accordion" south wall insulating interior shades that, along with a Franklin woodstove, made the house toasty warm in the snowy winters and nice and cool in the hot summers of Santa Fe. Proof of concept! I went on to design several other quite different solar houses in the Santa Fe area; "Sunstep," "Suncave," etc., which used the same simple direct gain design principles.

One day after completing "Sunscoop" in early 1974, Herman Barkman, "Buck" Rogers, Steve Baer (who had manufactured the thermo siphon water heater collector), and I were sitting in "Sunscoop" sharing a fermented beverage and talking solar. I said, "So, what is this type of design that I've built?" Buck replied, "Well, in mechanical engineering we call systems that use pumps or fans and electricity active systems, so I guess this must be a passive solar design." That was the first time I heard the term "passive solar" and credit Buck Rogers with coining it – kind of spacey don't you think? Today, passive solar design is known and practiced around the world. The solar pioneering days in Santa Fe were fun, exciting, and effective. Prior to 1973, when the OPEC oil embargo occurred, we were known as the solar "lunatic fringe." Later we became known as the "lunatic core" of passive solar pioneers.

Because of allergies, I relocated in 1977 to the coast of California. I made a conscious decision to try to make solar applications to architecture as simple as possible. That lead to a design technique that emphasized the shape and make-up of a structure for solar performance. I tried to avoid pumps, fans, collectors, and more complicated systems, when possible. I designed and built my own home, "Sundown," at the Sea Ranch. This house garnered a prestigious AIA, Sunset design award and a lot of publicity and opportunities from articles in *National Geographic*, the *New York Times*, *Mother Earth News* and *Solar Age*, to lectures at the Smithsonian Institute and universities across the country and Europe. This was a heady time; I began experimenting with climate design all over the United States. The whole concept of designing buildings that respond to various climates and aesthetically reflect the multitude of geographic regions became a passion. Luckily, many architectural commissions came my way and I was able to conceive and shape climate responsive designs for many climate zones. I continue this work focusing on adapting passive solar design principles to architectural styles from traditional to modernistic architecture primarily throughout California and Nevada.

Today passive solar design is celebrated internationally. *Natural Solar Architecture: A Passive Primer* was reprinted several times and printed in six languages. I have received letters and emails from around the world over the last thirty years expressing gratitude for making the case for environmental design and expressing the basics of passive solar architecture in an easy to comprehend manual. Exactly what I had hoped for! I don't know if Monsieur Sassi in Tunisia has read it yet. Maybe I'll send him a copy of this new publication.

Southwest view of Wright residence

South view of Wright residence

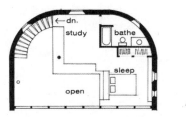
loft level

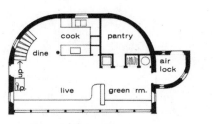
ground level

Plan of Wright residence (Sunscoop), Santa Fe, New Mexico

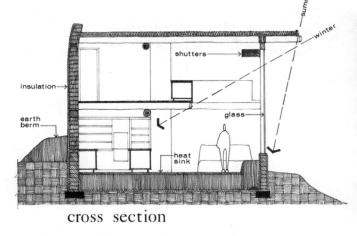
cross section

Cross section of Wright residence

Interior view of Wright residence

Interior view of Wright residence

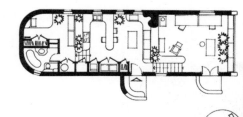

Floor Plan

Plan of Sunstep residence, Santa Fe, New Mexico

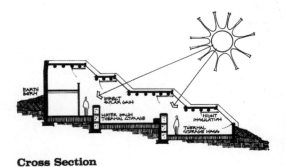

Cross Section

Cross section of Sunstep residence

Southwest view of Sunstep residence

Adobe construction, Sunstep residence

West view of Sunstep residence

Interior view of Sunstep residence

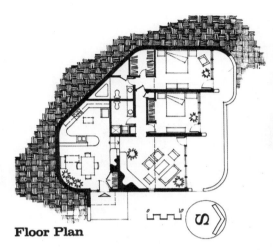

Floor Plan

Plan of Suncave residence, Santa Fe, New Mexico

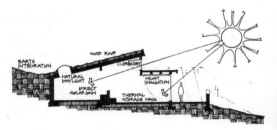

Cross Section

Cross section of Suncave residence

South view of Suncave residence

South east view of Suncave residence

Living room interior of Suncave residence

Living room interior of Suncave residence

Dining & kitchen interior of Suncave residence

Northeast view of Wright residence (Sundown), The Sea Ranch, California

West tower view of Wright residence

Floor Plan

Plan of Wright residence

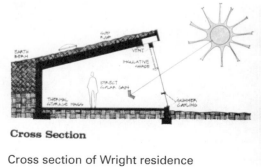

Cross Section

Cross section of Wright residence

Interior Wright residence

Interior Wright residence

The Present

During the last thirty years the ideas, tools, and examples which I presented in the original publication of this book have remained true or come-to-be. Passive solar architectural design has indeed become an international recognized science, rather than an art.

The American Solar Energy Society (ASES) has continued to convene conferences since the first passive solar conference of 1976 held in Albuquerque, New Mexico. At these conferences architects, engineers, scientists, researchers, designers, and solar nuts have presented all aspects of passive solar phenomena. The legacy continues. This year the American Solar Energy Society is holding its 37th annual solar conference in San Diego. Educators and scientists began to qualify and quantify passive solar performance characteristics. National laboratories conducted monitoring of prototype structures and test modules to isolate and identify the effective techniques and applications of various solar designs.

A number of educational publications, books, journals, magazine articles and films popularized the passive solar movement both in the United States and abroad. Edward Mazria's *Passive Solar Energy Book*, published in 1979 expanded on and refined the concepts of my primmer to reach thousands of professionals in the design and construction industry. Ed was a professor of architecture at the University of Oregon who was caught up in the enthusiasm of the passive solar wave. He, along with Douglas Balcomb, a scientist/administrator with the Los Alamos Scientific Laboratories solar division and others formed "Passive Solar Associates," a group who conducted workshops throughout the country reaching many educators, practitioners and builders to effectively spread the word and knowledge.

Many simulation routines and methods of predicting passive solar performance have been developed. Computer programs with sophisticated engineering parameters have been created for accurately predicting many different conditions and configurations. Techniques for simulating natural convection, thermal migration, natural daylighting, earth sheltering effects and other comfort

Wind generators

and performance standards have been made popular. A few of these software programs are: SUNREL at www.nrel.gov/buildings/sunrel/cfm/register.cfm, Bestest at www.eere.energy.gov/buildings/tools_directory/software.cfm/ID=85/pagename=alpha_list,

Sustainable Building Industries Council at www.sbicouncil.org/store/e10.php and BEopt at www.nrel.gov/docs/fy05osti/37733.pdf.

The California State Energy Commission (CEC) was evolved from the California Office of Appropriate Technology (OAT). Today it continues to enact standards and mandates for energy efficiency, which set the pace for state and federal programs with worldwide influence. Several creative innovators including authors Phil Niles and Ken Haggard, worked with the C.E.C. to publish *The California Passive Solar Handbook*. Starting in 1982 Jeffery Cook, of Arizona State University and Michael J. Holtz of the Solar Energy Research Institute (SERI) published the first passive solar journal for the American section of the international solar energy society (ASISES). The U.S. Department of Energy and the Department of Housing & Urban Development sponsor an ongoing annual international solar home decathlon program. Each year university students from around the world complete to design, build and transport for display on the mall in Washington, D.C. a passive and active demonstration house. This exciting program brings the fresh young minds of architecture and engineering students to focus on a practical cutting edge application of solar and sustainable technology. There is discussion about making this a regionally based competition leading to a national final winner. This is a great idea as far more people would be able to visit and learn from the competition. Sustainability needs to be a regionally applied concept. "Think globally, act locally" is the key to sustainability.

Building materials is another area that has been substantially improved and continues to evolve since the early 1970s. Many new building systems and items have emerged such as; structural insulated panels (SIPS), insulated concrete forms (ICF), straw bale, rammed earth, earth blocks, super insulation techniques, organic insulations, and low emissivity glazing.

Straw bale homes are being constructed throughout the USA and are being introduced to developing countries such as Pakistan, which recently suffered a severe earthquake that obliterated much of the traditional reinforced stone and adobe buildings. Structural insulated panels show promise in our country and world wide to replace standard wood frame and rigid concrete frame construction. There is current talk of developing a new "greencrete" material and forming system that could revolutionize affordable housing.

Innovative systems for achieving auxiliary heating, cooling, and ventilation for passive solar designs have emerged in the past three decades. Microprocessor controlled in floor radiant heating systems are widely used for heating and are now being promoted for cooling. Air to air heat exchangers allow efficient exchange of make up air for the tight super insulated buildings now in use. Ground source geothermal heat pump systems are now being used that use a small amount of energy specifically in solar electric powered to achieve complete heating and cooling without the use of any fossil fuels. On the near horizon are fuel cell/electrolyzers, which will use solar power to crack water into hydrogen and pure water. This technology could well be the answer to our long-term sustainable safe building and transportation systems energy needs.

Solar tubes and fiber optic cable daylighting devices are becoming popular for transmitting sunlight deep within buildings, light emitting diodes (LED), compact fluorescent lights (CFL), home energy monitor/controllers, on demand gas water heaters, phase change glazing, wind turbines, two-stage evaporative coolers, solar thermal water heaters, and many new solar electric photovoltaic collection devices are a few of the many newly developed energy efficient concepts that are being used today to fight the battle for energy independence and sustainability.

Jimmy Carter should be proud of his early efforts to make our country, and the world, aware of the need to change. George Bush was wrong. We are not addicted to oil. We have simply been seduced by corporate interests of the oil and automobile industries to take up bad habits. Just like with the tobacco industry, we, as a nation and world need to change our habits to achieve energy conservation and sustainability. The devices and techniques are available today, and now more than ever, it is time for the citizens of this planet space ship earth to evolve to sustainability.

I have changed the original title of this book in order to re-introduce the concepts, put forth thirty years ago, into the new energy conscious dialogue of today. The concept of "self sufficiency" has evolved into "sustainability" and I look forward to seeing this new green wave of thinking continue to survive and grow.

For the immediate future, my personal dream is to see photovoltaic and thermal solar collector systems once again installed on the White House in Washington D.C. This practical, symbolic gesture is as important today as the flying of the American flag, to remind all of us who we are, and what we need to do to demonstrate to the world who we are as a nation and what we stand for. The entire world is facing today's energy crisis and it is important for architects, engineers, and builders around the planet to work together in a collaborative way to create a sustainable future.

Peace,
David Wright, AIA
Environmental Architect
Grass Valley, California
dwright@netshel.net

March 3, 2008

Conceived profile of the United States White House with solar collectors (Circa 2009)

INTRODUCTION

Today, many catalogs of alternate-energy ideas, generalized solar manuals, and do-it-yer-self sufficiency guides proliferate. This passive solar primer will help fulfill the need for prerequisite knowlege of passive concepts for students, architects, builders, home planners, and survivalists prior to the undertaking of the ultimate logical process of designing a climatically oriented structure. It is meant for those of us who want to touch on the ABCs of solar thermal phenomena before tangling with highly technical manuals.

This is not a how-to book; it is meant to illustrate some of the concerns of passive solar design and at the same time tickle the imagination.

It is my hope that the basics offered in this book will aid people in their efforts to design energy-efficient buildings which are attuned to the environment, integrated with the landscape, beautiful to behold, and above all, in harmony with the whole of nature.

Dedicated to the world around us.

David Wright, AIA
David Wright Associates
Nevada City, California

1 ENERGY ETHICS

A True Tale

Prior to the fossil-fuel age and the Industrial Revolution, people depended on fire, animals, sun, wind, water, and themselves to get work done . . . and things got done. With the development of petroleum fuels, steam engines, electricity, and the like, people used these means to do work for them. . . . Much, much more work got done and no end was in sight for these relatively cheap tools. Fossil fuels, originally derived from the sun's energy, were used to heat houses, run automobiles, light cigarettes, and even produce suntans! People forgot about the things that they could do and that nature could do for them. They concentrated

on isolating themselves from nature's forces, allowing the machines and fuels to do as much as posible. . . . Many things were forgotten.

After a while, the natural environment became polluted and unsafe to live in because of the side effects of this new kind of work. The seemingly inexhaustible supply of fuel became more limited . . . and then the end was in sight. More effort had to be expended to acquire less and less fuel.

Suddenly, it was too expensive to drive cars, light cigarettes, take showers, and indulge in the energy orgy. People had to look around to see what they could do. Lo and behold, there were some easy and economical things that could be done without relying totally on the old machines and fuels. Although people had been sidetracked by a seductive servant, they had learned a few things. . . . Science had made astonishing discoveries about the physical world; industry had developed; marvelous materials and devices had evolved; and concepts of the world had been broadened.

People became receptive to the *Solar Age.*

It appeared silly and grossly inefficient to burn polluting fuel at temperatures in excess of 1000°F (538°C) in order to generate electricity and then send it hundreds of miles in order to heat water to 140°F (60°C)—all for a simple hot shower at about 100°F (38°C).

AGUA CALIENTE

It was far more economical, efficient, clean, and fun to hook up a flat-plate solar collector to a water tank on the roof of one's house. The water got just as hot and proved to be an excellent investment, and some even thought it felt a little better.

The same was true of heating or cooling a home; conventional fuels and machines were not always necessary. The more people used their imaginations and befriended nature, the simpler it became to get work done. A crank could often work a pulley as well as an electric motor could, and it provided good exercise.

As time went by there were more changes. Solar cells produced electricity, providing light, sound, and refrigeration. Wind machines pumped water and powered sailing ships. Solar conversion plants made clean, safe fuel for energizing industrial processes. . . . The alternatives were almost endless.

For some people it was difficult to change quickly. They still liked their old machines and the noises and smells they made while doing work. These folks had to pay more for less and less work. A larger and larger portion of their waking hours was allocated to the fossil fuel machines.

Many others liked using the natural methods and enjoyed paying less for more. They soon discovered many things they could do by alternative methods—such as sunbathing, growing food, drying crops, distilling liquids, cooking, pumping, generating, converting, transporting, communicating, and so forth.

They will live happily ever after. . . .

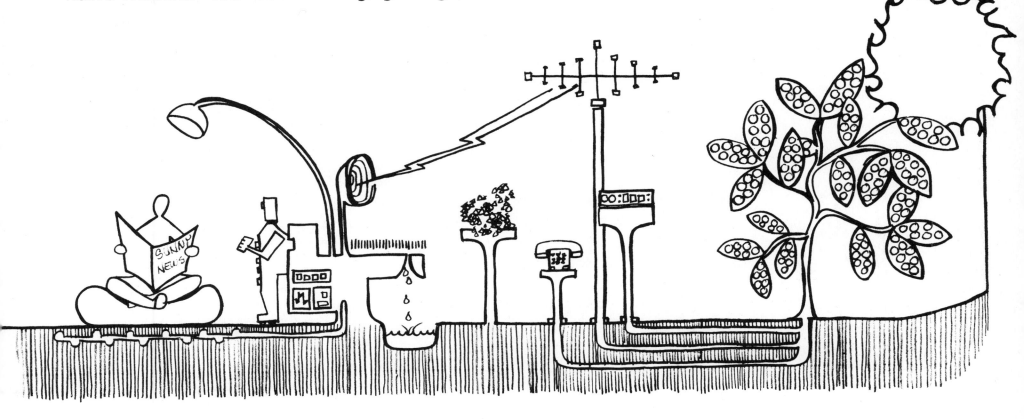

Solar Citizens

With the advent of the Solar Age and the rediscovery of survival basics other than dependence on fossil fuel, much emphasis has been placed on complicated methods of solar technology. Our civilization has evolved to a point of technological sophistication which should enable us to simplify our approach to dealing with many of the daily tasks in our world.

Until now, we have used stored solar energy, in the forms of petroleum, natural gas, wood, and hydroelectricity, to power nearly all of our machines for accomplishing work. Now that we are aware of the inefficiencies, side effects, and limitations of these forms of solar energy, we have begun to focus on relatively complex techniques of converting direct solar energy for doing even simple work.

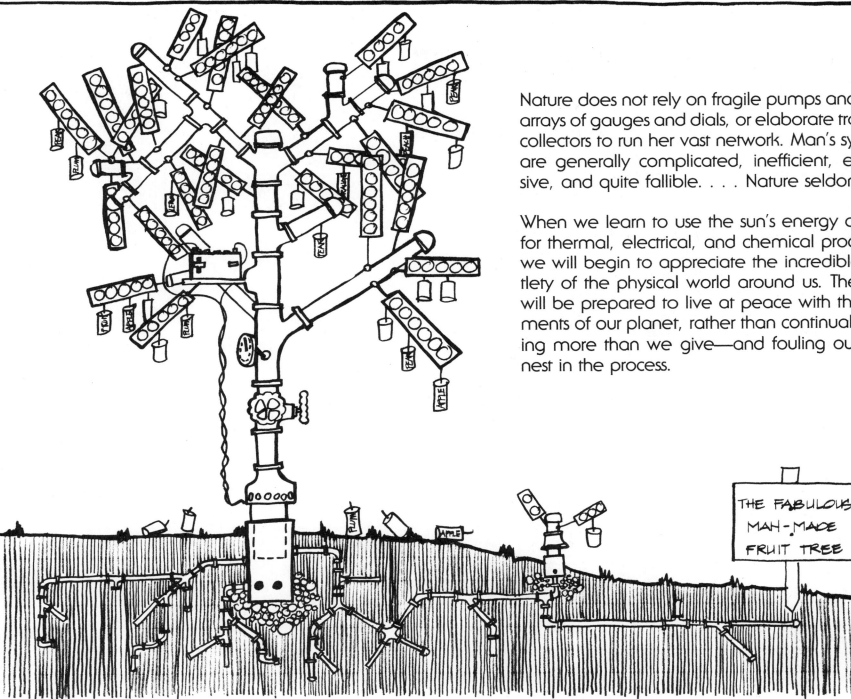

Nature does not rely on fragile pumps and fans, arrays of gauges and dials, or elaborate tracking collectors to run her vast network. Man's systems are generally complicated, inefficient, expensive, and quite fallible. . . . Nature seldom is!

When we learn to use the sun's energy directly for thermal, electrical, and chemical processes, we will begin to appreciate the incredible subtlety of the physical world around us. Then we will be prepared to live at peace with the elements of our planet, rather than continually taking more than we give—and fouling our own nest in the process.

Once we have recognized, identified, and made good use of the total spectrum of the physical potential, we will undoubtedly change the ways in which we live. Solar power will not be a mystery to us. Use of the sun's energy will be second nature, and the routine of life will involve few of the unknown elements that pervade our existence today. It is our destiny to become solar citizens. When our politicans, economists, engineers, teachers, and the rest of us attain solar enlightenment, our physical world, too, will change. Land use patterns, structures, forms, functions, and the environment as a whole will all be affected—*positively!*

The transition from the passé fossil fuel age to the new energy consciousness will not be easy, but we must change gears and operate on a more efficient plane. The idea of tacking solar collectors on an antiquated structure of another age and considering it a solar house is much like adding an internal-combustion engine to a horse-drawn carriage and calling it an automobile. It is a start, but we have more to learn before we are truly solar citizens in a solar economy.

Obviously, if we are to survive, we cannot continue the way we have since the Industrial Revolution. Returning to some primitive state is not attractive. Therefore, we must work at developing new patterns of responsibility and a code of ethics for dealing with our earthly biosphere.

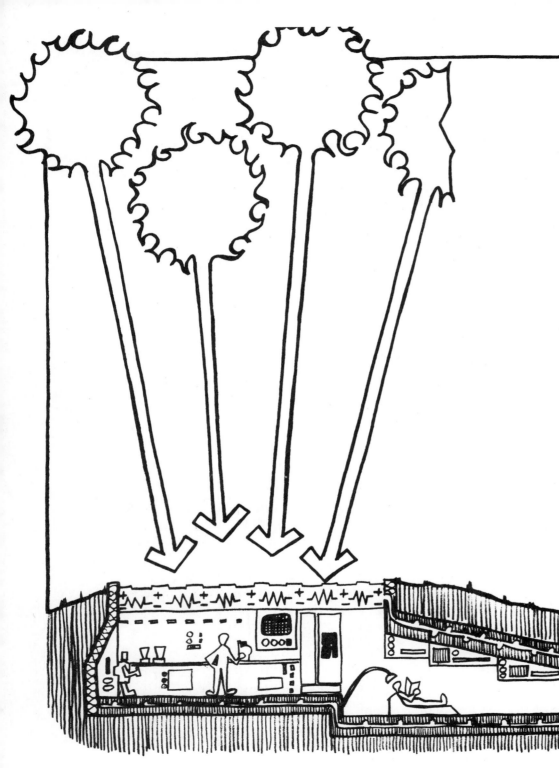

Each year over three and a half times the energy needed to satisfy all of the power requirements of an energy-efficient household falls on the roof of practically every dwelling. Until now, this handy resource has been virtually ignored, but the recognition of this fact alone should provide the stimulus for reevaluation of future design.

Solar power, with its democratic distribution throughout the world, is ours for the taking. We can accept the challenge and use it wisely, or we can continue to muddle along, denying the inevitable. The quality and quantity of solar energy is sufficient for human life support in most life zones. We must establish our priorities of energy use and learn to apply the needed type at the right location, at the right time, in the right way to sustain a balanced interplay of resource and demand.

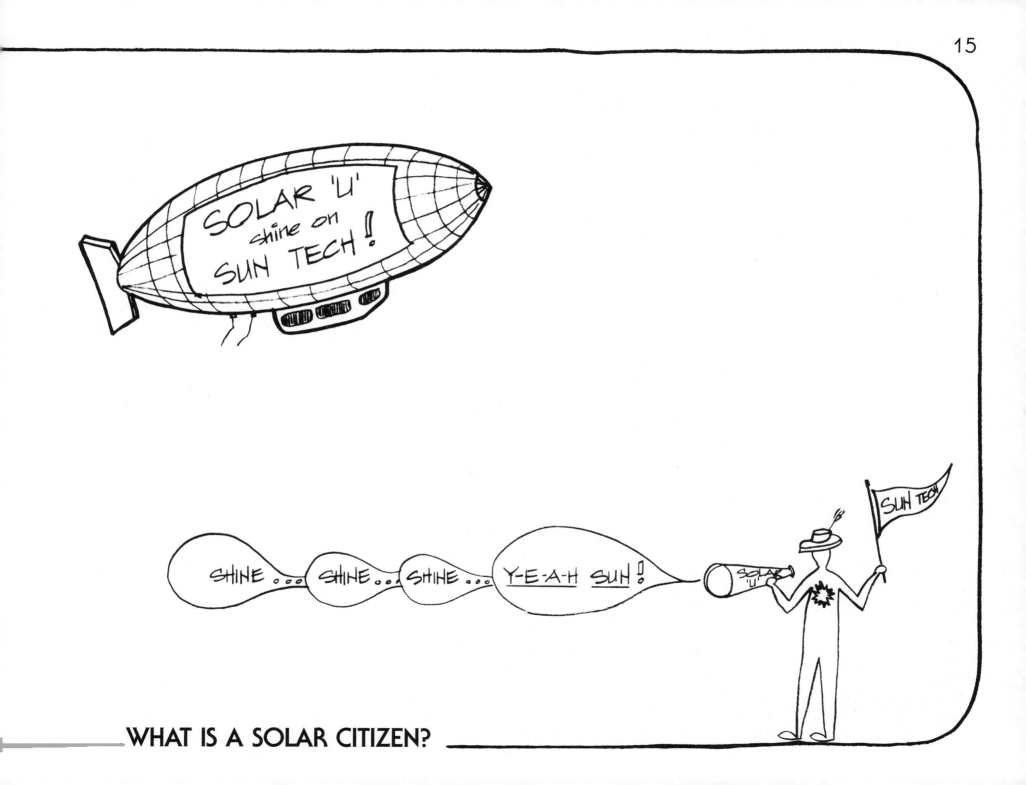

WHAT IS A SOLAR CITIZEN?

A Passive Attitude

One avenue for implementation of the solar-citizenship ethic is to approach the process in the most natural way. The passive solar concept is to allow nature to operate our systems with a minimum of mechanical inteference. We know that the potential for heating, cooling, and powering our dwellings, factories, and office buildings by nonmechanical means exists. Our ability to allow this to happen is limited only by our imagination.

It is far easier to move a heavy object by gravity than by brute strength. We must exert much effort to push or pull a load up a hill; coming down the other side is simply a matter of controlled descent. Nature provides the push and pull in many cases, as with the hydrological cycle,

winds, tides, gravity, and the earth's rotation. A sailboat makes the best of wind and current potential; all that is required is control. By applied knowledge and manipulation to keep the craft trimmed, great distances can be traveled with minimal effort and energy expense.

In most climates, the natural energies that heat, cool, humidify, and dehumidify structures are available throughout the year. The trick is to distribute these energies to the times they are needed for comfort. Since the weather does not adapt to our exact needs, our structures must do the adapting. Buildings can be designed to accept or reject natural energy and store or release it at appropriate times.

If we maximize the passive potential for each building in each climate zone, our need for off-site energy will be vastly reduced. In many places it is possible to design and build totally self-sufficient structures. In others, a great percentage of the needed support is available. The idea is to do your best with what's there, and then augment with active solar power, renew-able resource fuels, or conventional fuels—in that order.

On an individual basis, we can each look around and see what can be done. Many facts are available for our use. Today, this natural approach must be supplemented by intuition, estimation, guesstimation, and conjecture.

Tomorrow, applied engineering, physics, and architecture will better define the parameters of what can realistically be accomplished passively. But for now we should be aware that passive space-conditioning applications are potentially the most cost-effective, most efficient, and possibly most comfortable approach to worldwide solar energy use.

Passive acceptability requires insight into what makes us comfortable. Do we always need the thermostat set at 70°F (21°C) with a fifty percent relative humidity? Certainly not! Usually we associate comfort with the relative loss or gain of body heat. However, the sense of comfort involves many factors besides air temperature alone. Mean radiant temperature (MRT) and ambient air temperature are two distinct criteria for judging comfort, each somewhat affecting the other. We have all experienced being outside on a clear winter day when a sheltered thermometer may read 25°F (−4°C), but when standing in the sunlight we can feel quite comfortable, and perhaps even hot. The radiant heat from the sun is warming your body; the coldness of the air is really not the final determinant of comfort.

The same radiant comfort effect can be experienced in a building. Mean radiant temperature has forty percent more effect on comfort than air temperature. Thus, for every 1.4°F decrease in air temperature, a 1°F MRT increase is required to maintain the same comfort level. If the mass of a structure contains enough heat to register 75°F (24°C), then the air temperature can be as low as 58°F (14°C), and you can still feel comfortable. Conversely, with cold walls and floors and an air temperature of 75°F (24°C), one can feel chilled. The rate at which a body gives off heat to surrounding surfaces is the determining comfort factor. Humidity and air motion will affect comfort, but mean radiant temperature is dominant.

If the conditioning in the spaces in which we live, work, and play is allowed to flex with the weather conditions, our ability to survive is probably reinforced. Many of today's maladies are due to our isolation, of our own volition, from the environment for which we were designed.

For instance, lately we have been heating air and blowing it around the spaces we inhabit. Radiant heating is much more uniform, comfortable, and efficient. The noise, dust particles, pollens, and irritation associated with forced-air systems is tolerable only in terms of first cost economics—the price paid for the system.

To have a passive attitude toward space conditioning is to create comfort levels closely related to the most natural temperature/humidity balance for a particular climate and season. Maintaining an artificial comfort level not related to the outside conditions is unhealthy; think about the metabolic shock experienced upon leaving an overly conditioned space and walking outside into ambient conditions that are much different. Our bodies must struggle to adapt, and we experience undue strain, which sometimes leads to illness and malfunction.

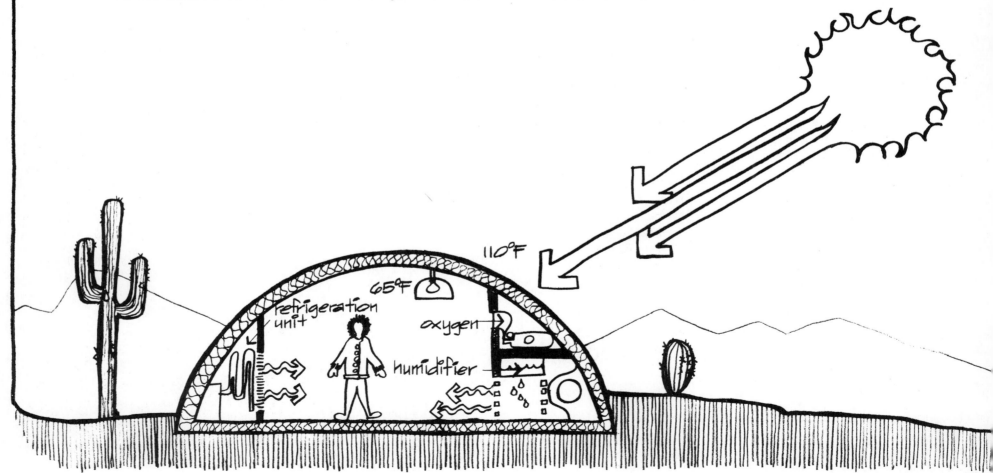

All space-conditioning systems involve the same basic chain of operation: energy collection, transportation, storage, distribution, and loss back to the environment.

Conventional systems collect oil from production fields, transport it to refineries, convey it to holding tanks, and send it to home furnaces where it's burned. The energy is then distributed throughout the house to heat the interior, eventually escaping to the outside as heat loss.

Solar heating systems, whether active or passive, act in much the same way. The sun's heat is gathered by solar collectors or the structure, transmitted to the heat-storage mass, held until needed, and then distributed to spaces for warmth, where sooner or later it passes through the weatherskin (building exterior). Obviously, solar heating is vastly easier and more efficient in terms of the total chain of operation.

conventional

active solar

passive solar

Solar space heating is less polluting, more economical, and healthier for our environment and economy than any other energy source. Valuable fuel resources should be saved for more important uses, such as materials, industrial processes, and transportation.

The use of materials reflects another facet of the passive attitude. It takes over three hundred times more commercial energy to produce a concrete block equal in volume to a sun-dried adobe block. The adobe block may not have all the structural properties of the concrete block, so use two or three adobes for bearing strength and save a bunch of energy!

Why chemically alter heavy materials with heat and great consumption of energy and then transport them long distances in order to construct buildings when most of the structural material is underfoot at each site?

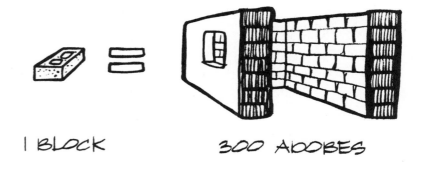

1 BLOCK   300 ADOBES

With some thought and development, we should be able to come up with organic binders which would permit the simple mixing of the earth on site, enabling us to build structures in place. We build dams, roadways, and runways out of earth and stone. We should be able to build megastructures with the same materials and techniques.

As suitable methods of passive solar space-conditioning for various applications are determined, appropriate architectural materials will be developed. It is conceivable to create a structure of integral thermal-storage mass with an adaptable transmittive/insulative weatherskin that will accept or reject and automatically store all externally incident heat energy or internally generated energy. With adequate and appropriate heat-storage mass, having constant temperature and variable thermal capacity properties, the building could absorb or lose large quantities of heat without changing temperature.

Novel materials with these and other characteristics are being developed by scientists, physicists, and system engineers in response to a heightened concern for efficient means of survival. As the new materials become a part of our architectural design palette, the traditional concepts of space conditioning, material use, and architecture will change.

This book illustrates passive solar space-conditioning principles on a single-family dwelling scale. Although the individual structure, housing one family, may eventually become uneconomical as a way of living, it is still very much with us throughout the world. At this time, the individual dwelling is a convenient and personal proving ground or test tube for experimenting with and refining the new solar concepts.

Many of the concepts that work on a small scale will also apply directly to larger structures. But it is important to understand that large complexes and megastructures have a different functional scale and require special solutions. Thermally, a larger structure will not react in the same way; and natural cooling, as well as shading, ventilation, and lighting, rather than heating, may be the design objectives. The potential for operating with natural solar means is perhaps greater in large-scale projects. However, at present, it is expedient to learn by experimenting on a smaller scale.

The basics of passive solar design in the following chapters are vital to implement natural solar architecture. Other rules-of-thumb, knowledge of thermal functions, and methods of use will continue to be discovered. As in all arts and sciences, the learning process is ongoing; each step forward is built upon preceding steps. It is hoped that the information included herein will provide one springboard for future advances into the solar field.

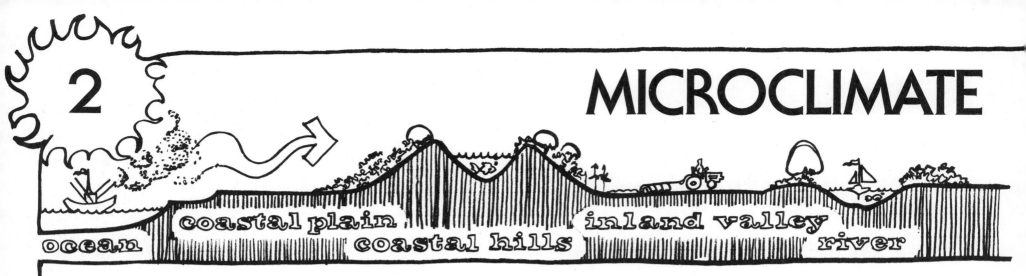

2

MICROCLIMATE

ocean   coastal plain   coastal hills   inland valley   river

Each specific piece of land is endowed with certain characteristics which establish suitability for various life forms. At a given stage of earthly evolution the forces acting on any one area will determine what forms of mammal, bird, insect, fish, or vegetable life are likely to generate, adapt, thrive, or degenerate according to their compatibility. Mother Nature does not allow a redwood tree to grow in the desert; nor is a barrel cactus likely to survive in an alpine forest. But man is more imaginative and adaptive than many species. Variances in stature, skin color, diet, culture, and so on enable people to survive in diverse places.

In the long-range scheme of things, man's struggle to survive in any place he finds himself—be it city, country, or outer space—will be governed by his ability to integrate his needs with the environment. The more attuned our habits are to the forces acting upon them, the less contrived the routine of survival. The simpler the methods of survival, the more harmonious they are with nature. Structures and life-support systems should respond to the demands of the environment, optimizing the potential of their elements.

DESIGN

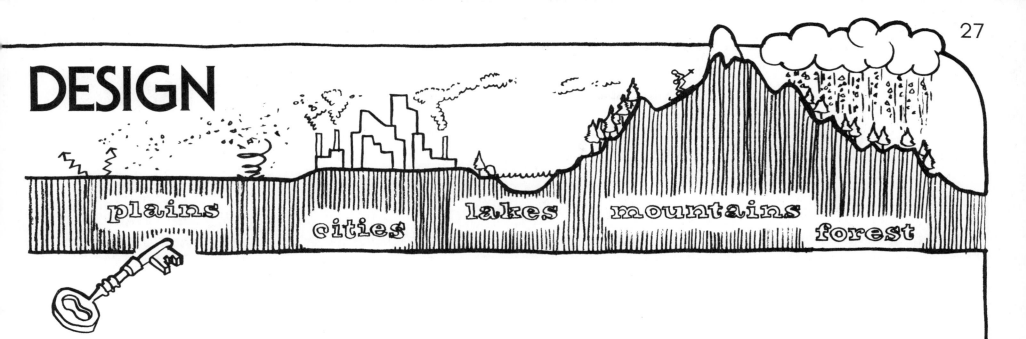

plains · cities · lakes · mountains · forest

The key to long-range survival is to minimize man's impact by balancing all things in the web of life while maximizing the potential of the natural elements. We need not go to the extreme of clear cutting a forest for material or fuel; neither is it necessary to treat forests, fields, and streams as inviolate. A happy balance is to use just enough to encourage proper regeneration. We should farm carefully, letting nature provide irrigation, fertilization, and insect control. Man's heavy-handed dominance seldom works in the long run.

When planning a structure it is important to evaluate all of the effects of the microclimate (i.e., the essentially uniform local features of a specific site or habitat). *Landscape and climate* characteristics will dictate the most suitable siting, orientation, form, materials, openings, and the like. The success of a design will depend primarily on the ability of the designer/owner/architect/engineer/builder to interpret the natural factors and to create architecture accordingly.

Landscape and climate dictate the rules!

Landscape Characteristics

The degree of *man's influence* changes a microclimate as surely as any natural factor. The effect of roads, buildings, dams, cities, farms, and so on exerts a presence and control of future usage. The task of designing to best integrate with nature becomes more difficult in proportion to the impact of man's presence. In high-density, urban situations the possibility of creating natural solutions may verge on the impossible due to vested interests, zoning, space and sun rights, building codes, and conflicting ideals. Cities should become prime targets for natural solutions; in many cases, only good can come from evolving them into cleaner and more efficient places.

urban   suburban

MAN'S INFLUENCE

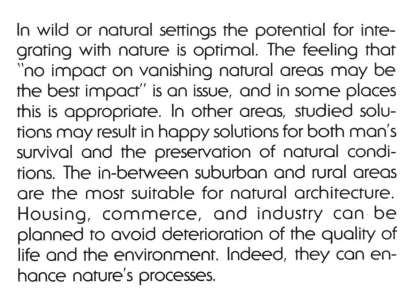

In wild or natural settings the potential for integrating with nature is optimal. The feeling that "no impact on vanishing natural areas may be the best impact" is an issue, and in some places this is appropriate. In other areas, studied solutions may result in happy solutions for both man's survival and the preservation of natural conditions. The in-between suburban and rural areas are the most suitable for natural architecture. Housing, commerce, and industry can be planned to avoid deterioration of the quality of life and the environment. Indeed, they can enhance nature's processes.

rural

natural

Each *land type*, from desert to mountain to sea-shore, exhibits unique features of soil, weather, and terrain that can be generally categorized. The outline of specific types and associated characteristics (opposite) is a sampling of the many varied areas man inhabits. It is clear that a type of structure well suited to one area and land type will probably not be suited to another without modification.

For example, two diverse areas call for very different approaches. In the desert, subsurface structures using the stable temperature of the earth's crust to balance the outside day/night extremes are logical. In the tropics, above-ground building is desired to allow cooling breeze circulation, to combat heat and humidity, and to avoid subsurface water.

LAND TYPES

prairie hills forest seashore
desert valley mountains tropic

Desert

- dry, cacti
- hot
- sunny
- sandy
- flat
- windy
- dusty
- flash floods

Prairie

- dry, grasses
- electrical storms
- dirt and clay
- flat
- windy
- winter blizzards
- summer drought

Valley

- green, grassy
- rainstorms
- good soil
- gentle slopes

- farming
- temperate
- subsurface water

Hills

- trees and grass
- soil and rock
- slopes
- cool winters
- wind protected

Mountains

- trees
- thunderstorms
- rocky

- steep slopes
- cold winters
- snow
- deep freezing

Forest

- many trees
- good soil
- varied terrain
- wind, weather protection
- shady
- good water

Tropic

- lush growth
- sunny
- humid
- tropical storms
- moisture
- hot
- rich soil
- flat
- mosquitos

Seashore

- moist air
- breezy
- moderate climate
- salty
- sloping
- sandy soil
- fog
- changeable

Soil types vary and combine widely. Any site is likely to contain several soil types at various locations and depths. Understanding the makeup and attributes of both surface and subsurface *soil conditions* is important when analyzing the pros and cons of drainage, percolation, bearing value, structural uses, stability, earthquake potential, heat storage and insulation value, planting, ease of construction, and so on.

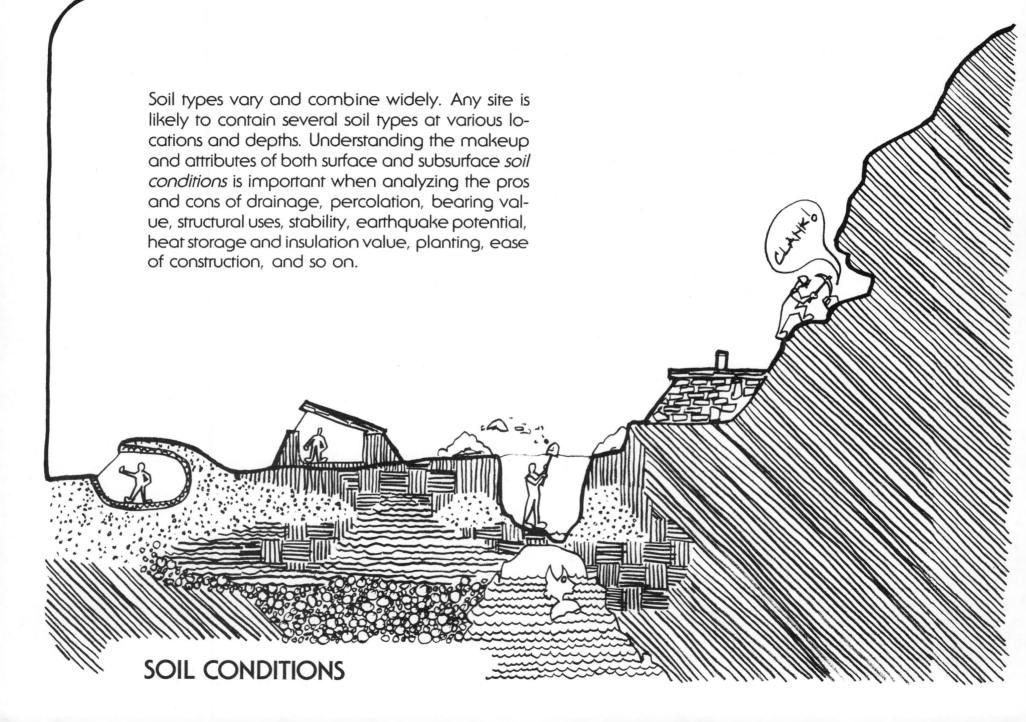

SOIL CONDITIONS

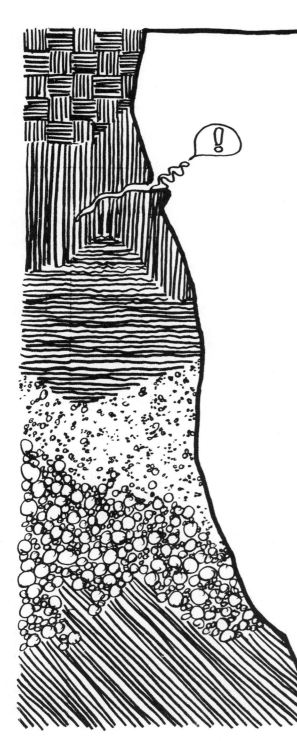

silt—fertile, expands and compacts, adequate bearing, easy digging, fair percolation, fair structurally, poor thermal capacity

loam—plantable, moldable, fair bearing, organic, compacts, fair thermal capacity, nice for worms

clay—expansive, hard, moldable and plastic, sticky when wet, poor bearing, poor percolation, fair structurally, good thermal capacity

sand—loose, grainy, heavy, good bearing, good percolation, needs to be contained, good thermal capacity

gravel—hard, heavy, loose, good bearing, good percolation, very good thermal capacity

rock—hard, heavy, solid, excellent bearing, good structurally, no percolation, excellent thermal capacity.

The hierarchy of plant life offers an extensive palette for the landscape designer to draw from. The many various types of *vegetation* can be used in very effective ways to modify the microclimate of a site. Grasses stabilize soil, retain rainfall, and harbor insects, birds, and small animals. Shrubs stabilize soil, make good ground cover and visual screens, and provide homes for many creatures. Deciduous trees provide summer shade and mulch for the ground, house birds, and channel breezes. Evergreens make good wind and snow breaks and visual screens, as well as pleasant music when the wind blows.

Generally, indigenous plant species adapt most readily, both visually and climatically, and require a minimum of care, feeding, watering, and maintenance.

VEGETATION

Grasses

- stabilize soil
- retain rainfall
- build soil
- harbor insects and rodents

Low Shrubs

- cover ground
- retain moisture
- mulch soil
- shelter small birds and animals

High Shrubs

- visually screen
- channel winds
- mulch soil
- shade ground
- provide flowers and berries that taste and smell good

Deciduous Trees

- mulch soil
- seasonal shade
- channel winds
- shelter structures
- bear fruit
- visually screen

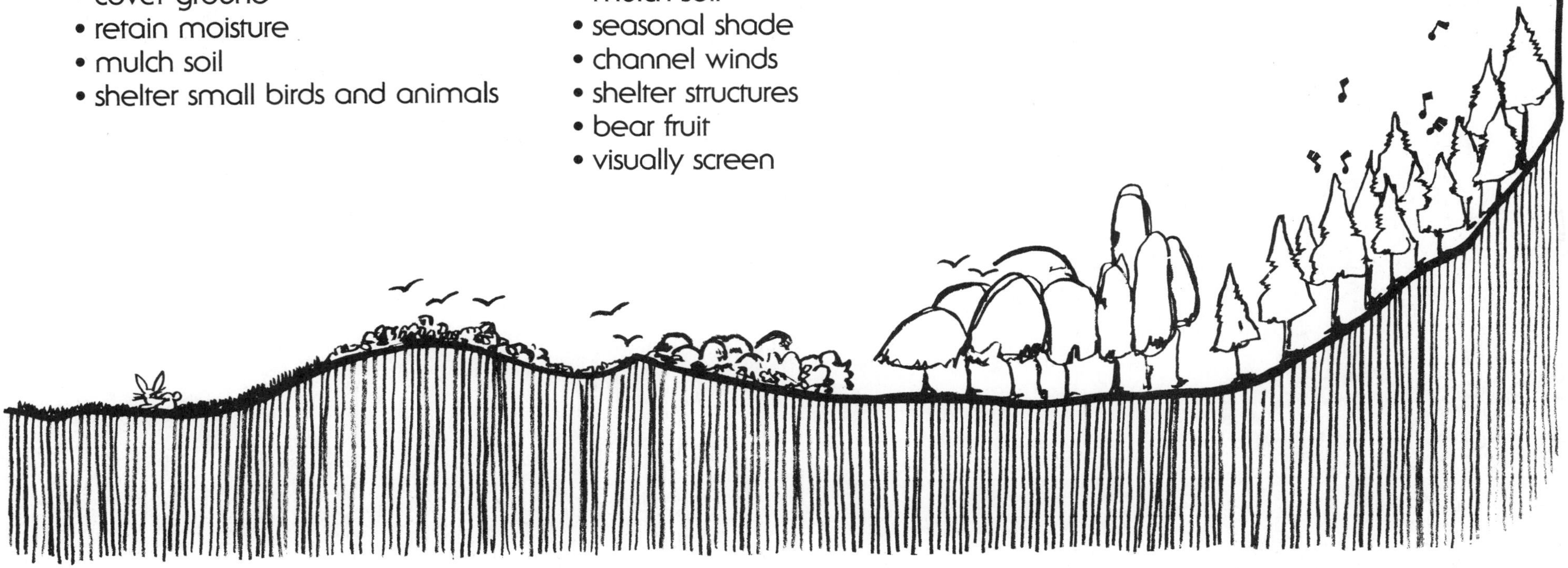

Evergreens

- cool breezes
- block winter storms
- visually screen
- retain soil
- add acid to soil
- shade ground

The contour of a site and adjacent lands will affect its viability for building in many ways. Drainage; solar exposure; wind, storm, and snow protection; ease of construction; visual impact on the land; and so forth are all dependent on the *profile* of the land. Each type of terrain suggests a kind of structure most suitable for maximizing the useful potential while minimizing the adverse.

Usually, the structure which least modifies the natural form of the land is preferred for protection from the elements and low visual impact.

Nature's housing systems are unobtrusive and harmonious with the landscape. Our ideal as builders should be to integrate our structures with the terrain—our egos are better fed if we are safe and warm rather than exposed to the mercy of the elements.

PROFILE

Each area or region is endowed with certain God-given material assets. These resources, indigenous to an area, are a part of the landscape. The shape and makeup of a structure should reflect and complement the material world at hand.

Any *material* that may be native to an area—such as timber, sand, earth, stone, adobe, and ice—is probably the best suited to interact with the local landscape and climate forces. Redwood dries out and splits away in the desert. Adobe melts away in damp climates. Earth, stone, and timber are abundant material assets requiring little fuel energy to convert to usable form.

It is wise to maximize the use of local and to minimize imported and high-energy materials. Certain man-made items, such as glass, electrical wiring, steel reinforcing, and insulation, are necessary for modern building. Wise planning will limit the amount and expense of these valuable technical materials.

In almost any location safe, inexpensive, low-energy materials are at hand. Construction techniques may have to be developed to build with adobe bricks, stone, earth berm, and sandbags. Yet, the potential for building cost-effective, modern structures with local resources may be our best option for energy efficiency.

MATERIALS

The water table of a site can vary from non-existent to excessive. The *quantity*, *quality*, and *location* of water regulate the suitability of land to support life. Water does not come from a pipe in the ground; it comes from watersheds and aquifers. In some climates one acre (0.004 km^2) of land will support one cow; other places with similar soil may require 100 acres (0.4 km^2) per cow. This is due to grass growth, which is due to moisture. The potential of any piece of land, watershed, or aquifer to support life is finite. The water crisis is real. Learn to respect this resource. It is like the air and the sun—fundamental to life.

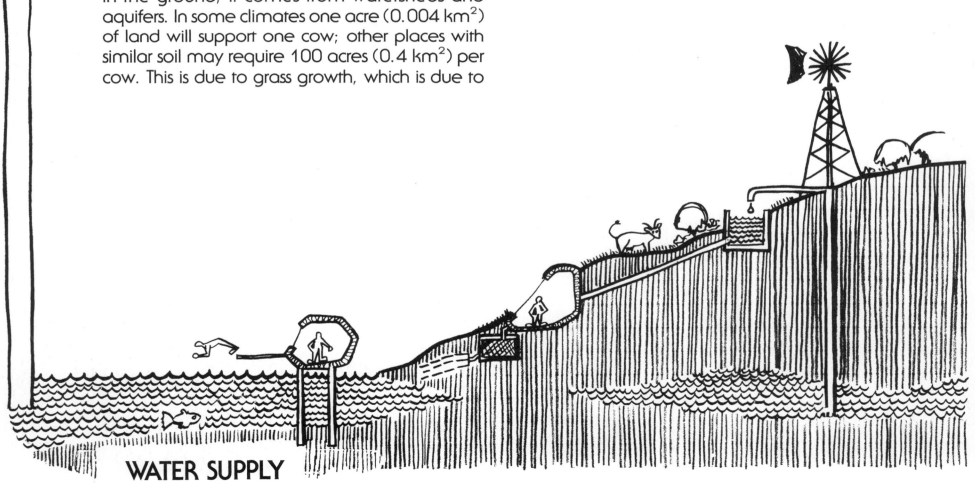

WATER SUPPLY

The *location* of water in relation to the surface of land is a determining factor in type of water supply, building location, surface drainage, vegetation, and so on. The *quantity* of water affects seasonal allocation, conservation techniques, waste-water treatment, population, and the like. The *quality* of water influences taste, appearance, type of piping, need for filtration and softening systems, tooth decay, and many other decisions.

Know where your water comes from and where it goes—you are what you drink . . . and how often.

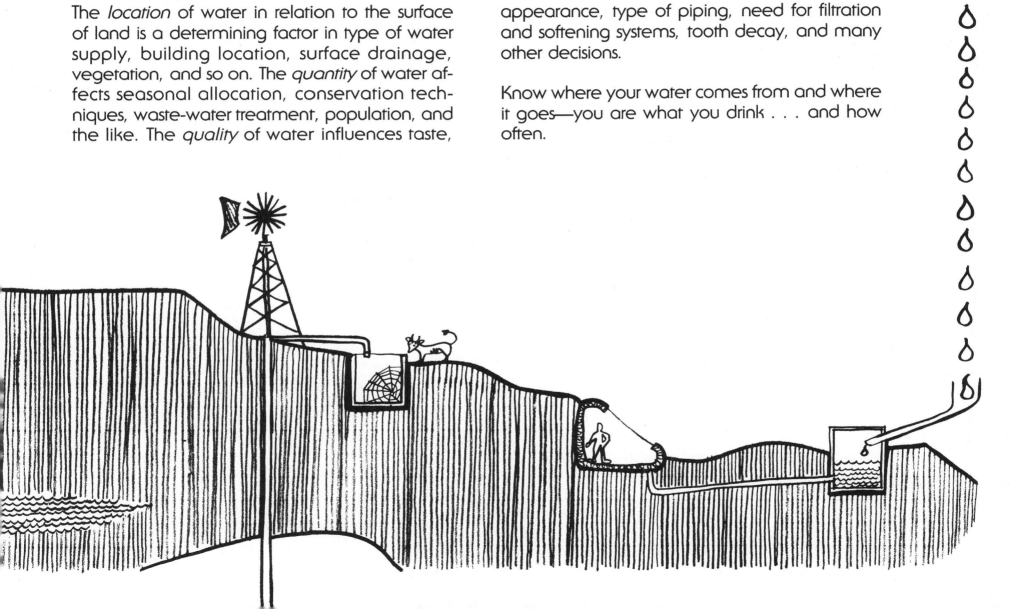

Location with relation to the equator is measured in degrees of north or south latitude. *Latitude* affects the landscape and microclimate design in several ways. Generally, the farther away from the equator, the colder the climate. This is due to sun angle and related weather conditions. Accordingly, the distance north or south of the equator should affect the type and shape of a structure as it does the characteristics of vegetation and other life forms. At the equator, a solar collector may be small and nearly horizontal. Going north, the area and angle will increase with latitude. A building at 50° north latitude may require the use of nearly all of its south-facing vertical walls to satisfy only a percentage of its heating needs.

The landscape should be visually different, as buildings change profile, size, and shape to comply with the elements. Knowing the latitude is another clue telling the designer what to do.

LATITUDE

N 75° 60° 45° 30° 15° equator 15° 30° 45° 60° 75° S

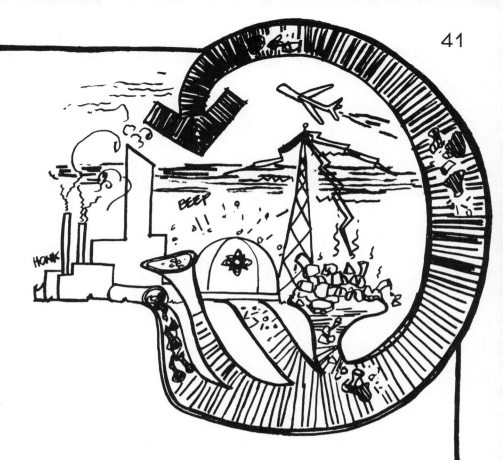

As surely as beautiful trees, rivers, mountains, valleys, and skies characterize our landscape, *pollution* affects our decisions, offends our senses, and ruins our health. Nature pollutes from time to time with forest fires, fouling the air and silt-mudding spring rivers; but this organic pollution is recycling waste or regenerating life cycles.

Only man fouls the environment by creating sewage-disposal problems, carcinogenics, smog alerts, fallout, electronic smog, and general systemic poisoning on all levels. The degree of pollution seems directly proportional to the density of human population. Our cities, skies, and rivers are always suspect of harboring unseen poisons. Inhabiting polluted places and systems is dangerous. Know how to recognize them. Correct and reclaim these areas when possible. Today's waste will be tomorrow's resource—recycle containers, compost sewage, control trash, and respect the air and water as the vital fluids they are.

POLLUTION

View is one of the first and last things considered when looking for land or an apartment, and prices generally reflect the quality of view. In today's world, pleasant landscapes and vistas are a vanishing species. Of course, as one wise man stated, "Beauty is in the eye of the beholder." Hence, not everyone needs to look at a national wonder all of the time. A designer can create small, interesting, subtle, and surprising sights virtually anywhere. It is desirable to find a microclimate that satisfies the yearning to behold beauty. Further, it is important to preserve and encourage nice views. Please don't block someone else's favorite spot. View is a matter of community responsibility; plant a tree, clean a yard, paint a house. Each new structure, garden, roadway, and sign becomes a part of the visible landscape, and it is the task of the designer to respect and harmonize with the surroundings. Mother Nature seldom makes mistakes with view. Man often does.

VIEW

1. Oil refinery to the west.
2. Power line across north.
3. View of lake to the south.
4. . . .
5. . . .
6.
7.
8.
9.
10.
11.
12.
13.
14.
15.
16.
17.
18.
19.
20.

start your own list!!

OTHER LANDSCAPE CHARACTERISTICS

Weather Characteristics

The microclimate as affected by its landscape characteristics is even further defined by its normal weather characteristics. Weather features and frequencies as they affect microclimate will differ from mountain to valley, north to south, and so on. Often a climate condition will vary within a short distance vertically or horizontally, and even this variation establishes a microclimatic difference. The weather on one side of a hill or valley may be quite different from the other and will require a special solution for optimum design. *Temperature* tells us much about microclimate.

TEMPERATURE

Temperature range is an indicator of required design. Depending on normal temperature records, heating or cooling may be needed to maintain comfort. The design, shape, and composition of a building changes considerably for temperature extremes. Window area, orientation, shading, exposure, and other variables are all adapted to the task of heating or cooling. A normally tolerable average temperature range is between 60 and 85°F (15 and 30°C). If the average falls above or below this zone, heating or cooling is generally desirable. Humidity, air motion, mean radiant temperature, and sunlight can improve or diminish this feeling of comfort.

People become accustomed to individual climates and temperatures. A comfortable warm to an Eskimo would be an intolerable cool to a native of the Tropics.

The amount of *sunlight* and clarity of atmosphere will vary the character of each microclimate. The quality and quantity of sun acting on a site will psychologically affect each person's physical comfort. A bright, sunny day is not necessarily desirable, especially after a few hundred days without rain. On the other hand, a break between cold winter storms will do wonders to warm spirits, as well as solar collectors.

Microclimate factors affecting sunlight intensity may include shading by trees, cloud cover, air pollution, latitude, seasonal patterns, and altitude. Designs for various microclimates might require extensive glass-collector areas or umbrellalike shading to take best advantage of the sun.

Sunlight has a hygienic effect—bringing it into our habitats at times helps nature keep us healthy.

SUNLIGHT

Wind, precipitation, sunlight, temperature, and humidity are all factors of the weather. *Weather cycles* are distinctive groupings of these elements. Each climate zone and microclimate receives its character and sustenance by the pattern of these cycles. The rythym of storms for an area establishes the climate pulse. When the pulse changes, the climate changes.

The weather is seldom normal. It is usually in a state of flux, seeming to change from year to year. Winter storms come in coveys— several days of storm may be followed by a sunny period. Gusty winds often accompany clear spring days; August rains interrupt the heat of summer.

To know these patterns of nature and to properly design to take best advantage of these interacting forces is the essence of microclimate design.

WEATHER CYCLES

The amount of *precipitation* in the form of rain, fog, snow, hail, and night moisture which delivers life-giving water to the land, does much to determine microclimatic character. Annual rainfall can be dramatically different within the same geographical area. Coastal mountains often receive three to four times the amount falling on coastal meadows. Mountains have a habit of rupturing clouds and benefiting from the contents, making the mountains greener and lusher than the neighboring lowlands. The amount and type of plant growth is directly related to precipitation. Vegetation, water resources, sunlight, erosion, and flooding are all microclimatic variations affected by the quantity and frequency of precipitation. Two forms of solar cooling are summer storms and fog—natural air-conditioning forces that occur in many parts of the world.

It just might be that the grass really is greener on the other side of the fence!

PRECIPITATION

The moisture contained in the air surrounding us is not always visible, as is most precipitation. *Humidity* is water moisture suspended in air and is measured as the percentage of the air saturated by water. At one-hundred percent relative humidity (RH) for a given temperature, the air cannot accept or hold additional moisture.

Microclimate comfort is directly influenced by humidity. Cold, damp air feels much colder than cold, dry air; and hot, damp air is stifling compared to hot, dry air.

When designing for humid microclimates it is prudent to allow air circulation, to consider dehumidifying, and to be aware of conditions causing walls to sweat and mold to grow.

Lack of humidity or very dry air causes excessive evaporation of moisture, resulting in dried skin, nosebleeds, and inhibited plant growth. A comfortable relative humidity range is generally between twenty and sixty percent. For example, at 77°F (25°C), with little air motion, the range of relative humidity for interior comfort would be between twenty and fifty percent.

18% RH   F   62% RH

75°

dry   humid

HUMIDITY

catch it

Air motion through and around a microclimate influences everything. Seasonal wind motions that bring winter storms and spring winds add to heat loss and affect storm patterns, but also make for good kite flying. Constant winds affect humidity and ground moisture, move soil and sand, and provide potential for generation of electrical energy. Daily wind thermals can be used to advantage for cooling and air exchange. In low-wind areas, air motion induced by solar collectors can cool or heat buildings.

Comfort may call for opening to, or shielding from, the wind at various times. Sheltered outside-activity areas, insulation from associated noise, and reduction of heat-loss surfaces may be integral in design for high-wind areas. Funneling of and orienting to prevailing breezes is desirable in warmer regions. By knowing the seasonal and daily wind patterns, the orientation and shape of buildings, fences, earth forms, and plantings can be planned to take best advantage of the forces of the wind.

screen it

AIR MOTION AND WIND

Location: Denver   Latitude: 39° 45'N   Altitude: 5280 ft.   Year: 1975

(Data taken from National Oceanic and Atmospheric Administration, NOAA)

Month	Temp.			Degree Days (65°F base)		Precipit.		Humidity		Wind		Sunshine			
	hi	lo	av	heat	cool	water	snow	am	pm	dir	spd.	clr.	p.cldy.	cldy.	%pos
Jan	46	17	32	1024	0	0.2	3.6	62	38	W	10.2	9	7	15	64
Feb	45	16	31	957	0	0.4	4.0	65	41	NW	9.7	10	5	13	55
Mar	50	24	37	852	0	1.2	14.3	64	39	NW	11.4	5	11	15	57
Apr	58	30	44	621	0	1.1	10.9	72	36	SW	10.9	9	13	8	79
May	68	41	54	332	3	2.8	6.1	71	40	S	11.2	4	17	10	62
Jun	80	49	64	85	69	2.1	0.0	71	36	S	11.0	15	7	8	70
Jul	87	58	73	0	246	2.8	0.0	64	33	S	9.5	10	20	1	73
Aug	86	55	71	4	192	2.0	0.0	58	27	S	9.2	16	8	7	74
Sep	75	44	60	195	39	0.3	0.0	61	28	SE	8.5	17	4	9	76
Oct	71	36	53	363	5	0.3	2.7	57	28	S	9.3	18	7	6	85
Nov	51	23	37	840	0	1.9	15.2	64	49	SW	10.0	12	8	10	75
Dec	51	25	38	843	0	0.5	7.3	63	55	SW	9.2	9	8	14	70
ave	64	35	49	6116	554	15.5	64.1	64	38	SSW	10.0	134	115	116	70

Daily, monthly, and annual *weather records* are available for most areas from national, state, and county climatological bureaus. Other local sources are agricultural agencies, newspapers, and airports. Old-timers often carry valuable microclimate information in their heads.

WEATHER RECORD

Acts of God

Above and beyond the normal landscape and weather characteristics is a group of special considerations we attribute to *acts of God,* which certainly are never welcomed as a part of the microclimate. Tornadoes, floods, earthquakes, forest fires, volcanos, landslides, tidal waves, hurricanes, and cyclones of devastating force occur infrequently and randomly. The likelihood of occurences in certain areas and even times when conditions are right are well known. Yet pinpointed accuracy of location and force is as impossible as is prevention.

Be aware of the possibility of these acts occuring wherever you are. In each case, careful planning and design of structures can lessen or minimize catastrophe. Do all you can do to understand and deal with these forces. After that, only prayer will help.

Acts of Man

The *acts of man* always modify the microclimate—planting a tree, building a house, or drilling a well all have an impact on the land. Sometimes the change is immediately visible. Many times the effect of what is done today may not be known for years to come.

It is important to know what the possible effects of our actions will be. Positive change is our goal.

Regionalism

The result of applied climatic design is a true *regionalism*. In the past, regional architecture and city planning evolved from climatic conditions, cultural habits and taste, use of indigenous materials, social structure, tradition, and a myriad of other factors. Regional styles in many instances have failed to adapt to change, have become illogical in today's world, or have been corrupted or forgotten in our rush toward technology, systemization, and sameness.

Many facets of traditional regionalism are worthy of preserving or readapting through microclimate design. If fully understood and applied, it is inevitable that landscape and climatic influences will generate a regional character with a type of architecture and community plan that best suits a geographical area. When supplemented with our vast knowledge of technical methodology and materials, this regional approach, modified and refined to suit present and future lifestyles, should provide the most logical solutions to habitat and community design.

Today, with our rich storehouse of history and technology, we have much to draw from. Rather than being guided by style, custom, or first-cost economics alone, it is vital, in terms of long-range survival and ecology, that man use systemic analysis to shape his environment. This process leads toward a balancing of the long-range interaction of man, his world, and the solar system.

We are now approaching general system overload because of the way we live and use our resources. It is time to reevaluate transportation, housing, communications, economics, farming, city planning, defense, and all other systems in the light of past mistakes, new limits, and future quality. Enlightenment or escape from this earthly condition for our species is perhaps possible, but not in the foreseeable future. In the meantime, we must strive to make each decision carefully and to make each action count, if we are to make a positive contribution to the overall scheme of things.

Each region must adapt in its own way!

3

NATURE'S DESIGN TOOLS

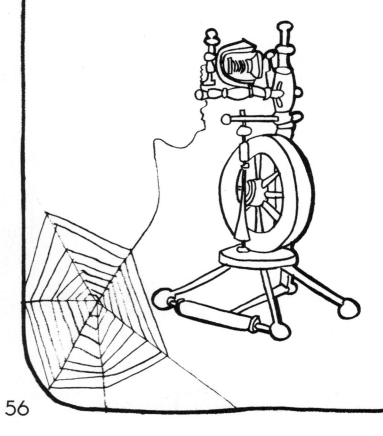

Each of these tools can be used to create passive solar designs. The goal of passive solar applications is to create structures that respond to the patterns of nature.

A building that passively utilizes the energy of the sun for year-round space conditioning involves three basic principles:
—it must be designed to accept or reject solar heat when called for
—it must have the thermal integrity to maintain internal comfort despite the range of climatic forces acting on its weatherskin
—it must incorporate the ability to retain the presence or absence of heat within.

Generally, these principles are applied by having solar gain surfaces of the right size and in the right place to selectively admit natural heat. Passive solar structures must be well insulated and must contain adequate heat storage mass. By the use of movable and flexible devices, the flow of energy can be controlled throughout the various conditions of all seasons.

It is possible, using the same materials, to create a building that will never be comfortable—or a building that will always be comfortable. An applied knowledge of *nature's design tools* is the key to successful *passive solar architecture*.

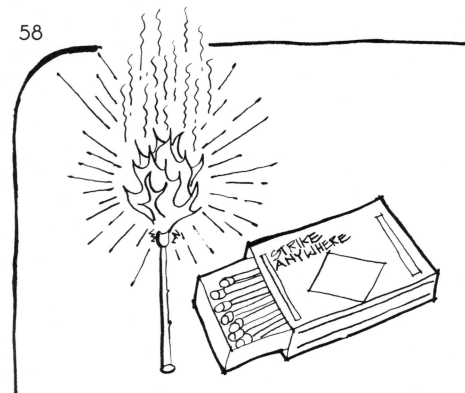

Thermal Factors

Energy can be neither created nor destroyed; when one form of energy disappears, another form always appears in equivalent quantity.

Heat energy cannot be lost. It can be converted to another form of energy (electrical, chemical, or mechanical) or remain as heat. It can be converted, stored, absorbed, moved, gained, and so on. In any system it will always be accounted for somehow. In buildings, the energy collected or generated will eventually be converted as work done or escape as heat loss.

FIRST LAW OF THERMODYNAMICS

Heat cannot pass spontaneously from a colder to a warmer body; when free interchange of heat takes place, it is always the hotter of the two bodies that loses energy and the colder that gains energy.

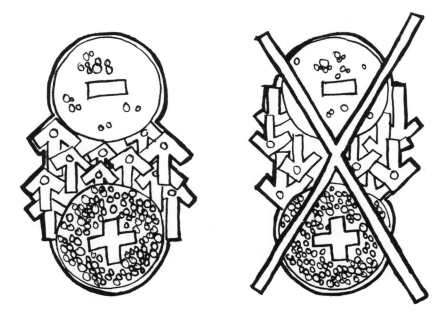

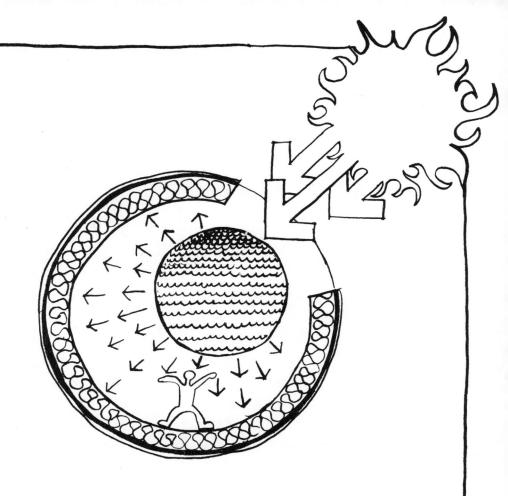

Heat will seek out cold. In passive solar design the heat absorbed or stored will constantly move to attain equilibrium throughout the mass of a building. Hot molecules of a substance can be thought of as excited, while cold molecules are still or quiet. By various methods of heat transfer, heat will constantly seek out cooler regions to share its molecular excitement.

SECOND LAW OF THERMODYNAMICS

There are three ways of transferring heat:

—*conduction*

—*convection*

—*radiation*.

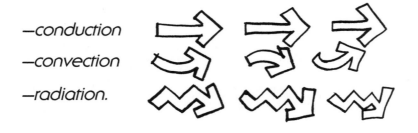

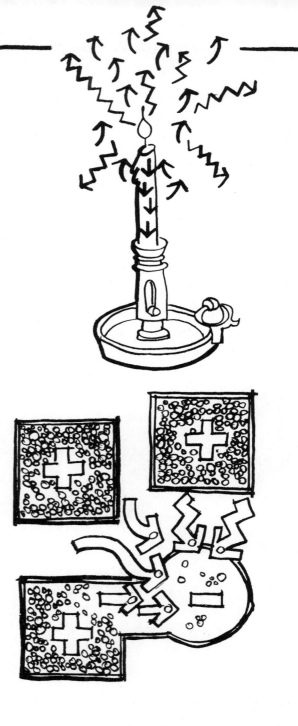

Generally, for natural transfer to occur, one body must contain more heat (+). According to the second law of thermodynamics, heat will travel to the cooler body or place (−). Many times all three methods of *heat transfer* will occur simultaneously. In passive solar design these elements of heat transfer are of prime consideration and should always be gracefully integrated with any concept. Natural transfer tendencies should never be denied; rather, they should be recognized and respectfully managed.

HEAT TRANSFER

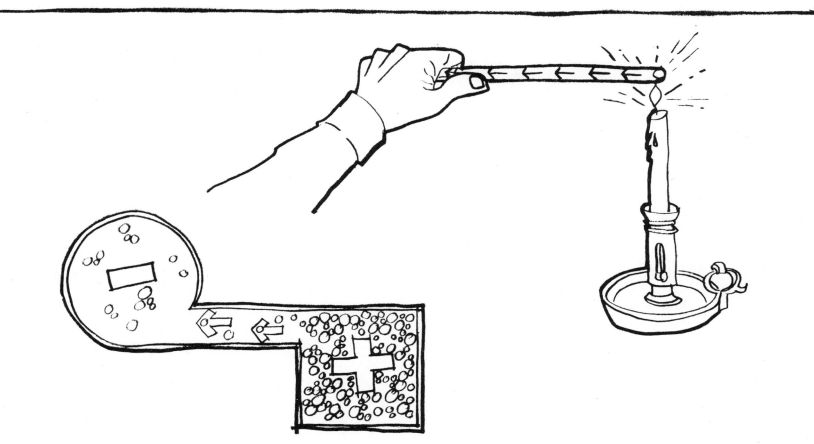

Heat energy travels from the candle, through the rod, to the hand, by *conduction*. Conductive transfer occurs between bodies in direct contact. Heated, excited molecules, bump into and transfer some of their energy into adjacent, cooler ones. The faster the rate of heat flow, or molecular interaction at a given temperature through a material, the higher its conductivity.

CONDUCTION

Heat energy travels from the candle (by air currents) to the hand by *convection*. In convection a flowing medium is necessary. Heat travels between two discrete places via a fluid, such as a gas (air) or a liquid (water).

CONVECTION

Heat energy is transmitted from the candle, through space, to the hand, by *radiation*. This transfer takes place without a medium. Radiant energy is transmitted as electromagnetic waves, which travel in lines through space and fluids until absorbed by a solid or reflected by a radiant barrier, such as silver or aluminum foil.

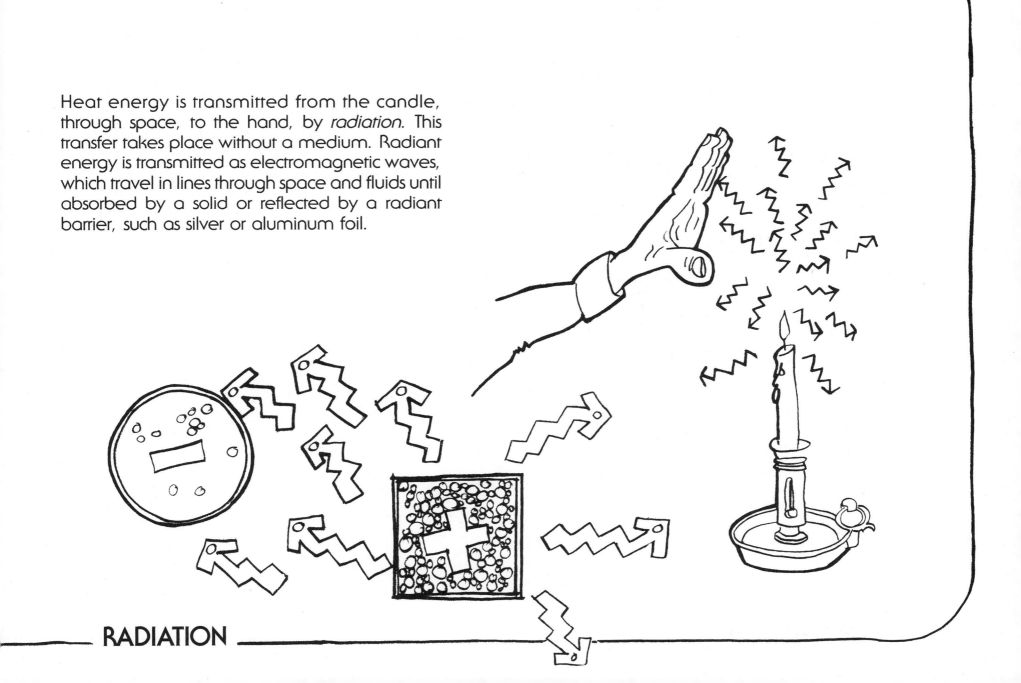

RADIATION

As a fluid is heated, the distance between molecules increases. With this volume increase or expansion and no change in mass, each heated molecule is buoyed up. Water, air, and many other fluids will *rise* when heated until contained or cooled. When cooled they contract and *fall* until equilibrium is attained.

In a hot-air balloon, heat energy is added to the air contained; the volume becomes greater and the trapped air lighter than the surrounding atmosphere, and it rises. Thermal convection occurs when a fluid is heated. In a closed-loop, solar water system the water is heated and it rises up the collector. The hot water stores in the tank. The relatively cooler water at the bottom flows down to the bottom of the collector for another trip. This rise and fall factor is experienced in many facets of passive solar design.

RISE AND FALL

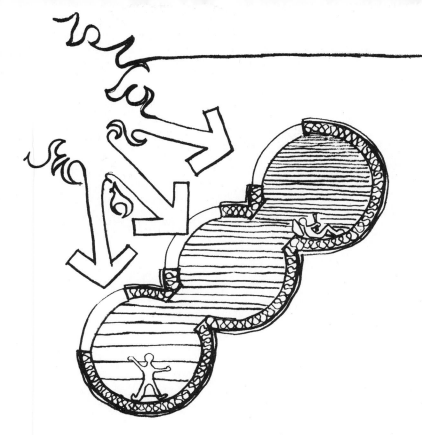

Heated fluids that have no natural flow circuit will tend to rise and stratify or layer in a given volume; the hottest fluid rising to the top and the coolest settling to the bottom, causing a vertical thermal gradient. Any surface or object in a space will be affected by the flow and layering of the air, storing more heat toward the top than the bottom. The liquid in a vessel will stratify with the warmest at the top. Actually, the warmest fluids are in a constant movement with the fluids at the heat-loss surfaces cooling and falling. Conversely, they warm at the heat-gain surfaces, rising and constantly mixing.

In passive solar design the effect of *stratification* can be useful in planning the placement of spaces and heat storage in relation to function. Various human activities require different temperatures for relative comfort—a person reading will require a higher temperature to be comfortable than a person running.

STRATIFICATION

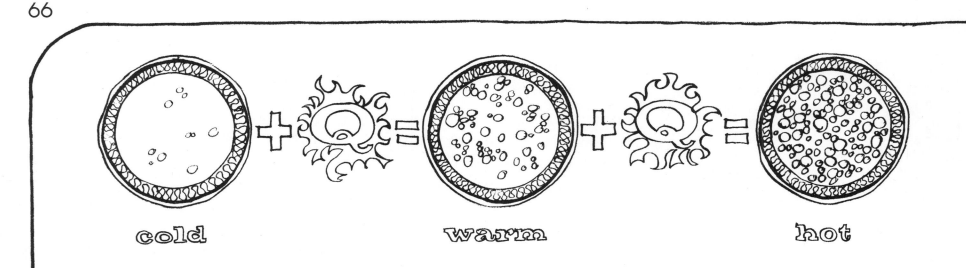

cold   warm   hot

Energy exists in six basic forms: thermal, electrical, mechanical, chemical, radiant, and atomic. In passive design, thermal energy and radiant energy are the states commonly utilized. Radiant sunlight energy is the initial form in which solar energy is delivered. It can be measured in *British thermal units* (BTUs). Heat energy, as stored in water or rocks, can also be measured in BTUs.

The scientific symbol for heat is Q. Heat content is measured quantitatively. A specific quantity of material, such as a pound of water, can contain different amounts of heat. As the *temperature*, which is a relative measure of heat, becomes hotter or cooler, the material will contain more or less heat energy. If you know the mass, specific heat, and temperature change of a material, you can determine the amount of heat stored or lost.

HEAT AND TEMPERATURE

All substances are capable of storing different amounts of sensible heat. The *specific heat* of a substance is the *amount of heat required to pro-duce a unit change in temperature per unit mass* (a constant for each material),

or: $$Q = C \times m \times \Delta t$$

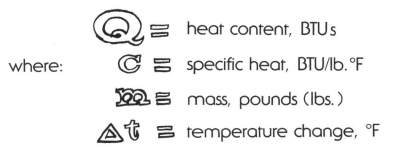

where:

$Q =$ heat content, BTUs

$C =$ specific heat, BTU/lb.°F

$m =$ mass, pounds (lbs.)

$\Delta t =$ temperature change, °F

Water has a specific heat of 1.0 and a density of 62.5 pounds per cubic foot (lbs./ft.³). It takes 1 BTU to raise 1 pound of water 1°F, as per the definition of a BTU. Dry sand has a specific heat of 0.19 and a density of 95 lbs./ft.³. Therefore, water holds $\frac{1.0}{0.19} \cong 5.3$ times more heat by mass than sand. It follows that:

$$\frac{1.0 \times 62.5}{0.19 \times 95} \cong 3.5, \text{ or:}$$

Water has approximately 3.5 times more heat content by volume than sand at a given temperature.

SPECIFIC HEAT AND HEAT CONTENT

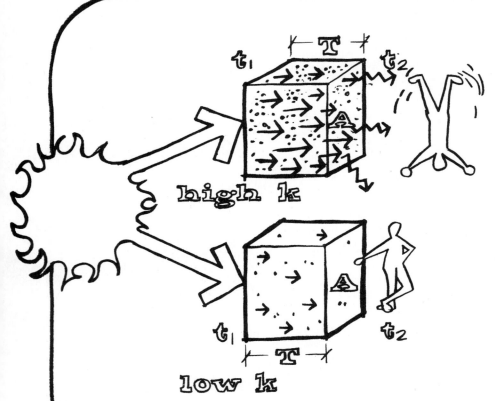

high k

low k

Thermal *conductivity* of a material is the time-rate transfer of heat by conduction, through a unit of thickness (T), across a unit area (A), for a unit difference in temperature (Δt). Or:

$$Q_c = A \times \frac{k}{T} \times \Delta t$$

Q_c = heat conducted, BTU/hr. T = thickness, inches

A = area, sq. ft.

k = thermal conductivity, BTU-in/hr.sq.ft.°F

Δt = temperature differential, $(t_2 - t_1)$, °F

The conductivity is caused by direct molecular interaction. Excited or hot molecules transfer some of their vibrational energy to their cooler neighbors.

A material with a good conductivity or high k has potential for heat transfer surfaces or heat storage:
    steel = 310, concrete = 12, water = 4.1.
A poorer conductor or lower k is generally more suited for insulation or resistance to heat loss:
    wood = 0.8, fiber glass = 0.27.

THERMAL CONDUCTIVITY

The gain/loss, rise/fall, expansion/contraction of heat energy is in all cases seeking a state of balance. In solar design the challenge is to achieve a state of *equilibrium* between heat supply and demand. For each system points of crossover between collection/loss occur; these are points of equilibrium.

Energy flows in a continual quest for equilibrium—hot travels to cold, heated molecules rise, and so forth. This will occur as long as there is imbalance. With the achievement of equilibrium the process will stop momentarily in a serene harmony, until the process reverses and starts up again. In a passive system, incoming energy in its quest for equilibrium will collect and store, seeking even distribution throughout the storage mass.

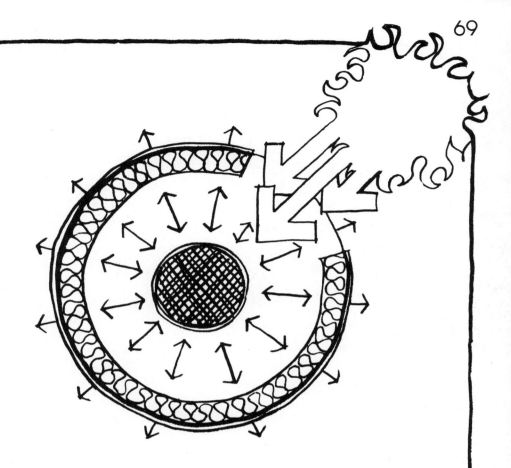

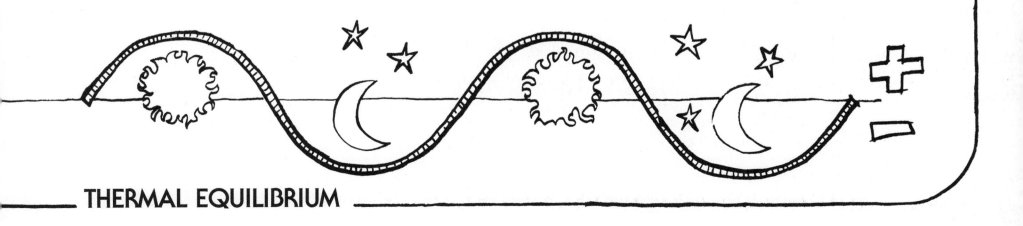

THERMAL EQUILIBRIUM

As the heat content of a solid, liquid, or gas is raised, the volume expands. The coefficient of thermal expansion assigns a factor to the relative rate of the expansion for each material per degree of temperature rise.

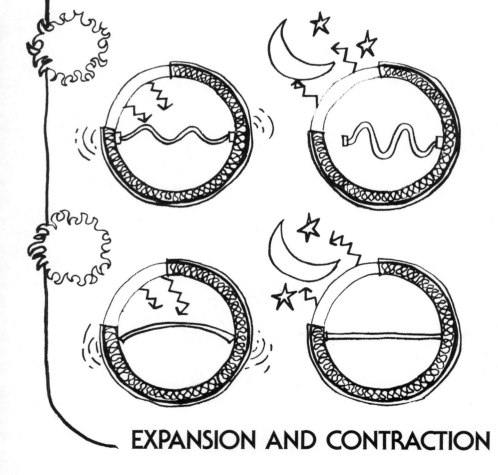

As the material *expands,* its dimensions change in all directions proportional to its volume. Conversely, as a material cools, its volume *contracts.* These changes in size are important in the operation of solar devices, especially in heat-actuated valves which silently open and close depending on the temperature.

EXPANSION AND CONTRACTION

Sensible heat is the thermal energy that changes the temperature, but not the state, of a substance. *Latent heat* (Ql) is the heat required to change the state of a material without changing the temperature. Materials exist in one of three states—solid, liquid, or gaseous. Some materials occur on earth in only one state. Others can be observed changing phase—water can be converted to ice or steam. Latent heat is added to ice to produce water and to water to produce steam; it is released when the process is reversed.

$$ice\ 32°F + Q_l = water\ \frac{32°}{212°}F + Q_l = steam\ 212°F$$

Various substances require different qualities of heat to change phase. With the addition or loss of latent heat the substance changes volume and heat content until the change is completed. Steam at 212°F (100°C) contains much more heat than water at 212°F (100°C). Thus, for a given mass and volume, latent heat, or the energy required to change phases, has a much larger potential in energy storage than sensible heat storage.

LATENT HEAT

Solar Factors

The sun, our nearest star, is a power plant in space fired by a nuclear fusion reaction. With a surface temperature of over 10,000°F, the hydrogen fuel sustaining the reaction is estimated to last a few billion years. It is our most dependable, ongoing source of usable energy.

The earth is a planet in orbit around the sun at a distance of about 93 million miles. Each day the sun provides more than a thousand times the energy ever used by humans. Solar energy is the source of energy and life forms on earth—coal, wood, gas, geothermal, wind, plastics, eggs, flowers, and people are all products of the sun. It has been estimated that the solar energy bathing the earth each hour equals the amount of energy contained in over 21 billion tons of bituminous coal.

THE SUN

As the earth orbits annually around the sun, its path is elliptical. Within this orbit, the earth rotates 15° per hour on its axis, which is tilted 23½°. The net effect of this perpetual circuit is our 24-hour day, 12-month year, the seasons, and the weather. In the northern hemisphere the sun is highest in the sky on June 21—summer solstice—the longest sun day

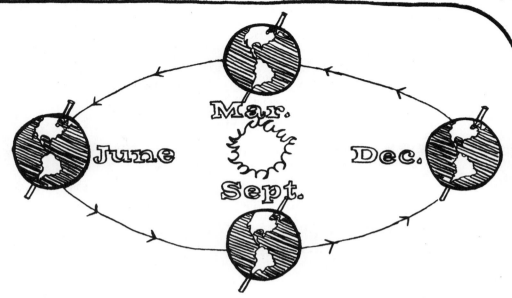

of the year. It is at its lowest point on December 21—winter solstice—the shortest sun day. The midpoints of the solar altitude are on March 21 and September 21—the equinoxes. Solar installations are oriented to take advantage of various aspects of the *solar year:* winter/spring heating, summer/fall cooling, year-round water heating, electrical generation, crop drying, desalinization of seawater, and so on. When designing it is important to accommodate to the sun seasons. It won't work the other way around!

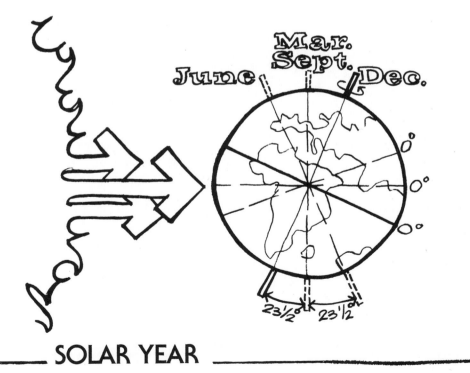

SOLAR YEAR

The sun, our cosmic clock, sets our seasons, years, days, hours, and minutes. A shadow cast by an object from the sun's rays can tell us if it is time to wake up, go to work, and plant, and the true geographic direction. At the two equinoxes, the shadow cast by a gnomon or a rod perpendicular to the earth's surface will be of the same length at a given hour of the day. The length of shadows at midday will tell you if it is winter or summer.

Sun time is also an accurate indicator of orientation. For example, to find solar noon determine the shortest shadow cast by a gnomon during the day. The direction of this shadow is a true north-south line.

The sundial is a clock with split-second accuracy, not affected by electrical outages, winding, mechanical failure, or daylight savings time. Who really needs to know the time at night or during cloudy weather? Hourglasses anyone?

SUN TIME

Because the sun appears to move in three dimensions, it is convenient to use two-dimensional geometry to understand its relative motion.

As the earth rotates at the rate of 15° per hour, the sun appears to move through our sky proportionally. It traverses a daily *solar arc*, which is the apparent path traced across the sky each day. Depending on the latitude north or south of the equator, each day the sun will rise at a different angle from true south and attain a different altitude in the sky from horizontal south. Only at the two equinoxes will the solar arch and the time of sunrise and sunset be approximately the same. This occurs about March 21 and September 21 each year. The shortest solar day occurs about December 21 (for 40°N latitude, approximately 20° angle on the ground and 9 hours), and the longest occurs on June 21(approximately 240° angle on the ground and 15 hours). The hours of diurnal traverse can be called solar time. A solar day is from noon to noon, or from zenith to zenith. The solar arch is always symmetrical around true south.

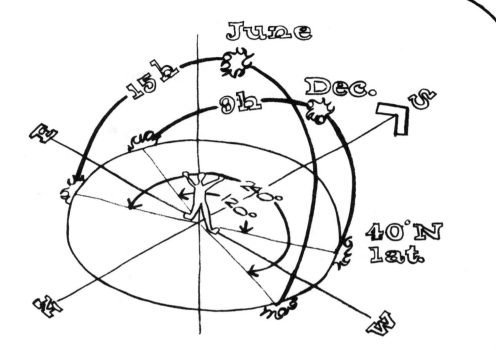

SOLAR ARC

Azimuth is the horizontal angle between the sun's bearing and a north-south line, as projected on a plane horizontal with the earth's surface. This angle, at a given hour, will vary each day throughout the solar year. The sun comes over the horizon at a different point each day, and the daily total azimuth angle will be smaller in winter, larger in summer. For any latitude, tables and charts can be used to determine azimuth hour-by-hour and day-by-day.

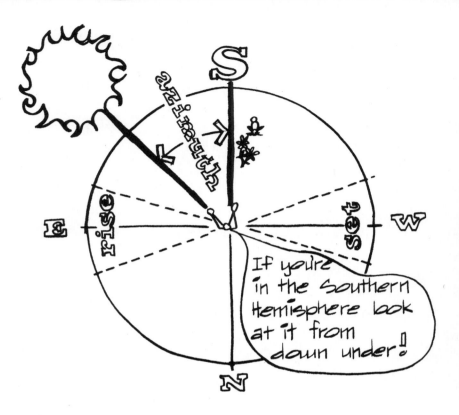

If you're in the Southern Hemisphere look at it from down under!

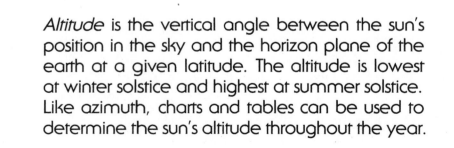

Altitude is the vertical angle between the sun's position in the sky and the horizon plane of the earth at a given latitude. The altitude is lowest at winter solstice and highest at summer solstice. Like azimuth, charts and tables can be used to determine the sun's altitude throughout the year.

AZIMUTH AND ALTITUDE

Altitude variation is an important facet of solar position and intensity. The sun changes altitude by about 47° from summer to winter solstice. The following examples are for solar noon at various latitudes.

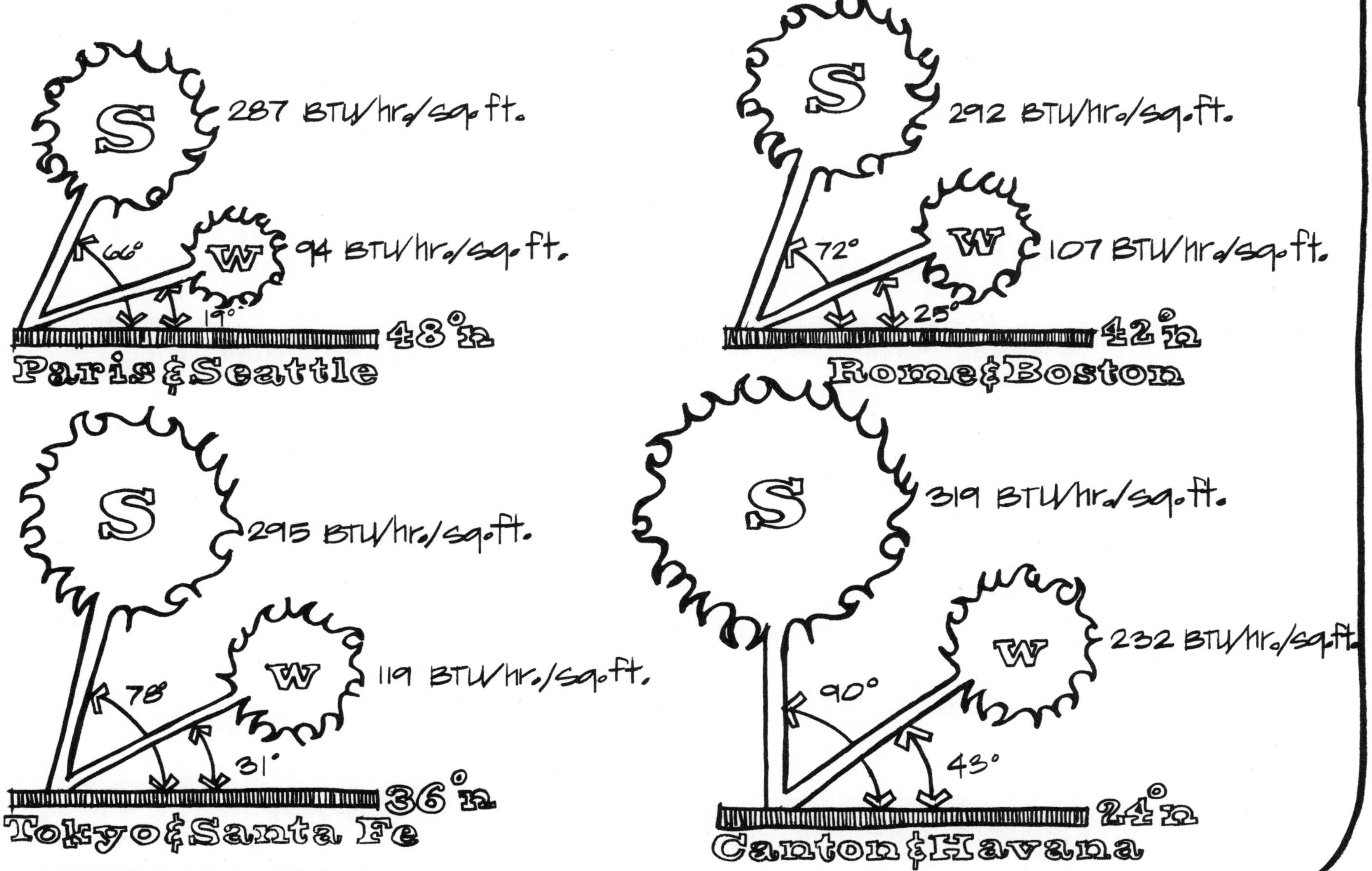

287 BTU/hr/sq.ft.

94 BTU/hr/sq.ft.

66°

19°

48°n
Paris & Seattle

292 BTU/hr/sq.ft.

107 BTU/hr/sq.ft.

72°

25°

42°n
Rome & Boston

295 BTU/hr/sq.ft.

119 BTU/hr/sq.ft.

78°

31°

36°n
Tokyo & Santa Fe

319 BTU/hr/sq.ft.

232 BTU/hr/sq.ft.

90°

43°

24°n
Canton & Havana

ALTITUDE VARIATION

The sun's energy reaches the earth radiantly across the nothingness of space. The amount of solar energy we depend on, or the *solar constant*, received at the outer space around the earth above the atmosphere is about 429 BTU/hr./sq.ft. (1.94 cal./cm^2/min.). Some of this radiation is reflected back into space—some is absorbed in the atmosphere by bumping into air molecules, dust particles, and clouds. By the time it reaches the surface of the earth, the amount of solar energy available varies between 0 to 330 BTU/hr./sq.ft. (1.49 cal./cm^2/min.), averaging about 225 BTU/hr./sq.ft. (1.02 cal./cm^2/min.), but depending on the time of day, latitude, season, and the weather. If you can see even a faint shadow, it is possible to collect useful solar energy.

Different wavelengths of radiation come to us from the sun—X rays, ultraviolet, infrared, and so on. But the largest portion of usable energy is in the visible light spectrum or shortwaves. Whenever there is light, solar energy is available.

SOLAR RADIATION COMPOSITION

ultraviolet

visible light 44%

infrared 53%

SOLAR CONSTANT

The amount of solar energy that bathes any surface area at any orientation can be determined by insolation data tables. The quantity of *insolation* (*incident solar radiation*) that should be expected to fall on collectors, windows, clotheslines, gardens, and the like can be calculated. Excellent data from the ASHRAE (American Society of Heating, Refrigerating, and Air Conditioning Engineers) *Handbook of Fundamentals* and other sources are available for surface angles at various latitudes, times of day, azimuth and altitude angles, and seasons. With this information you can determine the size and positioning of collectors and other solar-gain surfaces.

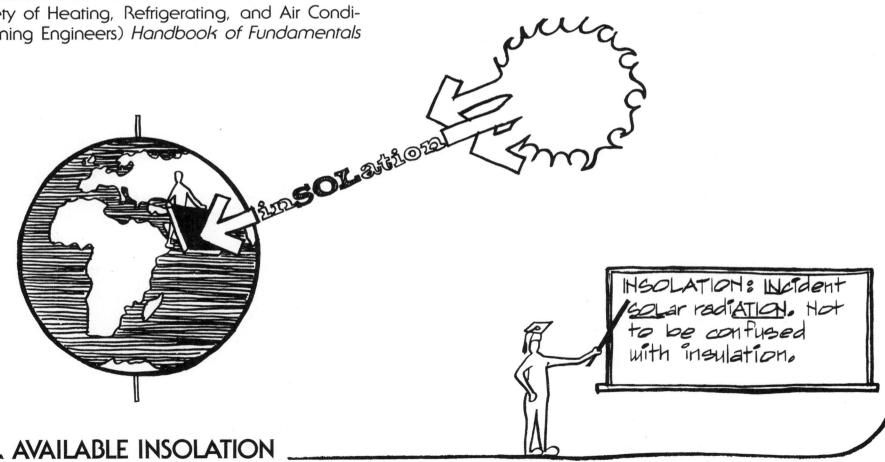

INSOLATION: INcident SOLar radiATION. Not to be confused with insulation.

AVAILABLE INSOLATION

Geographic location, which establishes sun angles and intensity due to latitude, determines the ideal amount of solar radiation available. In addition to this established figure, *percent of possible* must be considered before counting your solar eggs. In most locations throughout the world the percent of sun energy that annually reaches the ground will be considerably less than the amount possible with 365 clear days a year. Smog, cloud cover, dust, haze, and fog all reduce the usable solar radiation to between forty and ninety percent of the potential. It is important to determine the percent of possible sunshine factor for a given location before adding up your BTUs.

Location	% of Possible Sunshine/Year (%P)
Albuquerque	76
Boston	57
Chicago	59
Denver	67
Los Angeles	73
Miami	67
New York	59
Phoenix	85
Seattle	45

PERCENT OF POSSIBLE

Solar *orientation* is basic to passive design, but exact orientation is not too critical. Many factors affect collection, such as the weather, which can vary up to forty percent year to year. Deviation from true or solar south can vary 15° east or west, and the percentage of insolation decreases only two percent, leaving ninety-eight percent of the amount striking a south-facing vertical surface at winter solstice. But an orientation perpendicular to the sun's rays is the optimum orientation, and a tracking collector will maximize the capture of incoming energy. This is important for high-temperature systems, but is overkill for low-temperature passive systems. If perfect orientation is not possible and the energy is needed, simply increase collection area. For architectural applications, close is usually good enough.

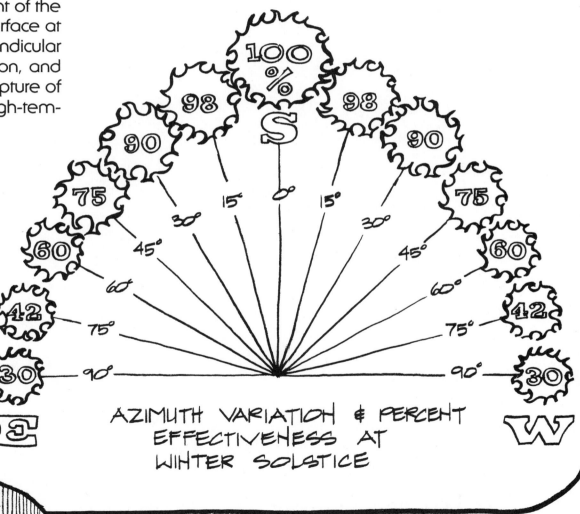

AZIMUTH VARIATION & PERCENT EFFECTIVENESS AT WINTER SOLSTICE

ORIENTATION

Interference with the sweep of sunshine as it traverses the sky is a factor to be considered in any building location. If, with luck, the sun makes a full day's pass with no *occlusion,* or interference, this factor is negligible, except for possible future building and tree growth. Most locations will have some shading to consider, particularly in winter, when the sun day is short and the sun's path is low in the sky. With excessive occlusion a site may be ruled out for solar use or solar surfaces might have to be sized larger or positioned differently.

The legal definition of solar rights and occlusion from neighboring properties, whether from natural growth or man-made objects, is an important concern. The use of sunlight should be a constitutional right; but this is a legal matter, ultimately determined by the courts.

OCCLUSION

Shading is an important aspect of occlusion. A plot of the *sunline* of any site can be made for each month by simple means. With a compass, transit or hand level, and sun path chart, you can plot the sunline and shadeline to determine how shading will affect the placement and solar gain of surfaces throughout the day and seasons. Trees, buildings, mountains, and so on will all cast shadows which may limit solar performance.

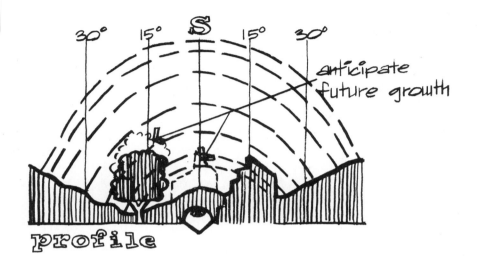

30° 15° S 15° 30°

anticipate future growth

profile

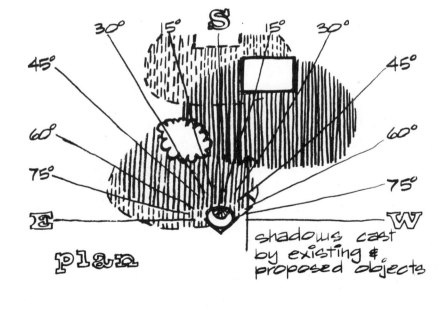

30° 15° S 15° 30°

45° 45°

60° 60°

75° 75°

E W

plan

shadows cast by existing & proposed objects

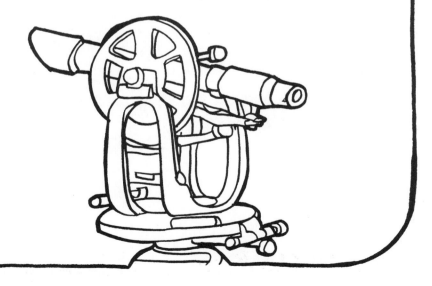

SUNLINE

At first glance, the geometry of solar architecture in relation to the solar angle seems clear cut—block the high summer sun and admit the low winter sun. Nature, however, complicates things a bit—we must compare seasonal demand to solar availability. The lowest point of the winter sun seems a likely place to aim a solar collector for winter heating, and this would be logical if the coldest day occured on December 21. The *weather* is generally not in time with solar intensity; it *lags* behind the sun by a month or two. Almost consistently, the coldest period occurs in January-March and the hottest in July-September. Consequently, if solar gain is maximized at winter solstice and minimized at summer solstice, the design will tend to overheat in late summer and underheat in late winter.

The weather will vary from year to year and season to season, so it is important to design for flexiblity to accommodate the fickle weather. Ideally, in a building most of the sun-angle geometry is fixed by architectural relationships, but fine tuning requires movable elements.

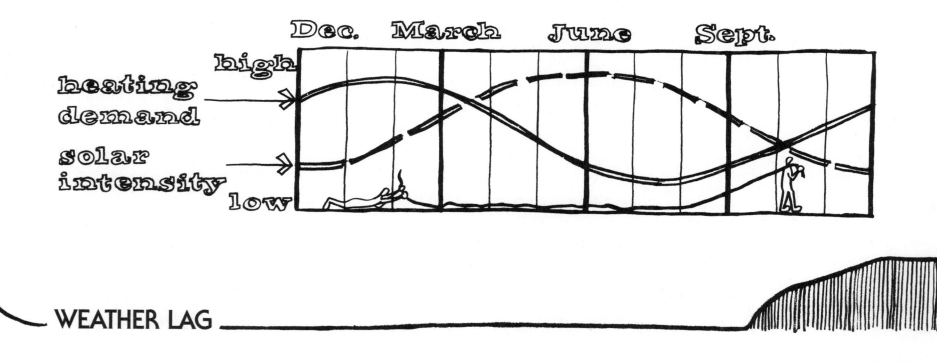

WEATHER LAG

Albedo is the ratio of reflected to received sunlight. This short-wave energy is similar to incoming energy from the sun and is significant in the total measurement of energy in many locations. The moon we see is a presentation of sunlight by albedo. Relfected sunlight from clouds, snow, sandy deserts, mountains, and bodies of water can be intensifying factors to the amount of energy received directly.

Reflectors use albedo when sunlight is bounced off them to solar-collection areas. Atmospheric scattering, earth *reflection* to space, and diffuse light are all albedo effects of sunlight reflected from atmospheric molecules. By capturing albedo we can get more than one hundred percent of the direct solar energy to a surface.

ALBEDO AND RELFECTION

Heat Loss

The loss of heat from a building is the villain which passive solar design attempts to control and balance. An effective solution requires an understanding of how a structure loses heat, how to control this loss, and how to offset the calculated *heat loss* with calculated heat gain. The methods of determining total heat loss are tried and true. Many manuals exist and most architects, engineers, and contractors are proficient in estimating normal heating demands of buildings. There is nothing mysterious about heat loss; you can figure out approximately how a building will function thermally before it is built. This step, though mathematically cumbersome, is a vital part of the design process.

The conventional heat-loss calculation method is to determine the average minimum outside daily temperature for the coldest period of the year, figure out how many BTUs will be lost from a building, and then install a heating system capable of maintaining a comfort level of 65 to 70°F (18 to 21°C). This is a reasonable approach if you can afford the gas, coal, oil, or electricity needed.

With passive solar design the approach is different. Conventional heating is relegated to the status of backup or auxiliary. The first concern is to design a structure that minimizes heat loss to the outside and eliminates wasted heat loss. When a satisfactory thermal tightness is attained, then solar heat gain and thermal storage are integrated to offset normal heating require-

ments. After the natural solar potential has been optimized, backup heating of active solar storage, wood stoves, or conventional heating can be sized for full tilt, ice-age cold spells when the sun doesn't shine for weeks. The most cost-effective idea is to provide partial backup until you experience the performance of the design and can determine what backup is actually needed.

FOR EMERGENCY ONLY

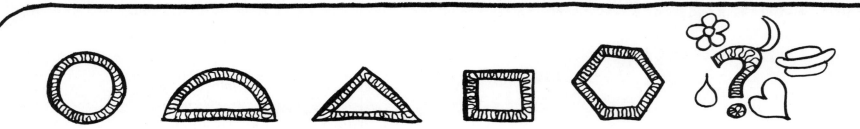

Each structure or complex of buildings has a *surface-to-volume* ratio. The less the exterior surface area to the interior volume, the lower the ratio. A low ratio indicates less heat-loss area per unit of usable space. A sphere is the geometric form with the least surface enclosing the maximum interior volume. Hemispheres, which sit nicely on the ground, make good sense thermally. However, domes, triangles, spheres, and question marks as forms do not necessarily make good use of materials, interior space, or money invested. Curved, triangulated, or bent surfaces are sometimes difficult to build, seal, and insulate. With rectangular or plane surfaces the goal is to minimize corners and joints. A building that is a simple box will have less heat loss for a given volume than a form with many corners, surfaces, and sides. Of course, simple box architecture may not fulfill functional needs and might be unpleasing to look at. The ideal approach for heating is to minimize the exterior surface area within functional, structural, and aesthetic requirements, whether on a single dwelling, multiunit complex, or urban scale.

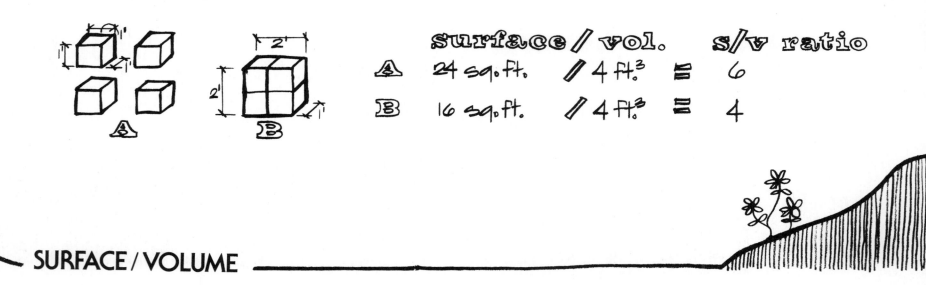

	surface	/	vol.		s/v ratio
A	24 sq. ft.	/	4 ft.³	≡	6
B	16 sq. ft.	/	4 ft.³	≡	4

SURFACE / VOLUME

The way in which a building intrudes upon the landscape and atmosphere will determine its thermal integrity. Each structure presents a profile to the world and the weather. Generally, the simpler the *profile,* the less its *exposure.* A well-insulated building with excessive profile can lose more heat per volume than a poorly insulated structure with a simple profile.

Profile is a combination of style, logic, structure, ego, function, and volume. Each building that is to have thermal integrity should reflect the climatic forces working on the land where it's sited. If a building is well designed, its profile will blend with the landscape and accommodate the weather.

Minimizing heat loss is one reason, and an important one, for simplifying exterior form. Minimum exposure to the north side where the sun never shines, burrowing into the surface of the earth to reduce outside surface area, orientating away from strong, cold prevailing winds and storms, and clustering structures—all of these help to reduce heat loss and satisfy an intuitive, yet often neglected, need for graceful repose on the land.

PROFILE AND EXPOSURE

Space acts as a void in the absence of thermal mass. Radiant heat tends to travel to voids or to places with less heat content. Consequently, heat that is radiated from an outside surface on earth will head for space and will keep going. Some radiation will be absorbed by the atmosphere before reaching outer space, but the greater portion will escape. At night, when the sun is not pouring solar energy onto the earth's surface, all surfaces radiate to deep space. Black and dark surfaces radiate best; light-colored surfaces radiate as well in the long wave, or infrared.

The clearer the night, the colder the outside temperature. This is due to *deep-space radiation.* Clouds act as a blanket inhibiting this radiant loss, absorbing some radiation from the earth and reflecting some back.

Nighttime loss of heat by radiation occurs throughout the year. Effective summer cooling can be accomplished by allowing mass surfaces to reradiate heat absorbed during the day to the night sky.

DEEP-SPACE RADIATION

Heat loss from a structure is affected by the climate and terrain factors acting on the site. These should be considered when selecting or designing for a particular building location.

chill factor—wind speed will make the effective or experienced temperature less than the actual thermometer reading, and is taken into account when establishing outside design temperatures

high altitude—greater altitude allows more deep-space radiation because the thin atmosphere allows radiative loss. High altitudes are usually colder

cloud cover—clouds, moisture content, pollution, and airborne particles act as insulation or a blanket, inhibiting radiation to space

terrain—cool air falls. Locating a building in a canyon or valley will allow colder air to flow around it

exposure—a building that is on the nonsolar side of a mountain or in the path of prevailing winds or storms will be more exposed to cold than one that is protected by hills or trees

moisture—damp air has a high heat-content capacity and will take more heat from around a structure than dry air

bodies of water—oceans and large lakes can act as heat sinks, containing more heat than land mass.

wind speed m.p.h.

thermometer temperature °F

	5	10	15	20	25	30	35	40	45	50
35	33	21	16	12	7	5	3	1	1	0
30	27	16	11	3	0	-2	-4	-4	-6	-7
25	21	9	1	-4	-7	-11	-13	-15	-17	-17
20	16	2	-6	-9	-15	-18	-20	-22	-24	-24
15	12	-2	-11	-17	-22	-26	-27	-29	-31	-31
10	7	-9	-18	-24	-29	-33	-35	-36	-38	-38
5	1	-15	-25	-32	-37	-41	-43	-45	-46	-47
0	-6	-22	-33	-40	-45	-49	-52	-54	-54	-56
-5	-11	-27	-40	-46	-52	-56	-60	-62	-63	-63
-10	-15	-31	-45	-52	-58	-63	-67	-69	-70	-70

CHILL FACTOR

COOLING EFFECTS

The term *degree days* (DD) is a convenient expression for denoting the annual heating or cooling demand in any climate. Historical temperature data are available for most areas where people build. To determine the degree days of heating, determine the temperature difference in degrees F between the interior [t = 65°F (18°C)] and the average outdoor temperature for each day of the year; then add these figures. This will give a quantative value for how cold a particular area is in relation to other places, and is a useful tool to let you know in what ballpark you are playing the solar game. In colder DD climates, extra insulation is required for successful designs. In climates with high DDs of cooling, insulation may be required only to keep heat out.

Location	Heating DD
Albuquerque	4348
Boston	5634
Chicago	6500
Denver	6283
Los Angeles	2061
Miami	214
New York	5000
Phoenix	1765
Seattle	5200

DEGREE DAYS

Design temperature, (to), for determining the temperature differential (Δt), is based on historical weather records, which are available for most climates through NOAA, United States Department of Commerce, Asheville, North Carolina. Temperature differential is the numerical indicator of the potential heat loss or gain through the fabric of a structure; and is the difference between inside design temperature, (ti), and the normal average low or high outside design temperature, (to).

For winter design conditions, interior temperatures range between 65 and 70°F (18 to 21°C). This is considered the normal comfort level. When you set your thermostat to a lower level, you are in fact changing the comfort level in order to save fuel.

Normal outside design temperatures vary widely by climatic zone. For each area, the (to) used by professionals for sizing heating and cooling systems takes into account day and night averages, chill factors, deep-space radiation, cloud cover, solar gain and intensity, and other climatic variables.

For heating:

$$\Delta t = t_i - t_o$$

$\Delta t =$ temperature differential

$t_i =$ interior temperature

$t_o =$ design temperature

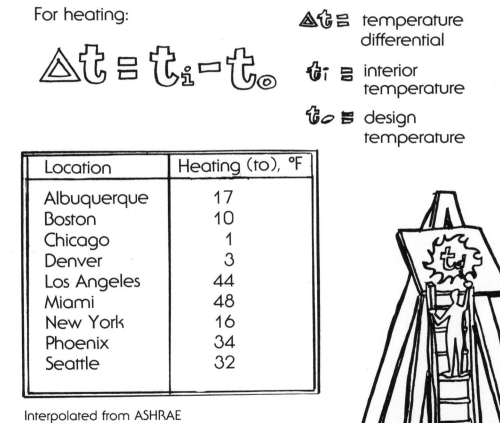

Location	Heating (to), °F
Albuquerque	17
Boston	10
Chicago	1
Denver	3
Los Angeles	44
Miami	48
New York	16
Phoenix	34
Seattle	32

Interpolated from ASHRAE *Handbook of Fundamentals*. Approximately 90% design conditions (design temperature that is satisfactory 90% of the time).

DESIGN TEMPERATURE

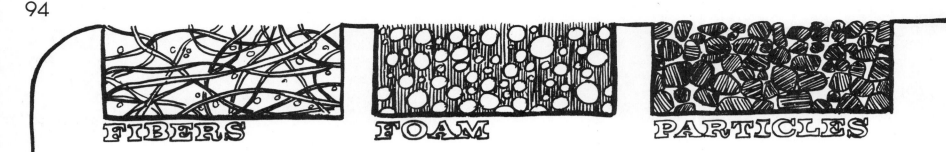

FIBERS **FOAM** **PARTICLES**

The *insulation* value of a *material* is primarily due to the quantity of air spaces or pockets separating the solid parts in the material. These air spaces stop the conductive transfer of heat directly through the material. The solid portion separating the voids should have a low heat conductivity. The more air spaces and the lower the conductivity of the solid between them, the better the insulation value.

The basic types of insulation are:

fibers—woven loosely to form a mat of materials with many air spaces, (fiber glass)

foam—air bubbles trapped in a solidified liquid like plastic (polyurethane, polystyrene)

particles—small pieces of material, loosely placed, allowing air spaces between (sawdust).

Insulation is used to keep heat out as well as in. Many materials can be used for insulation. Select the type suited to the job based on cost effectiveness, fire resistance, energy required to produce, structural practicality, ease of installation, and similar criteria.

Material	R/inch
polyurethane (expanded)	6.25
polystyrene (expanded)	5.26
cellulose (loose)	3.70
fiber glass (batt)	3.17
perlite (expanded)	2.70
cellular glass	2.50
earth (dry)	2.25
sawdust (loose)	2.22
wood (soft)	1.25
plywood	1.25
plaster	0.18
concrete	0.08
inside air film	0.62
outside air film	0.17

INSULATION MATERIALS

Every material in building has an *insulation value*. This value can be expressed as the coefficient of heat transfer (U) or the resistance to heat loss (R). These values are inversely proportional, or U = 1/R. The lower the U value, the better the insulation; the higher the R value, the better the resistance to heat loss. Resistance can also be expressed as the inverse of conductivity (K), or R = 1/K per inch of thickness.

Only R values are additive. Both U and K are absolute values for a given material, thickness, or composite and cannot be added to establish an overall value for a composite.

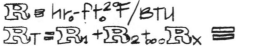

$$U = BTU/hr.-ft.^2 \, {}^\circ F$$
$$U_{total} = \frac{1}{R_{total}}$$

$$R = hr.-ft.^2 \, {}^\circ F/BTU$$
$$R_T = R_1 + R_2 \text{ to } R_x$$

$$K = BTU\text{-}in/hr.-ft.^2 \, {}^\circ F$$
$$\frac{1}{K_1} + \frac{1}{K_2} + \cdots \frac{1}{K_x}$$

Normally, these values can be found in tables stating r-per-inch thickness (t) or R per thickness given. Values for various materials, air spaces, air films, and so on are established, and can be used to calculate the coefficient of heat transfer for each heat-loss surface of a building. Tables are available in the ASHRAE *Handbook of Fundamentals* and other sources. Consulting a table is the first step in determining the heat loss or gain for the entire building.

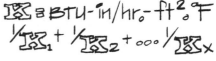

outside air film
1" wood siding
20# felt paper
5½" fiberglass batts
¾" plaster
inside air film

Material	Thickness	r	R	U
outside air	—	—	.62	
wood siding	1.0 in.	1.25	1.25	
felt paper	—	—	0.06	
fiber glass	5.5 in.	3.17	17.40	
plaster	.75 in.	0.18	.14	
inside air	—	—	.17	
TOTAL (Ur = 1/Rt) ——			19.7	0.05

INSULATION VALUES

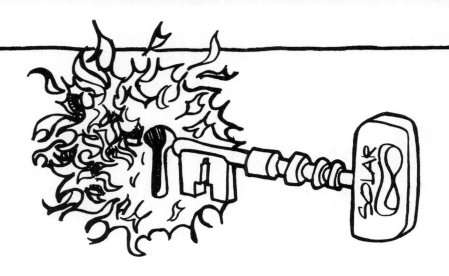

Wise response to daily and seasonal heating requirements is the key to passive solar comfort. *Flexible* or adjustable insulation of adequate resistance to heat flow should be provided for all exterior openings. Sliding-, folding-, blown-, or removable-insulation setups can be devised to prevent excessive heat loss or gain for any surface.

Ease of operation, durability, and visual appearance are as important as insulation value. Devices that are too large, cumbersome, or difficult to operate will inhibit proper usage. If a child can open and close shutters, chances are that the routine will become habitual and fun.

Seasonal operation of insulation devices may be needed only a few weeks or months each year depending on the climate. Shutters and panels can be removed and stored for much of the year. Flexible insulation can be manual or automated, but dutiful operation is necessary in order to attain optimum comfort and for the passive solar structure to be most effective.

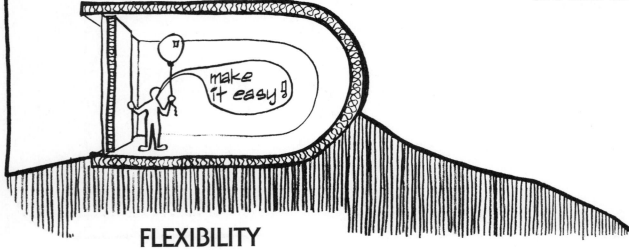

FLEXIBILITY

Flexible insulation can take many forms; select or devise the type most suitable to your design. Interior shades and shutters are less susceptible to the elements. Exterior devices can act as reflectors and may be required where thermal mass is adjacent to solar-gain surfaces.

A variety of winches, cords, pulleys, hinges, rollers, catches, and so forth that are commercially produced are suitable to a wide range of applications. Sailboat hardware is sturdy, weather resistant, and elegant. Door, window, and cabinet mechanisms suit many needs. Alternate-energy companies stock a variety of useful items. Your local building-supply store has many things that the manufacturer never imagined would meet your needs. Find something and try it!

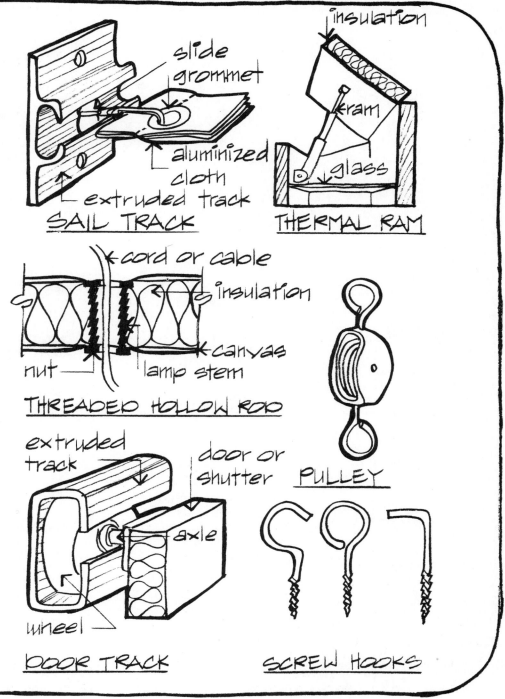

slide grommet

aluminized cloth

extruded track

SAIL TRACK

insulation

ram

glass

THERMAL RAM

cord or cable

insulation

canvas

nut   lamp stem

THREADED HOLLOW ROD

PULLEY

extruded track

door or shutter

axle

wheel

DOOR TRACK

SCREW HOOKS

HANDY HARDWARE

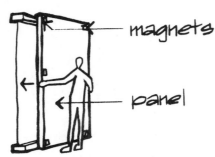

Nightwall

Foam panels, can be stored; attach with magnets to window frame.

Horizontal sliding

Sliding-door track stacks rigid panels to sides.

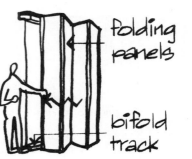

Horizontal folding

Bifold door action folds panels to side.

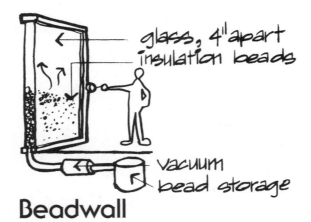

Beadwall

Foam beads are blown to fill double glass at night; emptied during the day.

Horizontal louver

Foam panels pivot open and closed.

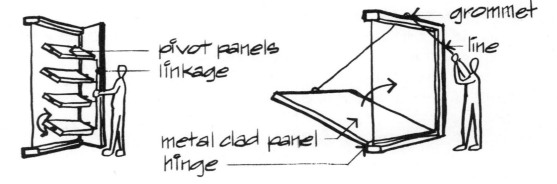

Bottom hinged

Outside reflective panel is pulled up; shut at night.

INSULATION DEVICES THAT MOVE

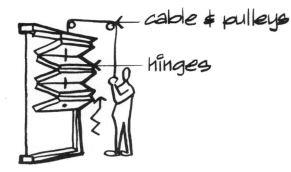

cable & pulleys

hinges

Vertical folding

Rigid panels fold up
to ceiling and down
to floor.

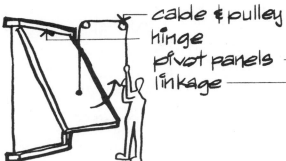

cable & pulley
hinge
pivot panels
linkage

Top hinged

Rigid panel hinges
up to ceiling.

Vertical louver

Foam panels pivot
open and closed.

overhead track
panels on
rollers

spring

Overhead rolling

Panels roll up to
or into ceiling.

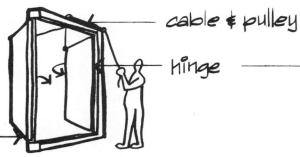

cable & pulley

hinge

Exterior side hinged

Outside reflective
panel is pulled in to
shut at night.

Interior side hinged

Rigid panel hinges
open to adjoining
wall.

MORE DEVICES

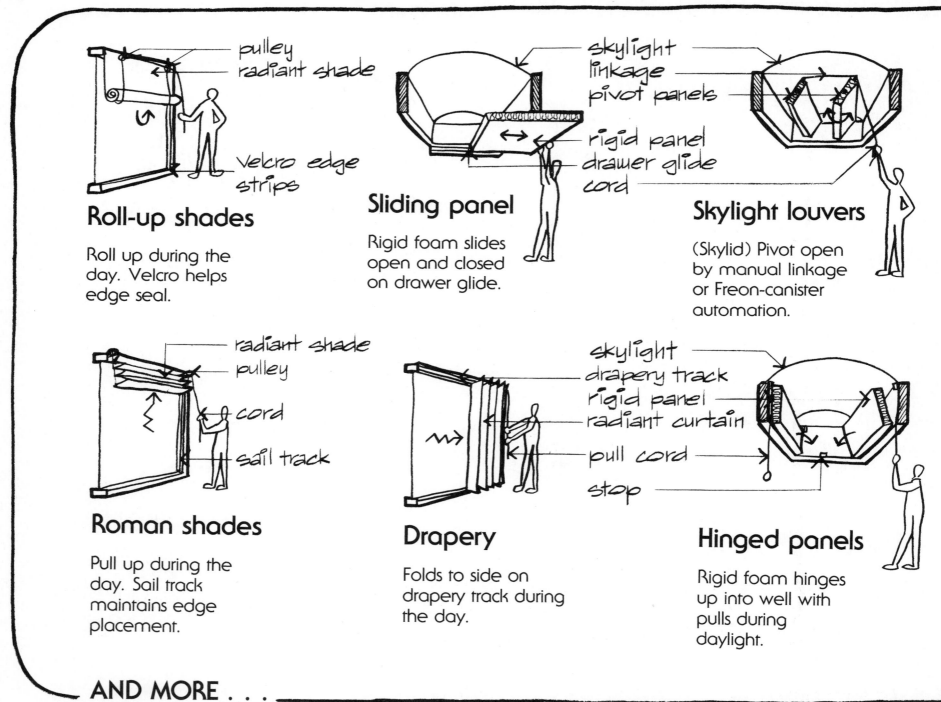

Roll-up shades

pulley
radiant shade
Velcro edge strips

Roll up during the day. Velcro helps edge seal.

Sliding panel

skylight
linkage
pivot panels
rigid panel
drawer glide
cord

Rigid foam slides open and closed on drawer glide.

Skylight louvers

(Skylid) Pivot open by manual linkage or Freon-canister automation.

Roman shades

radiant shade
pulley
cord
sail track

Pull up during the day. Sail track maintains edge placement.

Drapery

skylight
drapery track
rigid panel
radiant curtain
pull cord
stop

Folds to side on drapery track during the day.

Hinged panels

Rigid foam hinges up into well with pulls during daylight.

AND MORE . . .

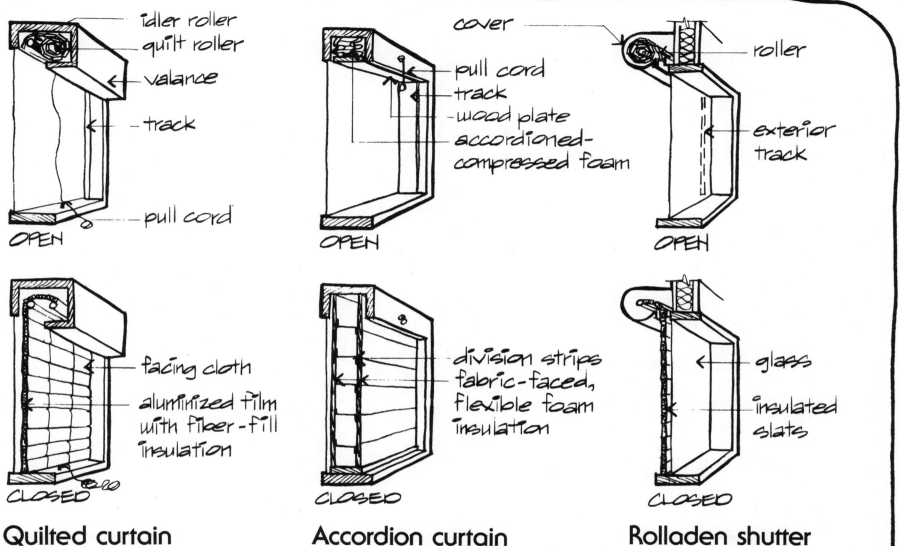

Quilted curtain

Rolls up during the day into valance.
Track holds edges in place.

Accordion curtain

Outer layers of foam compress and fold upward into valance during the day.

Rolladen shutter

Traditional in Europe, foam-filled metal slats insulate, shade, and secure window.

AND MORE

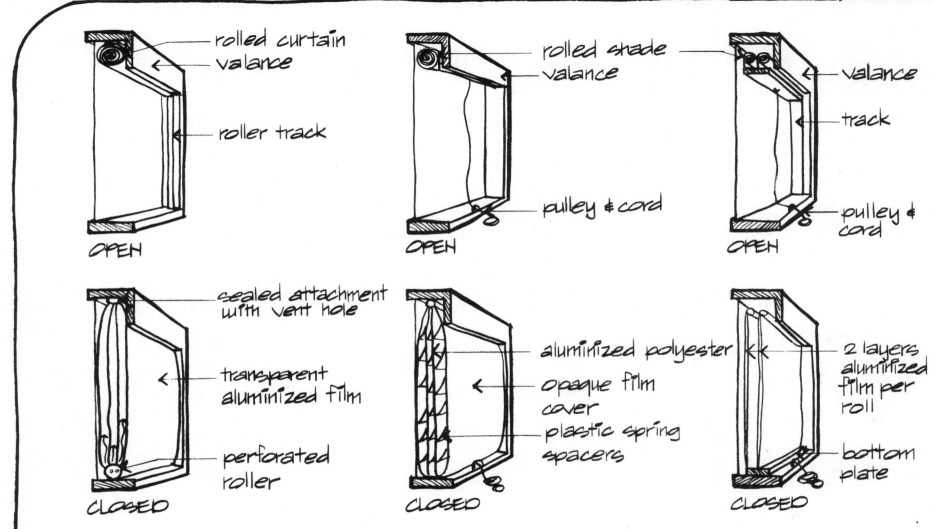

rolled curtain
valance

roller track

OPEN

rolled shade
valance

pulley & cord

OPEN

valance

track

pulley & cord

OPEN

sealed attachment
with vent hole

transparent
aluminized film

perforated
roller

CLOSED

aluminized polyester

opaque film
cover

plastic spring
spacers

CLOSED

2 layers
aluminized
film per
roll

bottom
plate

CLOSED

Self-inflating curtain

Layers of transparent film inflate automatically by convection when completely lowered.

Spring curtain

Pull down to insulate. Layers of radiant film are held apart by plastic spring spacers.

Multiroller shade

Ganged roller shades pull down at night.

STILL MORE

The *Thermos bottle* analogy is useful in understanding the goal of thermally tight structures. A Thermos bottle has a good surface-to-volume ratio, excellent insulation, tight seals at openings, a radiant barrier, and minimum doors and windows!

If a Thermos bottle is filled with enough thermal mass, such as apple cider, and is opened to the direct sun with the opening covered by a transparent membrane, heat will enter and warm the liquid. If you cover the opening with an insulated top, when the sun goes away it will be possible to have solar-warmed apple cider at all times.

It is also possible to reverse this procedure to keep the apple cider cool. By closing it during the day in a shady spot and then opening it up and exposing it to the cold night sky, you can have cold apple cider whenever you wish without refrigeration.

The same principle holds true for buildings: a well-designed, flexible, and thermally proportioned structure can maintain a comfortable temperature throughout the year in most climates.

thermal mass
radiant barrier
outer skin
insulation

seal

Where's the vacuum?

glazing

tap

THERMOS BOTTLE

Doors and windows are culprits responsible for considerable heat loss from structures. Because they open, have cracks around them, and are made of lightweight or transparent materials, they lose much heat by steady state and infiltration. Shutters are useful for insulating windows. However, doors do not facilitate the use of shutters. Instead, double sets of doors can be used in cold or hot climates to insulate and isolate the interior from the weather. An *air lock* is the space between two doors. In winter, when one door is opened, all of the heated air inside the rest of the building is not lost to the outside. Air locks also make excellent mud rooms for stamping off boots, removing heavy clothing, and storing outside gear. A greenhouse can act as an air lock. In hot climates an air lock will help keep interior spaces cool.

Air locks are used in submarines and space vehicles to keep from losing vital support substances. Today, the energy for heating and cooling buildings is valuable, and air locks help retain the invested energy.

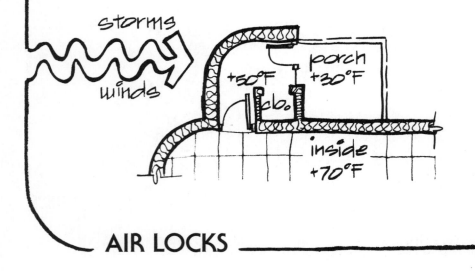

storms
winds

+50°F   porch +30°F

inside +70°F

AIR LOCKS

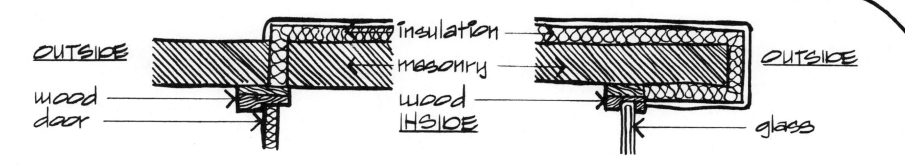

Thermal bridges to the outside are another consideration to be dealt with when designing a thermally tight building. Beams, walls, floor slabs, foundations, and the like should be insulated from the outside. An otherwise well-insulated house can lose a tremendous amount of heat by conduction through materials that are not properly separated from the outside.

A *thermal break* does the trick. For example, windows with metal frames and insulating glass can lose more heat by conduction through the metal frame than through the double glass! This should be avoided by using wood window frames or by insulating the metal frame's interior from its exterior. Even a relatively small air space, membrane, or insulation layer will help to break the thermal conductivity of concrete and masonry walls, steel or concrete beams, floor slabs, and so on.

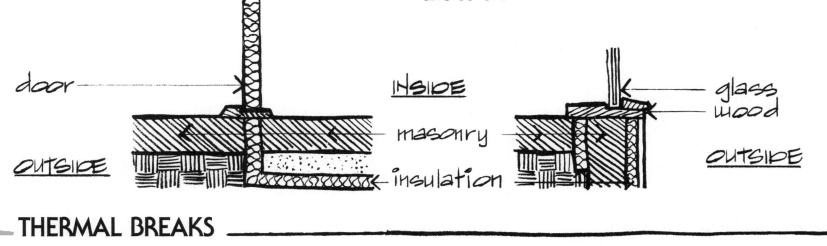

THERMAL BREAKS

A *radiant barrier* can act as the first line of defense against heat loss. A reflective metallic coating, such as aluminum, chrome, or silver, will reflect long-wave radiation. In passive solar design, radiation from heat-storage mass is the main heating mode. Conduction and convection are always present, but radiation to and from surfaces is what primarily affects comfort. To contain the heat within a building a combination of insulative materials and radiant barriers works best. Many conventional insulations have one reflective surface. Fire-fighting clothing is metalized to reflect the heat of fire, preventing it from reaching the cloth fabric and skin. Thermos bottles are reflectively coated on the inside of the glass container.

A radiant barrier with an air space in front of it can reflect up to ninety-five percent of long-wave heat energy before this heat is absorbed by insulation or glass and conducted to the outside. It is difficult to determine exactly how effective radiant barriers are because of the many factors involved. It appears that an air space bounded by aluminum foil will increase the thermal resistance approximately two and a half times, indicating that a ¼-inch (0.63 cm.) air space (r = 1.0), when lined with foil, attains an r equal to 2.5. It follows, therefore, that a curtain of four ¼-inch air spaces between layers of foil would have an R of 10.0! Radiant barriers are a valuable tool indeed!!!

RADIANT BARRIERS

Clear glass, which transmits up to eighty-seven percent of available solar energy and retains almost all the reradiated long-wave heat, is made from sand, one of nature's most common materials. Single glass has a resistance to heat loss (R) of 0.88. With double glazing R = 1.72; with triple glazing R = 2.77. However, each successive glazing layer reduces the amount of entering solar energy.

In addition to double glass, other materials have been and are being developed to transmit solar energy and yet attain significantly better R values. They include:

transparent foam—comprised of many tiny bubbles, which allow solar energy to penetrate and inhibit conductive loss back out through a maze of air spaces (R = 2.5 and above)

heat mirror—glass or plastic with a transparent, metallic, reflective coating on the inside of the exterior layer, adjacent to a dead-air space, preventing up to ninety-eight percent of reradiation and attaining an R of up to 4.0

film layers—polymers or plastics with high solar transmission that can be evenly spaced to create several air spaces; with solar transmissions of eighty percent, R values of 4.5 can be achieved

one-way transmission materials—prisms or concentration cells that allow the sun's energy to enter, trapping it to the inside in a way similar to primitive fish traps; R values of 3.0 and greater can be realized.

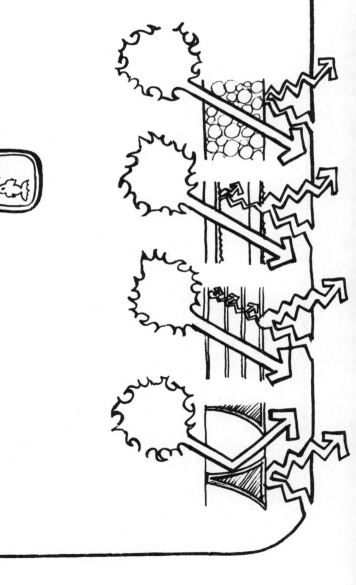

INSULATIVE-TRANSMISSION SURFACES

The *steady-state heat loss* from a building or space is the heat that is continually being lost through the exterior fabric. Each exterior surface (roofs, walls, windows, perimeters of slabs, floors) can be given a coefficient of heat transfer or insulation value (U). By multiplying this U value by the total surface area (A), by the temperature differential (Δt), and by the time in hours (h), the heat loss for each area (Qhl) can be calculated. This loss can be totaled per hour, day, or season, but is usually done on a 24-hour basis.

$$U \times A \times \Delta t \times h = Q_{hl}$$

pronounced delta tee

$U \equiv$ coefficient of heat transfer, BTU/hr./sq.ft./°F

$A \equiv$ area, sq.ft.

$\Delta t \equiv$ temperature differential, °F

$h \equiv$ time, hours

$Q_{hl} \equiv$ heat loss, BTUs

If heat loss is calculated through the floor or basement walls, the (Δt) changes. Temperatures below ground vary with location from 45 to 75°F (7 to 24°C); they are generally higher than winter outside temperatures.

STEADY-STATE LOSS

Room-by-room calculation is a convenient way to keep organized, check your figures, and size the heating requirements for each room. When the heat loss for each exterior surface area is determined, all the losses are added for a total heat loss value (Qhlt). It is this total loss that must be compensated for by some heat input (Qin), either conventional or solar, to maintain thermal comfort within a space. Many spaces may generate heat of their own; human bodies give off heat, as well as cookstoves, lights, refrigerator motors, and computers. The list goes on.

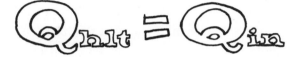

$$Q_{hlt} = Q_{in}$$

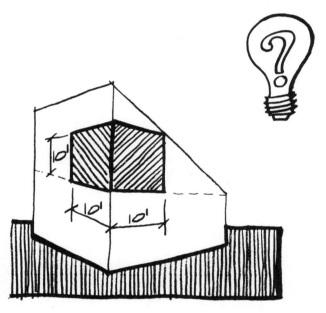

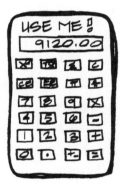

Example:

Assume a room with 200 sq. ft. of exterior wall area. The wall has a U value of 0.05, the outside design temperature is 32°F, the inside design temperature is 70°F, and length of time is one day, or 24 hours. So—

U = 0.05 BTU/hr./sq.ft./°F
A = 200 sq.ft.
Δt = 70° − 32° = 38°F
h = 24 hours/day

Qhl = U × A × Δt × h
  = 0.05 × 200 × 38 × 24
  = 9,120 BTU/day

Follow this procedure for each heat-loss surface in a space, and add them up. Then do each room the same way. Add up the room loss total for every room and you have a total steady-state loss for the building and are ready to tackle infiltration loss!

Buildings lose more heat at *night* than during the *day*. During the winter when the sun shines, solar gain adds heat energy. However, heat continues to be lost to the outside. Solar gain surfaces, such as windows, clerestories, and skylights, should be insulated when the sun doesn't shine to minimize heat loss. It is important when calculating heat loss to evaluate solar-gain surfaces differently than normal, steady-state, heat-loss surfaces. Windows, which are insulated during the night and overcast periods, can be assumed to be uninsulated and lose more heat during solar collection time. If solar energy is available for

8 hours during a winter day, the calculations should reflect 8 hours uninsulated and 16 hours insulated.

Example:

Assume a 20 sq.ft. window is insulated 16 hours per day, with 2-inch polyurethane shutters clad with ⅛-inch plywood and a 1-inch dead-air space. Using the data below, the losses are:

U uninsulated	=	.58 BTU/hr./sq.ft.°F
U insulated	=	.06 BTU/hr./sq.ft.°F
A	=	20 sq.ft.
Δt	=	45°F

Q	= $U \times A \times \Delta t \times h$	
Q day	= $.58 \times 20 \times 45 \times 8$ =	4,176 BTU
Q night	= $.06 \times 20 \times 45 \times 16$ =	864 BTU
Total daily loss, Qhl		5,040 BTU

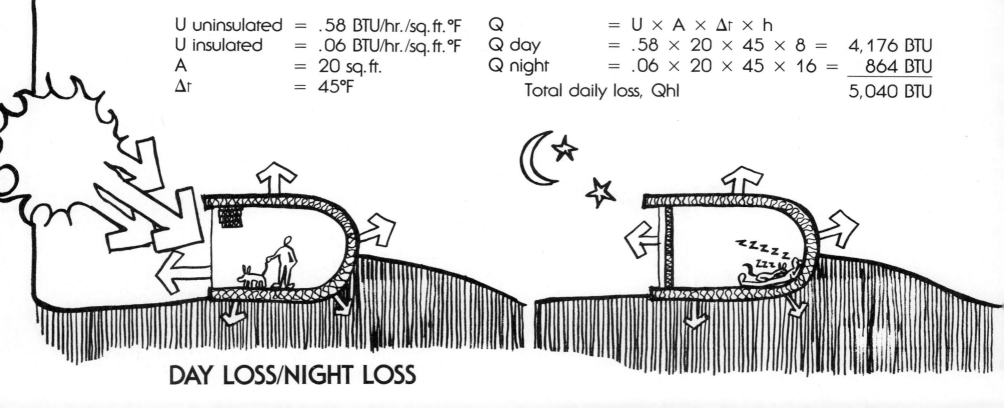

DAY LOSS/NIGHT LOSS

Heat loss due to air *infiltration* and air exchange is different from steady-state heat loss of a structure. Infiltration occurs at all cracks in a building and is due to pressure differences between the outside and inside, caused primarily by wind and temperature differentials. It is important to construct a building as tight as practical, by minimizing the number of cracks and by caulking all the joints where materials meet. Using doors and windows with good weatherstripping helps.

Building paper and vapor barriers reduce leakage through walls and roofs. Wind forcing air into a building on one side will force air out on the opposite side. Use of storm windows and good sealants, and reduced window area facing prevailing winds, all help control infiltration. Altitude, wind speed, and building height are factors that also affect the infiltration rate. Let it suffice that these factors are included in the generalized air-change-per-hour table.

Air change is the amount of room air which is exhausted and replaced by reconditioned or fresh air. Burning fireplaces, open doors and windows, mechanical exhaust fans, and similar conditions all contribute to the exchange. Some air change is required to provide air to breathe and to clear odors and smoke. The point is to minimize unneeded air exchange.

INFILTRATION

The *crack method* of calculating the infiltration is to sum all the lengths of crack around windows and doors and then multiply this total by a factor rating the tightness of type of crack. This method is questionable, since the factors are based upon subjective evaluation of the tightness of each crack, while leakage through the walls and other places is neglected.

Surfaces with exterior doors and windows	0	1	2	3
number of air changes per hour, h	.33	.66	1.0	1.33

$$Q_i = A_{hc} \times V \times \Delta t \times h \times n$$

Q_i = infiltration heat loss, BTU

A_{hc} = air heat capacity = 0.018 BTU/ft.^{3}/°F

V = space volume, cubic feet (ft.^{3})

Δt = temperature differential, °F

h = time of loss, hours

n = number of air changes per hour

The *air exchange method* applies a general factor to each space based upon the number of exterior surfaces with windows, doors, or skylights. This method factors in all typical leaks, and external effects with the exception of ventilation. The air-change-per-hour chart shown above assumes double glazing and good weatherstripping. By this method, the heat loss by infiltration for a space (Qi) is equal to the heat capacity of air (Ahc = 0.018 BTU/ft.^{3}/°F) (0.00029 cal/cm^3/°C), multiplied by the space volume (V) in cubic feet, times the temperature differential (Δt), by the time (h) in hours, and the number of air changes per hour (n).

AIR-CHANGE METHODS

skylight
window
900 ft.³

anc $= 0.018$ BTU/ft³/°F
V $= 900$ cubic ft.
Δt $= 70° - 25° = 45°F$
h $= 24$ hours
n $= 1.0$

Follow this procedure for each room or space, add each value for steady-state and infiltration loss together, total the whole can of worms, and you've calculated the entire heat loss of the building!

Example:

Determine the daily infiltration loss of a room having a volume of 900 cubic feet, a window on one exterior wall, and a skylight on the roof (ntotal = 1.0). The interior design temperature is 70°F and the outside temperature is 25°F.

$$Qi = anc \times V \times \Delta t \times h \times n$$
$$= 0.018 \times 900 \times 45 \times 24 \times 1.0$$
$$= 17,496 \text{ BTU/day}$$

$Q_{i(1)} + Q_{i(2)} + Q_{i(3)} + Q_{i(4)} + ? + ? + ?$

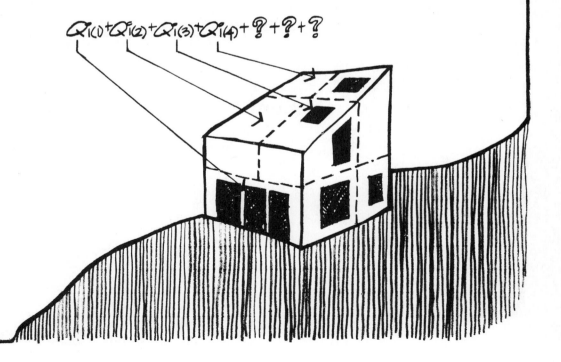

Traditionally, winter heat-loss calculations have been gross estimates and relatively simple approximations of the actual thermal performance of buildings. This has often been compensated for by oversizing heating units and, thus, the energy consumed to maintain comfort—an expedient approach due to the relative low cost of heating equipment and fuel. Summer cooling or heat-gain calculations, on the other hand, have been more sophisticated and complex, taking into account a wider range of thermal factors because air cooling is more expensive than winter heating.

With a new emphasis being placed on life-cycle cost of systems and the accompanying concern for fine tuning our ability to efficiently space condition buildings, new procedures will develop for more accurate determination of the actual year-round thermal performance. This will be of particular importance for passive structures.

One approach which should be updated and applied to annual analysis is the *sol-air effect,* or the calculation of solar radiation on, and air temperature at, a building's weatherskin. (See the *ASHRAE Handbook of Fundamentals,* 1981, page 265.) This procedure takes into account a number of factors:

—solar radiation on all building surfaces
—outside air temperature with relation to time of day and solar position
—building orientation
—exterior materials with relation to thermal mass, conductivity, color, texture, and movable insulation
—shading on all surfaces
—window placement.

SOL-AIR EFFECT

During cooling periods the sol-air calculations indicate the net heat gain into a building. This gain must be removed to maintain comfort. An interior design temperature for cooling is usually 75 to 80°F (24 to 27°C).

For heating periods sol-air calculations will usually total a net heat loss which is less than the steady-state and infiltration loss totals for a given 24-hour period. By subtracting the sol-air loss from the steady-state loss, the radiation effect on the weatherskin is known. By adding the direct gain through the solar collection surfaces to this sol-air radiation value, we have a good idea of the total solar-radiation impact on the building.

The important implication of sol-air analysis, other than determination of the thermal performance of a given building, is its usefulness in analyzing building shape, orientation, materials, and window placement suitable for best year-round performance for each site. Sol-air tables and charts facilitate schematic design analysis prior to actual design development—a valuable tool indeed.

Through dynamic sol-air analyses involving complex calculations, it can be proved that in most climate zones the optimum year-round solar orientation is slightly east of south.

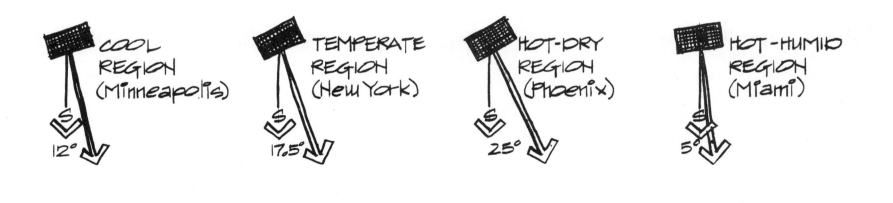

COOL REGION (Minneapolis) S 12° TEMPERATE REGION (New York) S 17.5° HOT-DRY REGION (Phoenix) S 25° HOT-HUMID REGION (Miami) S 5°

Calculating heat loss from a building is a well-established engineering procedure. Much is known about thermal phenomena. However, the procedure is fairly complicated, and it involves enough options and subjective decisions that no two analysts will come up with exactly the same total heat loss for the same building in the same location.

The goal is to be thorough and close to the potential performance of a given building. The values, tables, and charts for design temperatures are based on historical average weather and climate conditions. The weather as we experience it is seldom average. Floods, drought, severe cold, mild winters, hot summers, rainfall, and so on all conspire to elude normalcy. The world's weather is in constant flux and gradual change. Given these parameters, heat loss and thermal performance are at best calculated and educated estimates.

Use a consistent procedure and format for calculations. A checklist is a handy visual aid outline to help organize the process.

CALCULATING

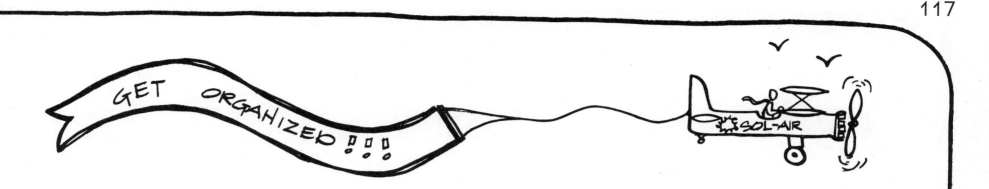

Heat Loss Checklist:

☐ 1. Determine inside and outside design temperatures and temperature differential (Δt).

☐ 2. Establish U values for each heat-loss surface.

☐ 3. Calculate area of each heat-loss surface.

☐ 4. Calculate steady-state heat loss for all surfaces. (Don't forget day loss/night loss and sol-air effect.)

☐ 5. Total steady-state heat loss (Qhlt).

☐ 6. Calculate volumes of rooms or spaces.

☐ 7. Select appropriate air-change factors.

☐ 8. Calculate infiltration heat loss by air-change method for each room or zone (Qi). (Is the sol-air effect useful?)

☐ 9. Total infiltration heat loss for building (Qit).

☐ 10. Sum steady-state and infiltration heat losses (Qhlt + Qit).

☐ 11. Evaluate total loss and reconsider loss areas and space volumes; are better insulation, fewer windows, and reduced volumes necessary? Revise if necessary.

☐ 12. You have now conquered heat loss. Treat yourself, lie back, and gloat before tackling solar gain, thermal storage, and auxiliary.

"trapped" within the space. This collected heat can be stored in a thermal mass to heat the interior, eventually to be lost through the envelope of the structure.

It is important to remember that although a structure may collect, trap, and store radiant energy, at the same time normal infiltration and conductive losses occur through solar-gain surfaces; and these losses must be considered in thermal calculations.

The *greenhouse effect,* which traps radiant energy, allows high interior temperatures in an automobile with its windows closed and heater off on a clear, cold day.

Heat Gain

The incoming radiation from the sun is primarily short-wave, high-temperature energy. Interior objects absorb this short-wave radiation and emit long-wave, or infrared, low-temperature radiation. A minor portion of these emitted long waves radiate back and strike the glass, heating it. The glass then reradiates this heat energy in all directions. Consequently, most of the heat is

GREENHOUSE EFFECT _____

In passive solar design terminology, more descriptive than solar home, solar energized, or sun heated is the term *suntempered*. The idea of orienting and shaping a structure to take advantage of seasonal sun angles and intensities, thus providing required heating, cooling, ventilation, and light, is basic. Suntempering is simply a design form which in winter allows the sunlight to penetrate and store and in summer blocks out the sun and permits ventilation, optimizing the natural solar potential.

The climate and weather of any location will dictate the type, amount, and flexibility of suntempering required. This is an attitude of accommodating and adjusting to the patterns of nature.

SUNTEMPERING

The size of a collection surface is dependent on several interacting factors. Basically, the type and size of a collector should be adequate to absorb and store the amount of heat energy required to make up for the daily average winter heat loss (Qhlt) of a building. In order to store energy for nonsolar days, more than make-up heat should be collected; a factor of 1.25 will allow a storage bonus of twenty-five percent each day the sun shines. In four days collection, a full day of reserve is stored. If a collection system is fifty percent efficient (e), transferring only half of the energy it receives (Qs) into storage, the *collector area* (Ac) must be increased accordingly to deliver the required amount of heat into storage.

Direct-gain systems deliver a maximum quantity of heat to a space. With adequate storage and insulation, this type of system will require the least collection area. Still, the idea of collecting a daily surplus is important. Excess heat can be eliminated by ventilation.

Q_s solar

collect store loss

transfer

$$A_c = \frac{Q_{hlt} \times 1.25}{Q_s \times e}$$

$Q_{hlt} \times 1.25$ distribute

Q_{hlt} = daily loss, BTUs

Q_s = daily solar available, BTUs/sq. ft.

e = system efficiency

A_c = collector area, sq. ft.

COLLECTOR AREA

Direct gain is allowing the sunlight to enter into a space before being intercepted. Greenhouses, solar floor/wall systems, and skylights are examples. Many people cannot tolerate direct sunlight for long—when designing, it is necessary to provide some shaded areas that allow relief from direct radiant energy. Some direct gain lends bright, sunny, green, fresh, and warm space to any building. Direct gain facilitates equal heat distribution throughout the thermal envelope.

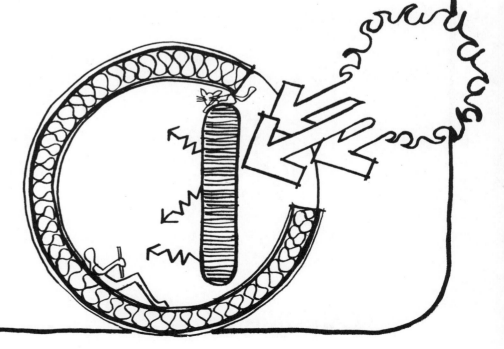

Indirect gain is the interception of the sun's energy before it enters the space. Solar masonry walls, water walls, collectors, Skytherm roofs, and the like are all indirect-gain systems. Allowance might be required to assure balanced distribution throughout the interior.

DIRECT AND INDIRECT

Virtually an infinite combination of collector positions are possible. The task is to select and integrate the type and placement that will be most suitable for the system.

Orientation for heating: the closer to perpendicular a collection surface is to the sun, the better the collection potential. However, for practicality, vertical surfaces are less likely to leak or cause troublesome glare and are structurally more economical. Orientation should be designed for best sun incidence. Thermal storage can be placed to take advantage of morning, midday, or afternoon sun.

Rooms have different patterns—morning sun is best for bedrooms, midday for greenrooms, afternoon for living areas. Normally, a collector area of twenty-five to fifty percent of the total floor area will be adequate, depending on local climate factors and the weatherskin.

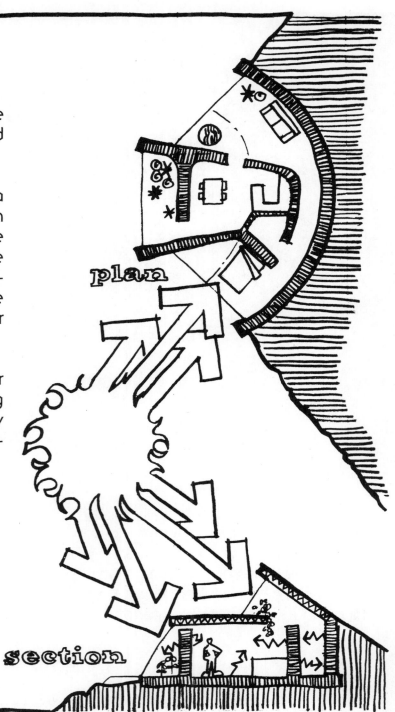

POSITIONING

Tilt for heating: an angle of latitude plus 15° is generally best for space heating. This optimizes collection and minimizes reflection. A deviation of up to 20° above or below this ideal angle will reduce insolation by less than ten percent.

For domestic year-round water heating, a tilt angle equal to the latitude is generally ideal. If winters are severe, aiming more toward the winter sun position with a steeper sun angle can be helpful. A rule of thumb is to plan ¾ to 1½ sq. ft. of collector per gallon of hot water capacity (or 0.02 to 0.04 sq.m per liter). Use of a heat exchanger will increase the collector area needed by about twenty-five percent. Twenty gallons (75L) of hot water per person per day is a reasonable consumption rate.

The same positioning angles apply to a solar window or any solar-collection surface.

latitude +up to 15°

The integration of a *greenhouse* or greenroom in an existing or new structure is a delightful solution to passive solar design. Freshened air, fragrant odors, and humidity, as well as heat gain, are all products of a well-designed space for planting, playing, and enjoying. When acting as a solar collector, a large portion of the collected heat energy can be transferred to the living space. A heat-storage mass between the living/green areas can effectively store heat if insulated by movable panels during sunless periods. It is important to use radiant Space Blanket-type shades for winter insulation and summer shading if required. High vents can exhaust hot summer air.

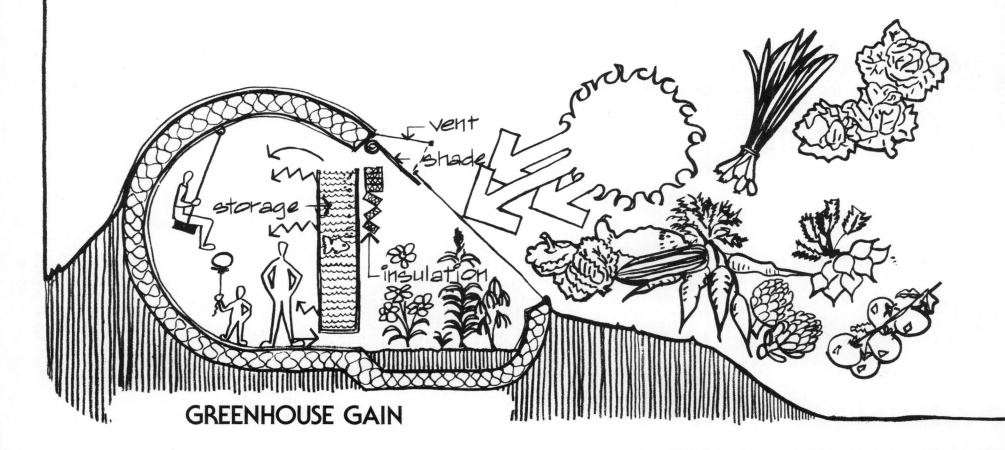

GREENHOUSE GAIN

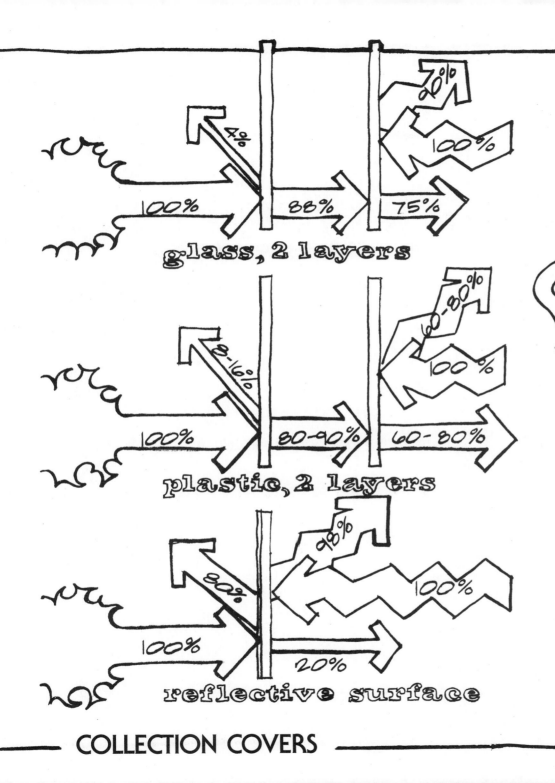

glass, 2 layers

4%
100%
88%
75%
100%
7%

plastic, 2 layers

2-16%
100%
80-90%
60-80%
100%
0-80%

reflective surface

80%
100%
98%
100%
20%

The sunlight-transmitting material which *covers* a solar window or collector is a subject that should be well studied. Before committing yourself, consider many factors, such as:

—initial cost
—life expectancy
—life cycle cost
—solar transmission, transparency, or translucency
—insulation value
—greenhouse trap effect
—resistance to damage
—thermal expansion
—ease of cleaning
—ease of installation and replacement
—maintenance
—visual appearance

COLLECTION COVERS

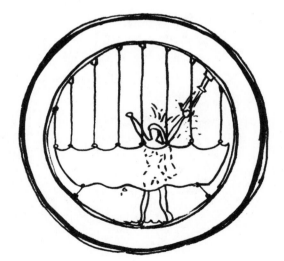

A multitude of coverings exists. The basic materials are glass or plastics, with the following general categories and qualities:

glass—permanent, transparent, ageless, breaks; generally a good choice

plastic film—ages, subject to weather damage, inexpensive, temporary

plastic sheet—ages, expands, expensive, scratches, break resistant

fiber glass—ages, expands, flexible, translucent, economical

transparent foam—ages, opaque, insulative, lower solar transmission.

TIPS

—Double coverings should be used in most climates, except where temperature differences between inside and outside are modest. In severe climates, triple coverings may be cost effective. An air space of approximately ½ inch (1.3 cm) between each layer will prevent convection and reduce heat loss.

—Caulking is important to reduce heat loss by infilitration.

— Most plastics do not trap long-wave radiation as well as glass—only ultraviolet-resistant types have any permanence. High temperatures as reached by flat-plate collector surfaces can damage plastics. Some special greenhouse/solar fiber glass has optical properties nearly equal to glass.

—Low-iron-content glass is preferred for solar transmission. It is relatively expensive and thus not cost effective. Reinforced or tempered glass is best for sloping or horizontal surfaces.

—Wood frames and mullions are preferable, as they lose much less heat by conduction than does metal.

—The space between homemade double glazing should be vented to prevent condensation.

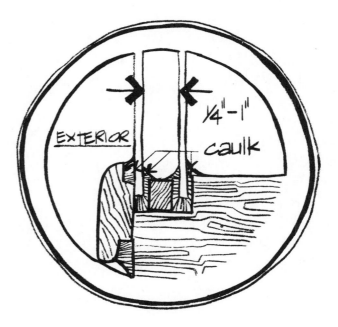

EXTERIOR

¼"–1"

caulk

In most passive-design schemes, the three means of *heat transfer* will be a part of the total method of heat gain. Convection occurs in air and water, conduction through solids, and radiation everywhere. The trick is to accommodate and integrate each to prevent overheating, cold spots, hot spots, discomfort, or wasted energy.

The transfer of heat normally requires some energy when moving or changing state. The least amount of exchange or transfer of solar heat gain is the most efficient, though possibly not the most suitable or comfortable.

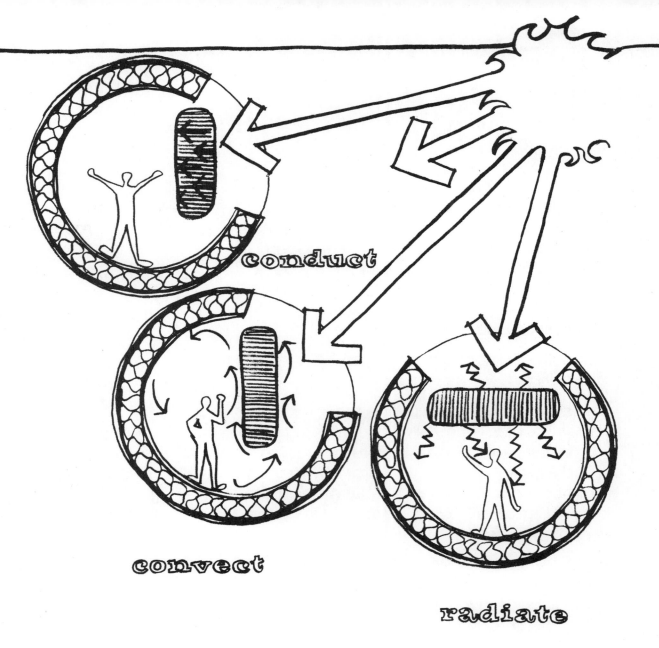

conduct

convect

radiate

GAIN TRANSFER

Heat *stratification* is the layering of temperature in a liquid, or gaseous volume; heat rises and causes higher temperatures at the top and cooler temperatures at the bottom. The tendency for heat to stratify can be nicely integrated into many passive designs. Indirect heating can be affected by allowing heat energy to flow by conduction, convection, and radiation to spaces not struck by sunlight. This type of thermal gradient can be easily controlled by ventilation and is particularly suited to heat low-activity or night-use areas, such as living and sleeping rooms.

STRATIFICATION

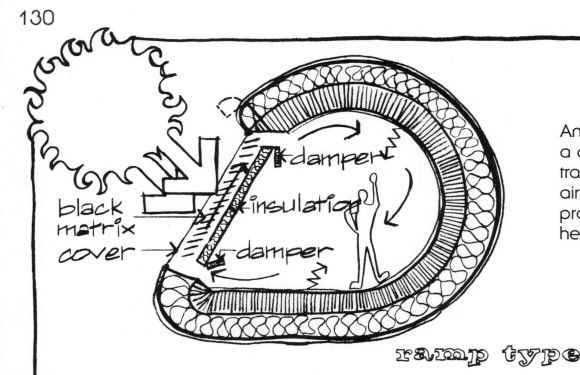

black matrix cover

damper

insulation

damper

ramp type

An open *convection*-collector *loop* system allows a dark surface, plate, or matrix to heat up and transfer heat to the surrounding air. The heated air rises up the collector and enters into a space, providing immediate space conditioning and heat distribution through the interior.

With the mass-wall type, the heated masonry mass will radiate heat when the sun no longer shines. It is important to integrate flow-control devices in order to prevent reverse action at night and to allow control of the heat gain. These systems are suitable for day-use facilities. The solar-masonry wall mass also works well in distributing heat over 24 hours and is ideal in cold climates with dependable sun.

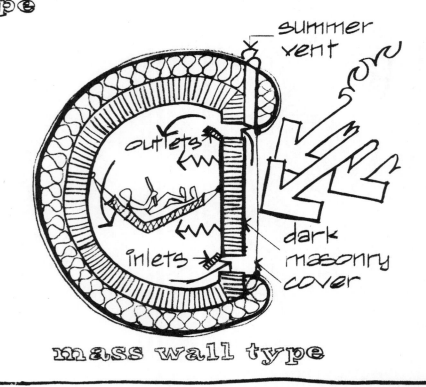

summer vent

outlets

inlets

dark masonry cover

mass wall type

AIR-CONVECTION LOOP

An insulated solar trough with a transparent cover and a metal-mesh matrix will permit air to rise by convection, picking up heat as it tumbles up the ramp to exit at the top. The heated air then flows through a low-friction storage mass of water containers or rock, where it transfers its heat and falls as it cools to return to the bottom of the collector.

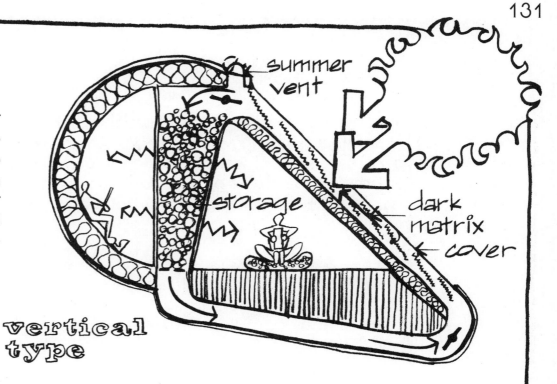

vertical type

A *chimney* of this type will convect whenever the sun shines and is self-balancing, going faster or slower as the intensity of the sun varies. It is important to prevent reverse action at night by control dampers and to cover or vent the chimney during summer. Proper proportioning of collector cross section and area to storage position and volume can be determined by scale-model trial and error.

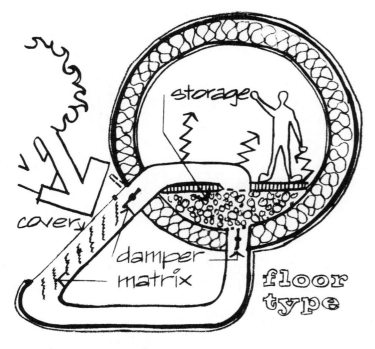

floor type

AIR-CHIMNEY LOOP

Convection direction can be controlled throughout a structure by ducting damper controls, and airflow passages. Another control idea is to allow the thermal properties of different heat-storage masses to regulate convective flow to various spaces.

By placing storage mass (such as water-filled, black-steel drums) with greater specific heat, conduction, absorption, or mixing values in one space and a material with lower values (such as

brick masonry) in another, heated air will first seek out the best absorbing mass when free convective flow is allowed. When the water achieves a uniformly higher temperature than the masonry, the heat will then flow to the mass with the next lowest temperature.

The proper use and placement of phase-change materials, super-conductors, or heat pipes could dramatically influence convection direction and heat storage distribution.

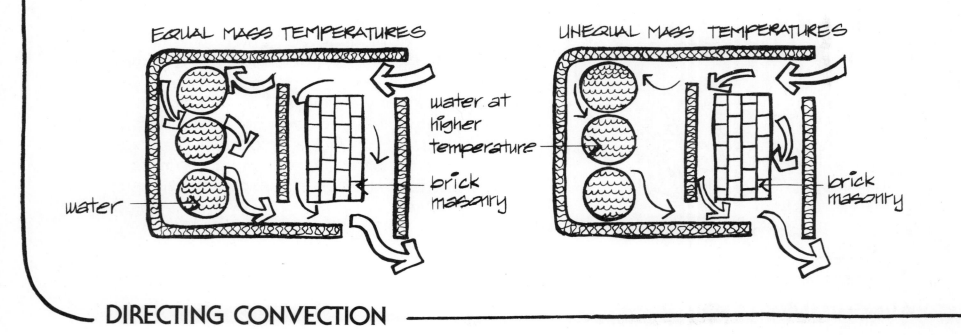

EQUAL MASS TEMPERATURES   UNEQUAL MASS TEMPERATURES

water at higher temperature

brick masonry

water

brick masonry

DIRECTING CONVECTION

Gravity convection is a handy term for describing the rising of heated air and the falling of cooled air in a heat-transfer loop. It can be visualized in a system which distributes heat to isolated thermal-storage mass or to rooms that do not have direct solar or conductive-heat gain.

Every structure experiences gravity convection in some way. The trick is to allow the associated heat motion to naturally distribute incoming heat where it is needed.

GRAVITY CONVECTION

Flat-plate *liquid* collectors, as in water heating systems, can *thermosyphon* (convect) naturally. By placing a storage tank inside a space or running a large-diameter tubing grid in a floor mass, such as sand, earth, or concrete, the fluid heated in the collector will rise and circulate through the storage mass. It loses heat to the mass as it travels, cooling and falling to return to the bottom of the collector.

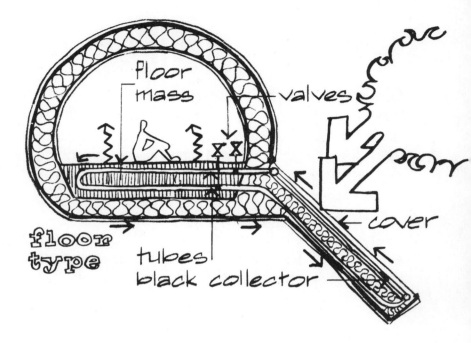

floor type

floor mass
valves
cover
tubes
black collector

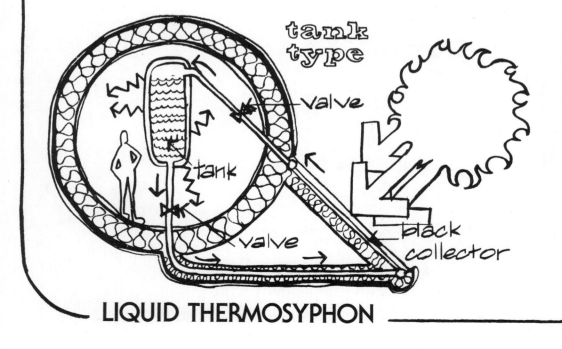

tank type

valve
tank
valve
black collector

Tubing sizes must be large to minimize friction loss, thus encouraging convection. Check or control valves may be required to prevent reverse syphon at night. Collectors should be covered or drained and vented in summer to prevent self-destruction. In cold climates an antifreeze solution must be used.

LIQUID THERMOSYPHON

one-way valve

control damper

18" min.

one-way flapper

Loss of collected solar energy can happen by reverse convection or *back syphonage*. Natural convection liquid or air collectors can reverse their normal flow direction at night and actually lose more energy to the outside than they collect. One way of preventing this is by proper elevation of the heat-storage mass above the collector. Sometimes it is difficult to predict if reverse flow will occur without experimentation. Also, the greater the temperature differential between storage mass and outdoor air, the greater the potential for the heat to migrate out.

Another way to prevent reverse action is to install one-way valves or dampers on the hot flow line into storage. These can be either automatic or manual. One-way flow valves and lightweight gravity dampers will operate without power— one less thing to remember or maintain. If these controls are closed during solar collection time, bypass loops or venting should be incorporated to prevent collector self-destruction.

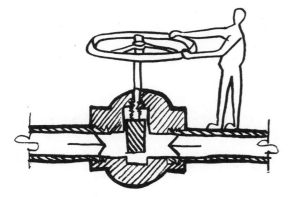

BACK SYPHON

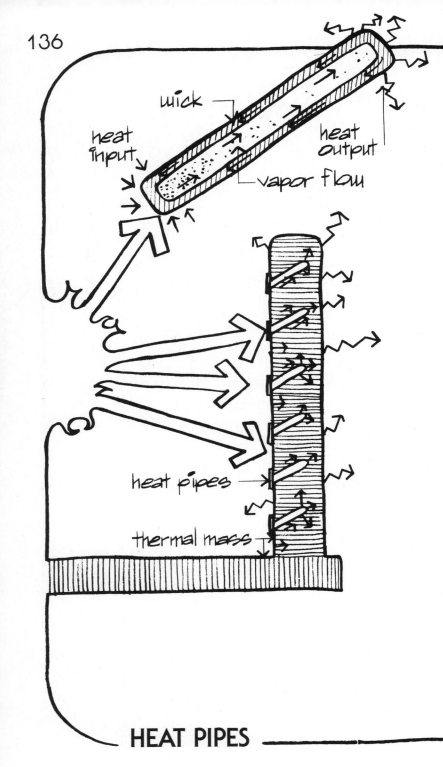

wick

heat input

heat output

vapor flow

heat pipes

thermal mass

The *heat pipe* is a sophisticated passive device for transferring heat from one point to another. It consists of a sealed tube which is evacuated and partially filled with a working fluid such as Freon. When heat is applied to one end of the tube, some of the fluid evaporates and expands, flowing to the unheated end where it releases latent heat by condensing. The condensed fluid returns to the point of heat gain via a wick in a constant flow, heat-transfer loop.

The heat pipe is self-balancing; the more heat applied the faster it works. Since gravity is necessary for fluid flow-back, a slight tilt is required; otherwise, if leveled or tilted the wrong way, the fluid will not flow back for more heat. Thus, the process is unidirectional and will not reverse or lose stored heat.

This tool can be used effectively to conduct and bury heat deep inside a thermal mass where it needs to be stored, quickly removing incoming heat from a space. Getting heat into storage can prevent overheating and greatly increase heat distribution.

There are many potential uses for heat pipes in passive systems.

HEAT PIPES

Another device which relies on natural physical properties to collect and distribute solar energy is the *Thermic Diode solar panel.* Each panel is composed of a thin outer layer for solar collection and a thick inner storage layer, both filled with water and separated by insulation. As the outer collection surface is heated, the water rises and flows through a unique unidirectional flow valve to the heat-storage layer. This oil-and water-filled valve is the main feature of the panel's design. Whenever energy is available and the heat storage layer is cooler than the collector surface, heat transfer will occur. However, when energy is not available for collection, the valve prevents the heated storage from reverse syphoning and losing heat to the outside.

By altering the directional flow from inside to outside, the Thermic Diode solar panels can be used for cooling. This device also offers great potential for a wide range of applications.

water
oil

flow valve
storage layer
insulation
collector surface

THERMIC DIODE SOLAR PANELS

Reflection of solar energy onto collection surfaces can boost the amount of incident radiation on a fixed area. A surface with high reflectivity, such as polished aluminum or white crushed rocks, can reflect approximately eighty percent of the incident radiation. A white roof or light-colored slab in front of a collection surface can also reflect a significant quantity of radiant energy. This approach can effectively reduce collection area by increasing the energy striking the collection surface.

When reflectors act as exterior insulating or shading devices, cost reduction and increased flexibility is possible. A reflector that is adjustable can adapt to various sun angles and seasonal demands.

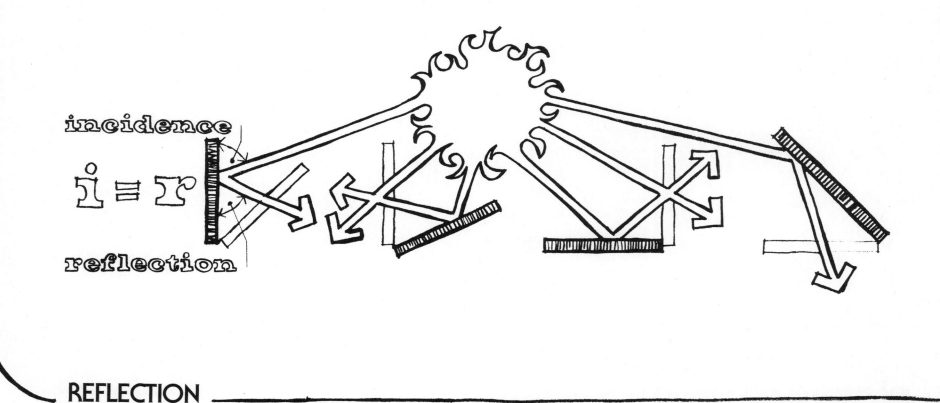

incidence

$$\stackrel{o}{i} = r$$

reflection

REFLECTION

Collection surfaces exposed to direct sunlight should absorb a maximum amount of energy. Various *colors* will absorb different amounts of light. Black will absorb nearly all light (ninety to ninety-eight percent). Conversely, white will reflect nearly all wavelengths, absorbing little (fifteen to forty percent). All other colors are somewhere in between, in proportion to their shade, darkness, pigment, value, or tone.

Faceted or finned surfaces are desirable for the transfer of heat to or from a transport fluid, as in a heat exchanger, air collector, or solar masonry wall. Perforated or folded surfaces, such as metal mesh or corrugated metal, permit a maximum of surface area for a minimum of collector area. Once sunlight has been absorbed and is reradiated as long waves, it is blind to color; white will absorb as readily as black.

Darkened metallic surfaces generally conduct incoming solar energy most effectively, getting heat away from the surface and into the transfer fluid. The cooler the collection surface, the better the efficiency for absorbing incident solar heat.

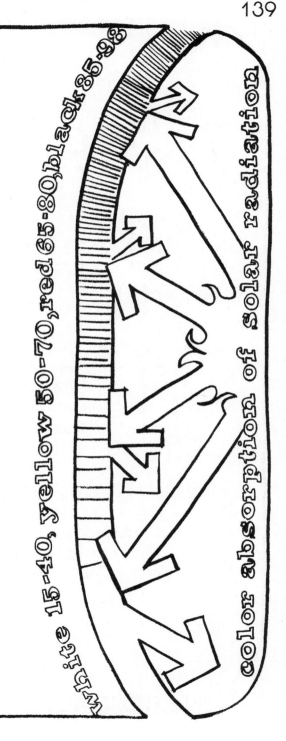

color absorption of solar radiation

white 15-40, yellow 50-70, red 65-80, black 85-98

SURFACE COLOR AND TEXTURE

Heat Storage

Heat sink is engineering jargon for a place where heat energy is dumped or stored. The solar-energy community uses this term to denote where collected (sun) heat is stored until needed.

Heat sponge, Solar Battery, and *heat reservoir* are other descriptive words. The terms most fitting for passive design are *heat storage* or *thermal mass*. Whatever you call it, every solar system needs a place where the sun's heat can be absorbed and held until needed.

Heat-storage or *thermal mass* should be selected for its storage capacity and cost effectiveness. It can be either a structural or a nonstructural part of the building. In any case, thermal storage should be contained within the fabric of the structure, or below it, in order to make use of lost heat. Once selected, sized, and installed, the storage should ideally remain variable until tested. Too little or too much thermal mass can cause a building to perform unevenly, by heating too quickly or never heating completely.

Too much heat storage can be too much of a good thing.

THERMAL MASS

Thermal inertia can be thought of as the heat action of a material or a structure. A flywheel effect in mechanics is the mass/velocity interaction that illustrates the axiom, "an object in motion tends to stay in motion," until it hits something! A heavy flywheel by its momentum tends to equalize the speed of machinery.

Heat storage can act as a thermal flywheel. If an insulated structure with a large thermal mass contains 10,000,000 BTUs (2,519,900,000 cal.) at 70°F (21°C), the addition or loss of a few hundred thousand BTUs will not vary the inside temperature too much. This concept has a potential for both heating and cooling.

Traditional adobe structures utilize this effect, even without exterior insulation, to equalize heat loss and gain through a wall. By spreading the action of exterior hot and cold over a long period of time the adobe reduces interior temperature extremes.

THERMAL INERTIA

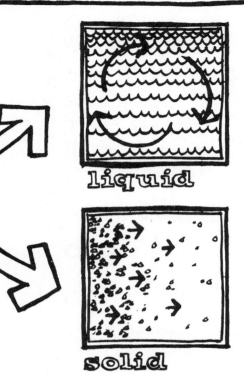

liquid

solid

Material	Conductivity (K_2) BTU-in/hr./ft^2/°F
adobe	4.0
brick	5.0
concrete	12.0
earth	6.0
sand	2.3
steel	310.0
stone	10.8
water	4.1
wood	0.8

The way in which a storage material absorbs heat and distributes it throughout its mass is important. Concrete can hold a lot of heat. However, because it *conducts* energy, it takes a relatively high or sustained temperature differential to penetrate throughout. Water, on the other hand, will absorb and *mix* heat more effectively because it conducts and convects. As sunlight strikes a water container, the molecules at the surface are heated; they then rise and are replaced by cooler molecules. The net effect is distribution of heat throughout the container. But heat stratification can cause temperatures to vary up to 50°F (28°C) from top to bottom.

The higher the conductivity of a material, the greater its ability to absorb heat and distribute it throughout its mass. A material of high conductivity, which may be good for thermal storage, is a poor insulator—heat-storage mass alone should not be considered as insulation.

CONDUCTIVITY AND MIXING

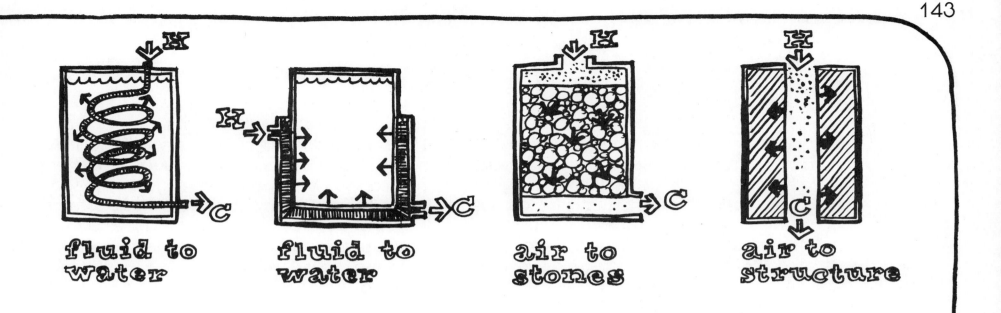

fluid to water   **fluid to water**   **air to stones**   **air to structure**

Where direct gain into a conditioned space is impractical or in colder climates where water freezes, solar heat must be transferred from one place or material to another by *heat exchange*. A heat exchanger can transfer energy from a nonfreezing fluid (antifreeze, air) to a storage material (water, stone, concrete, and so on). An exchange surface should have adequate exposure area of the heated transfer fluid to allow a maximum heat flow. With liquid exchangers a low corrosive piping, such as copper or plastic, should be used. Air collectors do not require expensive piping and can effectively exchange heat to rocks, sand, earth, water, and structural mass. In all natural convection systems, the heated transfer fluid must enter the exchanger at the highest point and exit low.

HEAT EXCHANGE

Thermal mass can be used two ways—*structurally* and *nonstructurally*. Structural mass, which helps hold a building up, can act as heat storage. This approach is appealing for new construction; the double investment of both building fabric and heat storage can take advantage of gracefully integrating two functions at once. Massive structural elements, such as stone, concrete, brick, and adobe, when thoughtfully placed and properly insulated, can successfully fulfill heat storage in passive solar design.

Nonstructural thermal storage is useful for refitting existing buildings, increasing or decreasing thermal capacity of any building, or permitting seasonal flexibility. Nonstructural elements, such as barrels of water or fiber-glass water tubes, should not be installed where they are likely to be subjected to snow, earthquake, wind, or structural loading. Any heavy mass should always be adequately supported at the top and bottom.

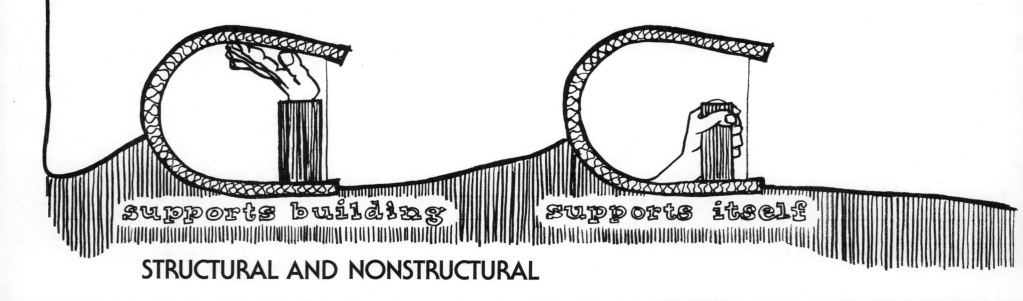

supports building   supports itself

STRUCTURAL AND NONSTRUCTURAL

hollow tube   stack sack   stone wall   wire gabion   cavity wall   earth block   rammed earth

Solid thermal mass, which can be structural or nonstructural, comes in many forms. The basic structural types are commercially produced materials—poured and precast concrete, brick, steel or fiber tube containers, abode blocks, concrete masonry units, and the like. Noncommercial materials, such as sand, earth, gravel, clay, stone, and so on, can be stacked in plastic and fiber sacks, compacted, used to fill wall cavities, contained in wire gabions, or laid to make a wall. They provide low-cost, energy-efficient storage. Perforated or porous stone walls, tubes with rocks, and rock-filled gabions can act as

thermal wicks by conveying warm air through the voids and across all surfaces, distributing heat throughout the mass.

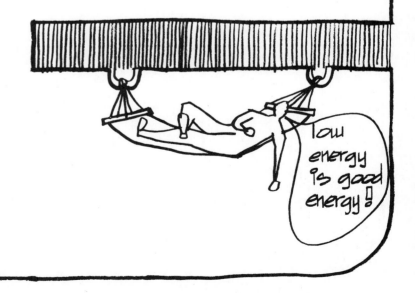

low energy is good energy!

SOLID THERMAL STORAGE

Liquid-thermal-storage vessels deserve special consideration. Water, brine, and other liquids that can be held in an infinite variety of containers offer cheap, flexible, and efficient mass-heat-storage possibilities for both new and existing buildings. Commercially produced, salvaged, and custom-built containers can be used. One should consider cost-to-volume ratio, attractiveness, durability, lifetime, structural ability, ease of draining and filling, patching and replacement.

Metal containers such as drums, tanks, pipes, cans, and culverts should be of homogeneous or compatible materials to prevent electrolytic action. Corrosive inhibitors should be added to metal water vessels to prevent rusting out. Salt brine and other highly corrosive liquids belong in corrosion-proof containers. Any vessel should be sealed airtight to pre-vent loss by evaporation. Avoid using flammable and highly toxic fluids for heat storage inside a building.

The glass and plastic jars, jugs, and bottles that you've been collecting from time to time and then throwing away can be recycled as heat-sink containers. Place them in bins, walls, or partitions, under floors, or anywhere heat can get to them.

LIQUID THERMAL STORAGE

Plastic membrane can be made into watertight bags to line most any structural cavity. Select long-life plastics, and avoid prolonged exposure to sunlight, as ultraviolet degrades most plastics. Flexible bladders, such as inner tubes, waterbeds, weather balloons, and hot-water bottles can be supported by wood or earth forms.

Fiber-glass tanks and tubes can be nicely arranged, painted, covered with plaster, or screened to create attractive surfaces.

Many waterproof containers, such as pipe, well casing, culverts, and tanks, can be purchased at reasonable cost per volume. Salvaged pressure and shipping vessels such as water heaters and propane tanks are sometimes free for the asking; take them home and clutter up your yard until you find a use for them. Remember, your imagination is the only limit.

When materials change from a solid to a liquid state and vice versa, they change phase. The best known *phase-change* material is water, which becomes ice at 32°F (0°C). Phase change involves the absorption or release of large quantities of latent heat energy. For instance, to change 1 lb. (or 1 g) of water from 36 to 35°F (or 1°C), only 1 BTU (or 1 cal.) of energy is released. But to go from water to ice or from 33 to 32°F (or from 1 to 0°C), 143 BTUs (or 79.8 cal.) are necessary. Thus, a large quantity of la-

tent heat is absorbed or released within the narrow temperature range of phase change.

Eutectic salts change from solid to liquid at various specific temperatures. Salts store a large quantity of heat by volume, around 90 BTU/lb. (50 cal./g) at phase change, but are usually toxic, corrosive, and have a limited life cycle ability. Thermocrete and other structural materials containing Glauber's salts offer a tremendous potential for storing heat in the fabric of a building.

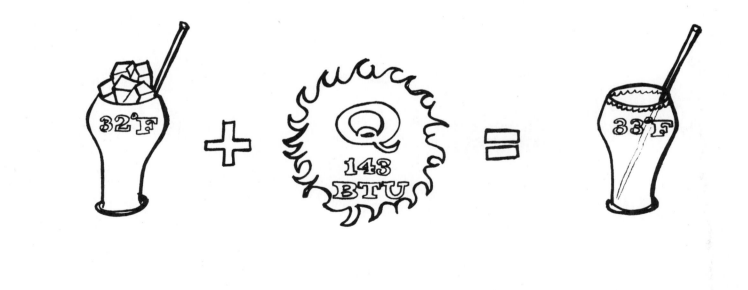

PHASE CHANGE

Material	Melting Point °F	Heat of Fusion BTU/lb.	Density lb./ft.^{3}	Heat capacity BTU/ft.^{3}
water (ice)	32°	143	62.5	8940
paraffin	35–115°	65–90	48–56	3200–4600
salt hydrates	55–120°	70–110	90–115	7200–9900

Paraffin, which absorbs about 75 BTU/lb. (42 cal./g) upon melting, is a phase-change material. It corrodes, burns, evaporates, changes volume significantly, and should be held in glass containers. All phase-change material should be tightly sealed to prevent evaporation, with allowance for expansion. Flammable materials should not be installed within habitable structures unless approved by local officials.

Other materials, such as honey, sugars, pitch, and tars, might be combined with binders such as cellulose, sand, metal, or conductive fibers to change temperature ranges, cycle life, and heat-to-volume ratios. The use of phase-change materials for permanent heat storage is still experimental, and considerable development can be expected. Who knows? Maybe reversible metallized Jello is the answer!

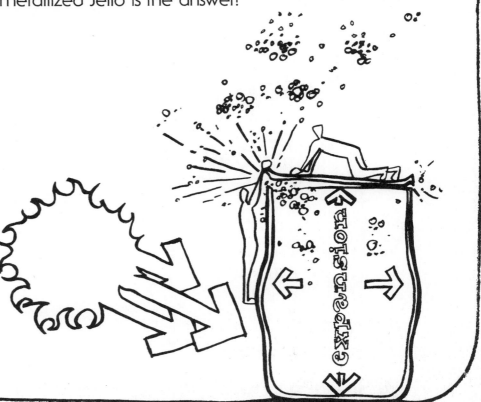

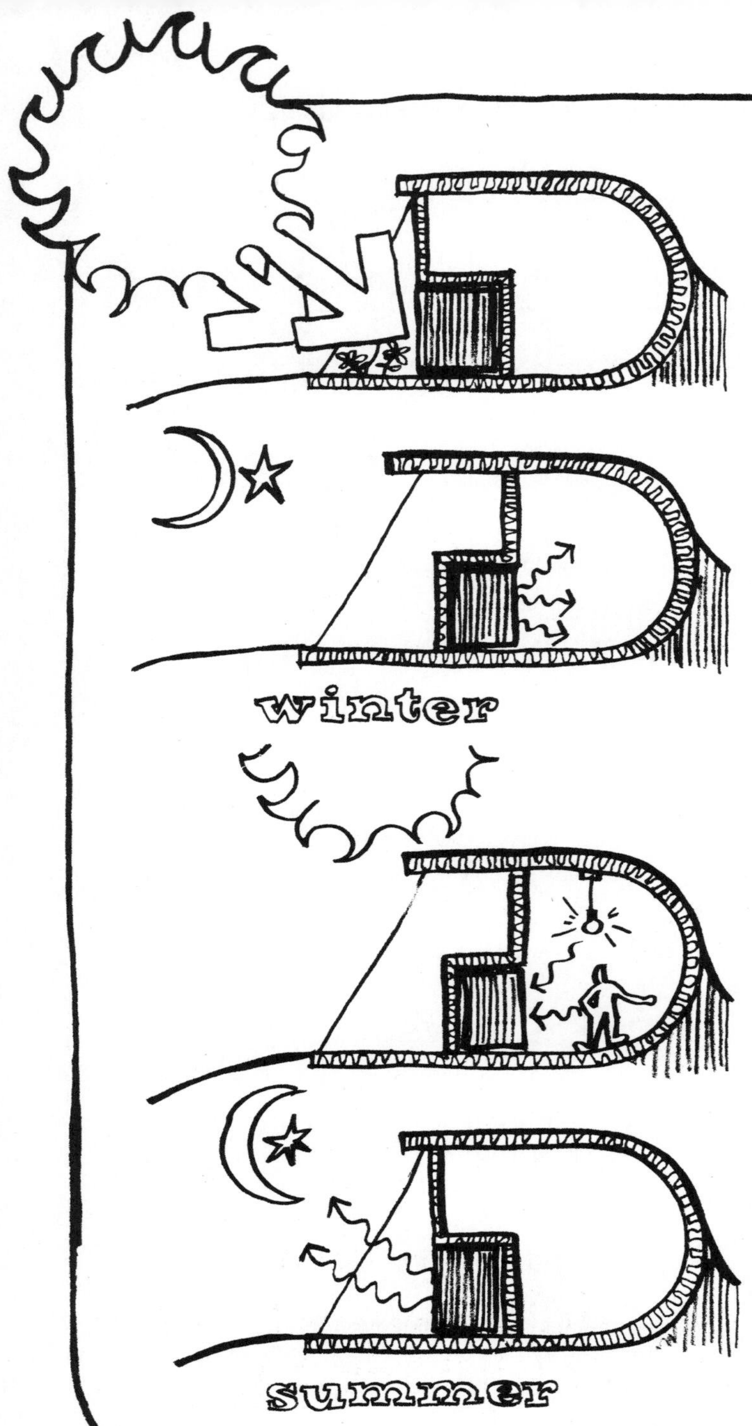

Seasonal and daily isolation/exposure of thermal mass is an integral function for passive heating and cooling. For heating, the storage mass should be exposed to absorb the winter sun; but at night or sunless times, it should be isolated from exterior heat-loss surfaces. Cooling operates conversely by isolating the mass from the hot summer sun and then at night exposing it to the outside sky for deep-space radiation.

Isolation of heat storage can be achieved by a variety of methods and apparatuses: opening and closing insulative devices, location of mass to take advantage of seasonal and daily sun angles, flexible shading devices, and movable heat sinks.

Faithful operation of control devices can keep thermal storage tempered for all seasons.

winter

summer

ISOLATION OF STORAGE

Certain areas in a building require different heat demands for functional comfort. Kitchens generate heat all year and can be self-heated in winter, perhaps requiring ventilation in summer. Bedrooms need not be heated above 60°F (15°C) for sleeping comfort. High-activity areas require less heat *storage* than areas *where* more passive activities take place. Living rooms *need* heat during the evenings and holidays. Pantries, root cellars, and storage areas should be isolated to subsurface ground temperature. Greenhouses need to be maintained at between 50 and 75°F (10 to 24°C) for optimum plant growth.

In planning room locations for a building it is prudent to evaluate the heating and cooling needs of each area before attempting functional organization. Heat storage should be located appropriately.

STORAGE WHERE NEEDED

Thermal mass, as affected by ambient air temperature, can work anywhere within a building for passive heating and cooling. However, ideal location can maximize performance. For heating, a storage mass, regardless of its conductivity, will be most effective when exposed directly to winter sunlight. Interior walls or upper floors are probably the best for heat retention and distribution, as all radiated heat will pass through a living space rather than being lost through an exterior surface or to the ground. Other *placements* may absorb heat better, hold up the building, or enclose it from the out-of-doors. Ceiling storage can take advantage of thermal stratification, absorbing heat from the air during the day, and radiating it downward at night. Floor storage is nice to the feet.

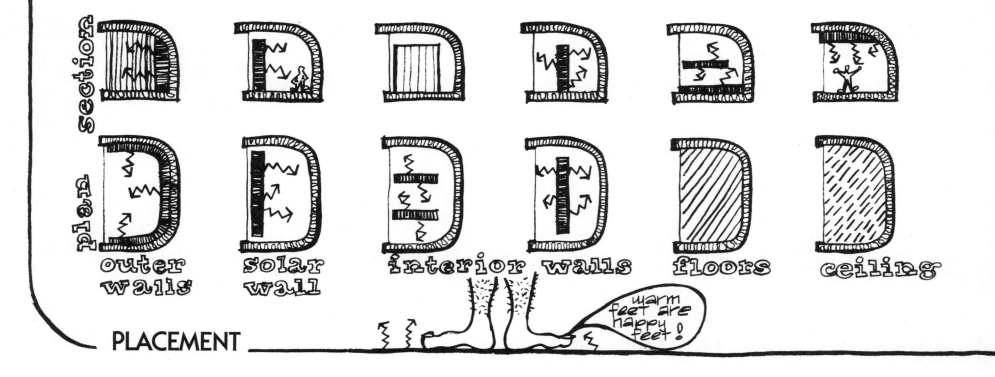

plan   section

outer walls   solar wall   interior walls   floors   ceiling

warm feet are happy feet!

PLACEMENT

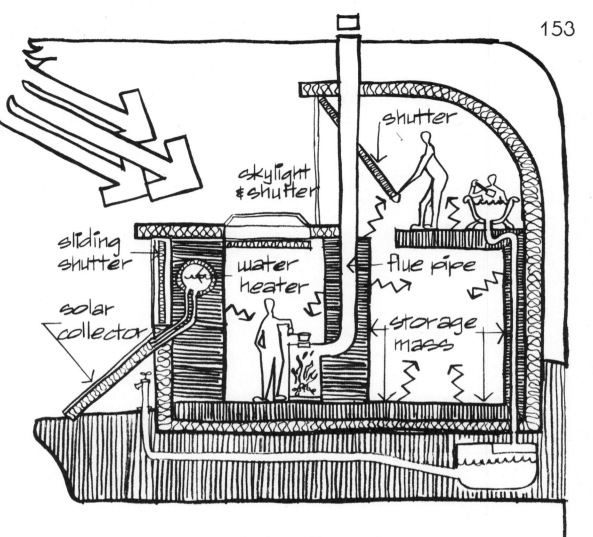

There are several ways of heating interior mass. Direct winter sun, natural convection, stratification, or collectors will all work. Generally, solar absorption surfaces should be dark in color and have sunlight fall on them directly. Heating or emission surfaces can be any color.

For any design, different combinations of thermal mass placements will allow variation in space, function, and heating requirements.

The location of heat generation devices, in or adjacent to thermal storage mass, will help to capture heat that may otherwise be lost. It can equalize the intensity of heat generated, during cooking or backup, by storing some for later. Try to incorporate fireplaces, stoves, water heaters, and hot-water-supply and waste lines near or into storage mass.

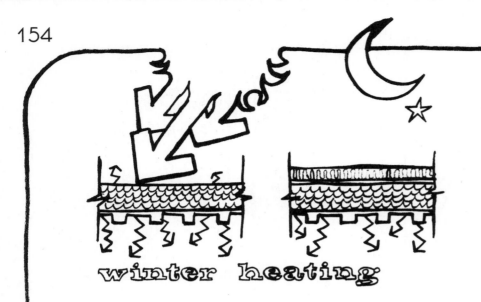

winter heating

summer cooling

Thermal *roof storage* mass offers a unique solution to passive heating and cooling. The Skytherm approach of installing water bags above or below a metal or concrete roof structure takes advantage of a little used exterior surface. By covering and uncovering the thermal mass with movable insulation, buildings in many climates can be totally heated and cooled. This thermal flywheel system distributes heat evenly throughout buildings. It can be manually or automatically controlled and requires little maintenance. Structural loading and the potential of freezing or leaking detract somewhat from the waterbag idea. However, water tubes, concrete, or even earth roofs with enough mass and insula-

tion can act in much the same way. Many existing types of structures throughout the world can take advantage of roof mass and movable insulation.

ROOF STORAGE

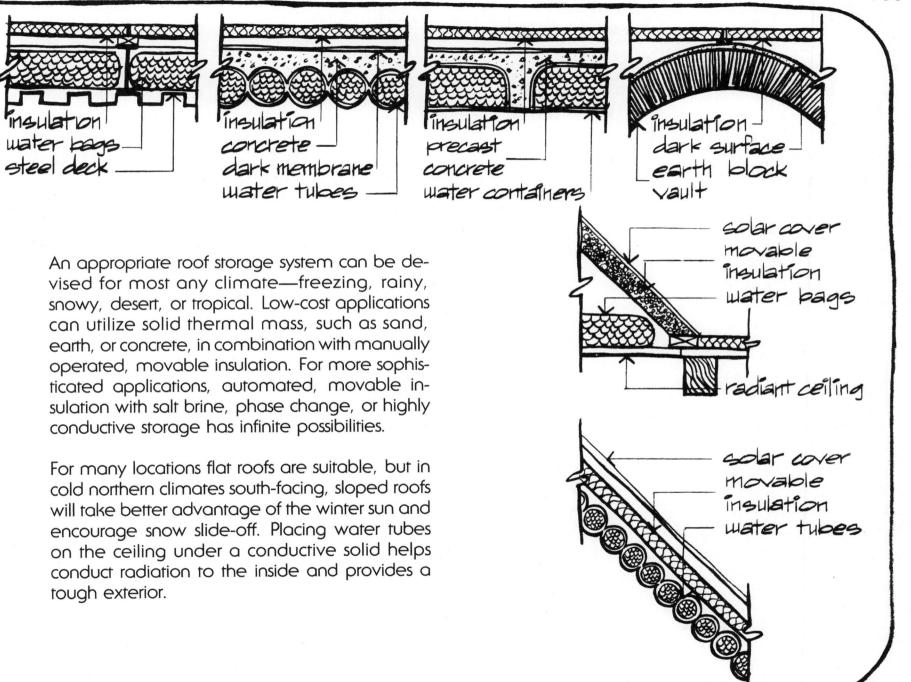

insulation
water bags
steel deck

insulation
concrete
dark membrane
water tubes

insulation
precast
concrete
water containers

insulation
dark surface
earth block
vault

solar cover
movable
insulation
water bags

radiant ceiling

solar cover
movable
insulation
water tubes

An appropriate roof storage system can be devised for most any climate—freezing, rainy, snowy, desert, or tropical. Low-cost applications can utilize solid thermal mass, such as sand, earth, or concrete, in combination with manually operated, movable insulation. For more sophisticated applications, automated, movable insulation with salt brine, phase change, or highly conductive storage has infinite possibilities.

For many locations flat roofs are suitable, but in cold northern climates south-facing, sloped roofs will take better advantage of the winter sun and encourage snow slide-off. Placing water tubes on the ceiling under a conductive solid helps conduct radiation to the inside and provides a tough exterior.

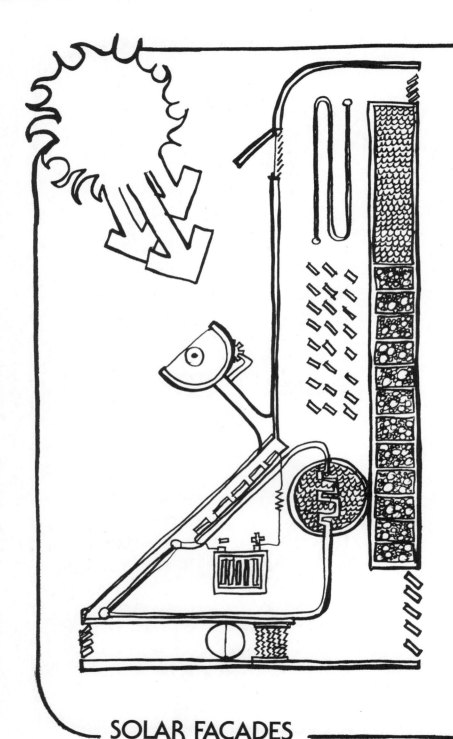

Solar facades, south facing with winter sun exposure, are popular for their unique ability to take advantage of seasonal solar angles. The mass incorporated behind the solar transmission surface (glass, fiber glass, plastics, one-way materials, collectors, and so on) is in an optimum position for intercepting the sun's energy before it enters the habitation space. Consequently, the mass controls excess light, glare, and heat loss/gain to the interior.

The potential use for solar walls is tremendous. Solar cells, thermal storage, collectors, thermal chimneys, glazing, and many other devices can take advantage of this handy vertical surface. Storage mass, such as solar water walls, solar mass walls, Solar Battery tubes, phase-change mass, and so on should be suited to the functional and climatic demands of each structure. It is wise to reserve some surface for future development and ideas.

SOLAR FACADES

The idea of *portable heat storage* is a titillating concept. A vessel could be placed in an ideal collection position during solar time and then moved to a variety of interior spaces when and where space conditioning is needed. This process can be reversed for cooling.

This method of putting mass storage where it is best suited could eliminate fixed collectors and thermal storage, perhaps freeing the design of architecture. Maybe heat sinks could be carried around, taken to work, or even lent to a friend.

PORTABLE STORAGE

The *heat storage capacity* (Qst) over a specified temperature range is a product of specific heat (c), density (d), and mass per unit volume. When selecting a storage mass, the objective is usually to contain as much heat as possible per unit volume. However, cost, performance, and practicality must be considered. Water, with a specific heat of 1.00, is generally a good choice because it has a high heat-capacity-to-volume ratio (q). Its problem is containment. Another material—concrete—is structural; thus, it is attractive, despite a lower heat-capacity-to-volume ratio and high energy cost required for manufacture. Earth, adobe, stone, and sand are excellent choices because they can be structural, don't leak, require little fuel energy to produce, and are dirt cheap!

Material	(c) BTU/lb.°F	(d) lb./ft.^{3}	(q) BTU/ft.^{3}/°F
adobe	0.22	90	20
brick	0.20	120	24
concrete	0.16	144	23
earth	0.21	95	20
sand	0.19	95	18
steel	0.12	489	58.7
stone	0.20	95	19
water	1.00	62.5	62.5
wood	0.45	35	15.6

Q_{st} ≡ total heat storage, BTU's
V ≡ volume, ft.^{3}
d ≡ density, lb./ft.^{3}
c ≡ specific heat constant
Δt ≡ temperature differential; °F

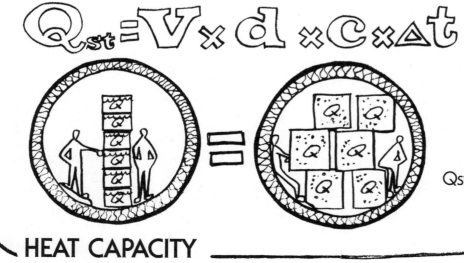

$$Q_{st} = V \times d \times c \times \Delta t$$

If the temperature of 10 cubic feet of water rises 8°F during a day, the water will have absorbed:

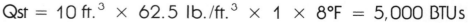

Qst = 10 ft.^{3} × 62.5 lb./ft.^{3} × 1 × 8°F = 5,000 BTUs

HEAT CAPACITY

Sizing the amount of heat *storage* mass required for a structure varies with the performance desired. In passive design the objective is to incorporate adequate thermal mass to minimize over- or under-heating during normal weather conditions. With inadequate capacity a building will gain more heat than it can absorb; the effect is overheating during solar periods and overdependence on auxiliary heating during nonsolar periods. With too much capacity a structure will take days to charge up by solar and may suck up the auxiliary heating when it's most needed.

An adequate design ratio is enough mass to carry a building, with a given daily heat loss (Qhl), in a given climate, for the normal duration of sunless days. For instance, if storms generally average three days, allow enough storage so that when charged to 85°F (29°C), the temperature will not drop under 65°F (18°C) over the three-day period. Nature often schedules longer storms, and, after three days, auxiliary heating may be needed. But in most climates, seventy to ninety percent long-run, passive solar heating can be achieved.

$$Q_{st} = Q_{hlt} \times D$$

Q_{st} = total heat storage, BTUs

Q_{hlt} = daily total heat loss, BTUs

D = days of storage

SIZING STORAGE

When designing a solar house or system, it is of value to determine the *percentage of solar heating* anticipated. This process is helpful when comparing different systems for cost effectiveness and suitability in various locations.

All calculations should be based on standard engineering data for local conditions. The following information is required for equivalent comparisons:

Climatic

—degree days of heating, (annual)
—altitude, feet
—percentage of possible sunshine, %p
—latitude, degrees
—outside design temperature, °F
—available insolation, BTU/day

Building

—shading factors, %
—floor area of building, sq. ft.
—volume of building, cubic feet
—heat loss of building, BTUs

System

—area of collector, sq. ft.
—angle of collector, degrees
—collector orientation, degrees
—inside design temperature, °F.

PERCENT OF POSSIBLE SOLAR

To determine the percentage of solar heating (%s), first calculate the total building heat loss (Qhlt) for the average ninety-percent design temperature (to) for a typical day of each month during your heating season. Then find the percent of possible sunshine (%p) for each respective month and calculate the amount of possible solar energy collected and stored (Qss) for each month; taking into account mitigating conditions, such as occlusion (of) by shading, screens or mullions, collector cover transparency (tf), system efficiency (e), sky haze (hf), and ground reflectance (gr).

Now divide the daily amount of solar energy received, stored, and available for use (Qss) by the total heat loss for the typical day of the month under consideration (Qhlt). This gives a percent of solar heating (%s) typical for that month. By summing the total monthly losses and dividing by the sum of the monthly solar gains, your average annual percent of solar heat (%Sa) can be determined.

To help unscramble the verbal analysis let's look at some equations which will set the story straight.

The amount of solar energy available and collected for a typical day is:

$$Q_{ss} = A_c \times of \times tf \times Q_s \times R_f \times e \times hf \times gr$$

where:

Q_{ss} = solar energy collected, BTU/day
A_c = collector area, sq. ft.
of = occlusion factor
tf = collector cover transmittance
Q_s = incident daily insolation, BTU/sq. ft.

R_f = radiation factor = $0.30 + 0.65\ (\%p/100)$ where $\%p$ = monthly aver-age percent of possible sunshine

e = system, efficiency
hf = sky haze factor
gr = ground reflectance

To determine monthly and seasonal averages:

$$\%S_{mo} = 100(Q_{ss}/Q_{hlt})$$

$$\%S_a = \frac{Q_{ss}(nov) + \ldots Q_{ss}(x)}{Q_{hlt}(nov) + \ldots Q_{hlt}(x)}$$

$\%S_{mo}$ = percent solar heated for typical day each month
Q_{hlt} = total heat loss, BTU/day, for typical day each month
$\%S_a$ = percent annual solar heated

Example: Assume a building located in Colorado (elevation 7,000 feet) at 40°N latitude, has a floor area of 1,250 square feet and an interior volume of 10,000 cubic feet. Because of its tight construction and efficient volume, the building loses only 12 BTUs per hour, per square foot of floor area, during a typical December day. Due to the greenhouse effect, thermal storage absorption, interior surfaces, and movable insulation, system efficiency is seventy percent. The vertical collector, double glazed, totals 420 sq. ft., fifteen percent of which is mullions and framing. So—

$$Ac = 420 \text{ sq. ft.}$$
$$of = 0.85 \text{ (mullions, etc.)}$$
$$tf = 0.76 \text{ (dbl. glass)}$$
$$\%p = 65 \text{ (typ. Dec.)}$$
$$e = 0.70$$
$$Qs = 1,646 \text{ BTU/day/sq. ft.}$$
$$hf = 1.05 \text{ (winter condition)}$$
$$gr = 1.30 \text{ (snow)}$$

$$Qhlt = 12 \text{ BTU/hr.sq.ft.} \times 1,250 \text{ sq.ft.} \times 24 \text{ hours/day} = 360,000 \text{ BTU/day}$$

$$
\begin{aligned}
Qss &= Ac \times of \times tf \times Qs \times Rf \times e \times hf \times gr \\
&= 420 \times 0.85 \times 0.76 \times 1,646 \times \\
&\quad (0.30 + 0.65 \times (65/100)) \times 0.70 \times \\
&\quad 1.05 \times 1.30 \\
&= 308,305 \text{ BTUs/typical December day}
\end{aligned}
$$

$$
\begin{aligned}
\%Sdec &= 100 \, (Qss/Qhlt) \\
&= 100 \, (308,305/360,000) \\
&= 86 \text{ percent solar heated for December}
\end{aligned}
$$

Now repeat the process for each month of the heating season; add these up, divide the totals, and you have the seasonal average!

Shading

Comfort can be maintained in almost any climate through passive measures. Where cooling is desired at various times of the day, seasons, or even throughout the year, consideration must be given as to the appropriate method. Hot and dry, hot or humid, windy and dry, windy and humid, and other prevailing conditions dictate the approach to be used. Often a combination of shading, cooling, and ventilation should be integrated to satisfy seasonal or daily variations.

Shading the exterior, interior, and surrounding areas of a structure is the first line of action to reduce the temperature buildup due to ambient air or solar incidence. By limiting the amount of heat buildup in the thermal mass of a building, the job of cooling is reduced. A structure that is properly designed for its climate will need little, if any, conventional equipment to achieve comfort for most uses.

In some cases, buildings in cooler climates that generate heat from lighting, machinery, equipment, or occupancy loads will require cooling or ventilation throughout the seasons instead of heating.

The *planting* of trees, bushes, or vines in appropriate places can adequately shade structures in many climates. When attempting to cut solar gain into a building, it is important to interrupt the sun's energy before it strikes the glass or walls. Once the heat has penetrated the envelope of a structure, it must be removed from the interior, which may require additional unnecessary steps.

Evergreen trees planted to the north of buildings act as buffers, helping to block winter storms, wind, and snow. Further, they can act as evaporative coolers, lowering the temperature of air passing through the branches and needles. They also shade the ground around buildings, preventing heat buildup in the earth and thus modifying the microclimate. Glades and oases illustrate this effect in hot climates.

PLANTING

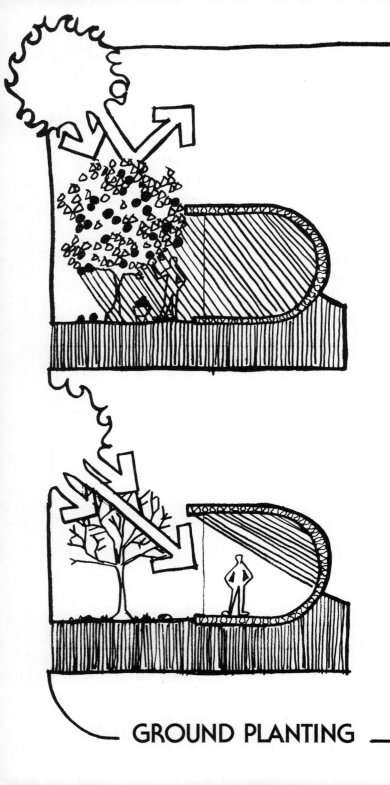

Low shrubs, bushes, and grasses are advantageously planted around buildings where a view is desired. They reduce reflection of solar energy from roadways, walks, patios, sand, or bodies of water. These shrubs, when watered in the morning, will cool air passing by, evaporatively cooling the area around a structure and reducing secondary heating effects.

Deciduous trees, such as fruit and ornamental types, are particularly suitable to *planting* on the south, east, and west sides or in courtyards of buildings. Their spring, summer, and fall foliage interrupts the flow of solar energy before it strikes the ground, window, or wall surfaces. These species defoliate in the late fall, and the loss of leaves allows the sun's heat to warm collection surfaces, as well as the ground, heating the earth around structures, melting snow and ice, and evaporating surface water.

Vines and climbers can be planted to shade east, west, and south facades. Planter boxes on roofs and walls create hanging screens of foliage, shading windows and walls. A lattice or trellis will accommodate climbing plants to form a similar screen, blocking the sun yet allowing cooling breezes to flow through.

GROUND PLANTING

west   east

Sod roofs or rooftop vines are valuable in many climates. A properly constructed roof, when covered with earth and planted, may never wear out. The earth prevents the injurious effect of sunlight, wind, freeze/thaw, and wet/dry cycles on the moisture membrane.

In dry climates irrigation of *roof planting* will do much to cool a structure through evaporation. A moist roof will lose the heat it absorbs during the day to the night sky. Roof planting should be well-irrigated to prevent the shallow roots from drying out and to prevent fire danger.

Fruits, flowers, grasses, and leafy things make life a bit more beautiful. We should encourage their growth in and about our habitats, particularly where they help to maintain comfortable temperatures. For the most part, plants are nice to look at, have pleasant odors, freshen and moisturize the air; and some are good to eat—let's be friends with them, invite some into your home. Take a flower to lunch this week!

ROOF PLANTING

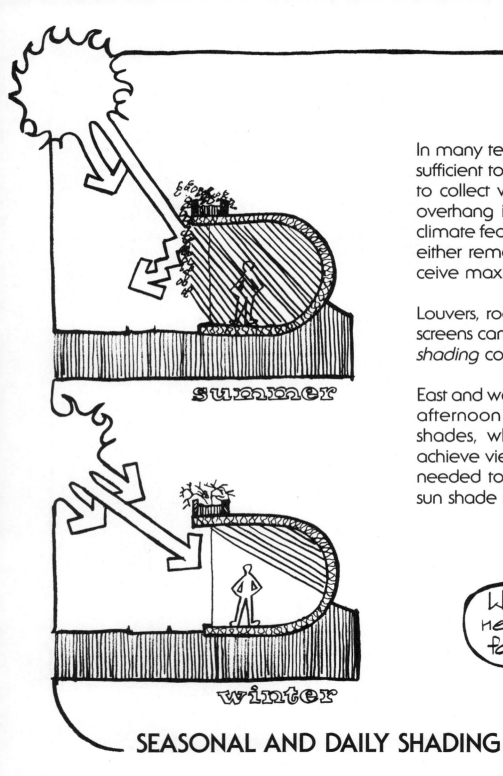

summer

winter

In many temperate climates simply interrupting solar gain is sufficient to prevent overheating. A solar facade that is used to collect winter sun for heating can be shaded by a roof overhang in the summer. Depending on the latitude and climate features, this overhang might need to be adjustable; either removable or retractable in winter and spring to receive maximum sun.

Louvers, roof overhangs, vertical shades, and other such sun-screens can be designed to accommodate various *seasonal shading* configurations.

East and west facades, which experience direct morning and afternoon sun, might require shading. Usually, vertical shades, which can pivot, roll, or fold up, are desired to achieve view, openness, and ventilation when they are not needed to block the sun. Seldom is a fixed or permanent sun shade satisfactory throughout all the seasons.

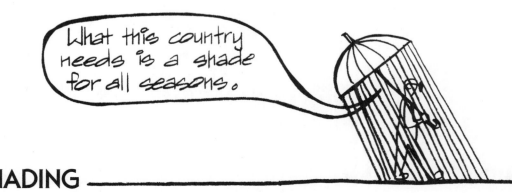

What this country needs is a shade for all seasons.

SEASONAL AND DAILY SHADING

Spaces in a building will have varying shading requirements. A bedroom with southern exposure may need only ventilation during the day. Offices, kitchens, and other rooms might have to be shaded all day long, while other spaces may need to be shaded only in the morning or during the afternoon.

In most climates the western or afternoon sun is the hottest. Thus, extra shading on the west side of a building may make best sense. On the east, less shading may be desired to allow morning sun to take away the chill of the night and wake up the household.

Depending on the interior function and exterior orientation, the method, frequency, and type of shading should be appropriately adapted and designed to meet the daily and seasonal demands.

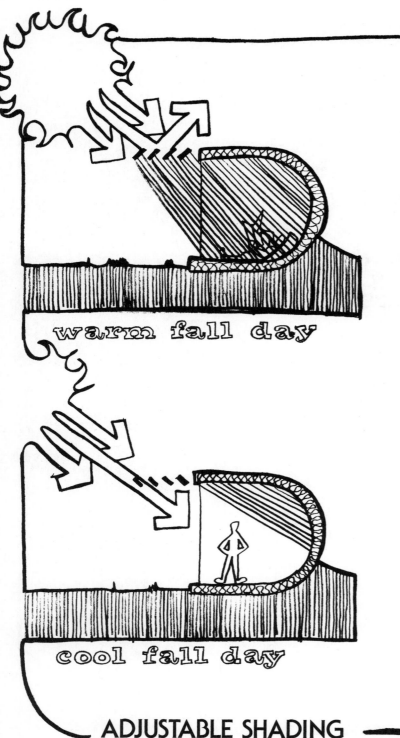

warm fall day

cool fall day

The weather varies from year to year and week to week. It is wise to design shading devices that are adjustable. Fixed overhangs, louvers, or sunscreens should only be installed at positions of permanent advantage and augmented with adjustable devices to suit the changeable conditions.

Vertical and horizontal louvers can be opened to take best advantage of any part of the day or season. Automatic controls, such as Skylid devices or heat drivers, can be adapted to permit the louvers to track and block out the sun all day long, thus accommodating both view and shading at any given hour.

Next time you see a baseball game notice the players' caps—the shape and angle of the bill may indicate the player's position with relation to the sun.

ADJUSTABLE SHADING

A shading device that is an extension of the *roof* plane of a structure is a simple way of blocking the sun. However, some drawbacks of adding exterior shading devices are that they are susceptible to the elements and that the risk of looking added-on, tacky, or too busy might affect the building's appearance.

Generally, in the northern hemisphere *overhangs* on the northern exposure are not practical, except in very warm climates, where the roof acts as an umbrella, shading the walls and ground around a building.

South shading is usually the most effective way of preventing summer heat gain, and, of course, east and west shading may be required to satisfy local conditions.

Certain minimal fixed overhangs are practical, and when supplemented by adjustable panels that slide or fold out as needed, the roof and its extension can be the first line of defense against intense summer solar gain.

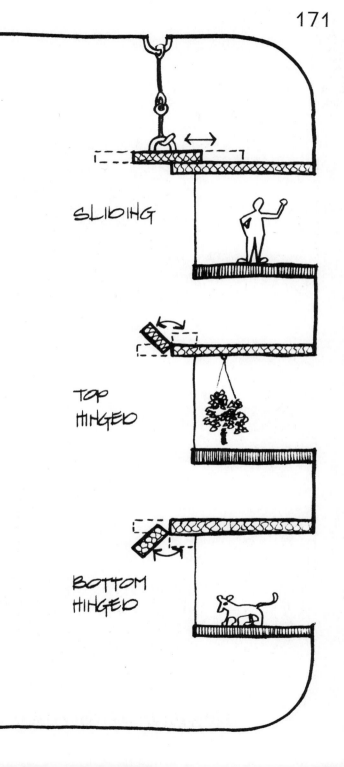

SLIDING

TOP HINGED

BOTTOM HINGED

ROOF OVERHANGS

shade poles
roof poles

adobe
bearing poles

BEAM OVERHANGS

The Pueblo Indians often extend the logs which support the earth roofs of their homes out beyond the exterior wall. During winter the unobstructed sunlight flows on and into the south wall, storing warmth for the night.

In summer, when the sun is high in the sky, a variety of things can be laid across or hung from these projecting *beams* to shade south walls and openings, thus preventing excessive buildup of heat stored in the walls. Branches, blankets, poles, drying fruit and vegetables, or any number of things can easily be installed or removed as needed on this solar control system.

Certain vines on south trellis *overhangs* are almost perfect seasonal shading devices. They lose their leaves regularly when the heating season begins—and in the spring the leaves pop out with the warmth.

Louvers, or light-control slats, can be arranged in a multitude of configurations to handle almost any situation.

Fixed louvers can be installed where the need for view and sunlight control is continual. Louvers allow breezes to pass, while limiting solar gain and glare.

Removable or adjustable louvers are used where seasonal or daily solar control is needed. The adjustable type lend themselves well to shutting out or accepting the sun, breeze, or view. For exterior installation, metal or treated wood is recommended to withstand wind, ultraviolet, rain, drying out, and snow.

Vertical louvers work well for admitting breezes, allowing view, and blocking the sun for certain periods of the day. To act as a sunscreen all day, they must be adjusted occasionally. They work best on east and west exposures when fixed.

Horizontal louvers can shade all day in summer while facilitating view and air motion. They work best on southern exposures. They can be set at any pitch, from vertical to flat.

Insulated louvers, which can be either horizontal or vertical, help prevent heat loss from buildings when closed.

vertical

horizontal

LOUVERS

Screens made of wood lath, metal strips, concrete block, clay tile, and so on are effective for cutting the amount of sun's heat reaching a surface or an area. They should, of course, be made of weather-resistant materials.

When placed vertically, horizontally, or at an angle, screens can reduce solar gain to the degree desired by correctly sizing, spacing, or angling the matrix material.

Screens not only have the advantage of interrupting solar gain, but also reduce glare, pass breezes, filter light, allow controlled views, and cast intricate, playful, shadow patterns that continually change.

Many screens can be removed and stored easily where advantageous for seasonal uses.

SCREENS

Automated louver systems, using electronic-controlled motors or phase-change driving fluids such as Freon, can be very effective for controlling solar gain into and on a structure. Even in large commercial buildings, heating and cooling loads can be decreased considerably with very little expenditure. Thoughtfully designed configurations of louvers to expose, shade, or insulate wall surfaces could minimize space-conditioning equipment need. A computerized control of exterior fins, panels, louvers, and so on could automatically adjust heat gain or loss window by window, room by room, and wall by wall, to achieve zone control for functional needs, occupancy use, and temperature variation. This would allow total flexibility throughout a complex structure—admitting heat when needed, ventilating when necessary, and closing off solar gain, noise, wind, heat loss, and glare, when required.

Heating and cooling structures and spaces by this means can substantially reduce the operation time of heating and cooling equipment and can lower the building's energy requirements.

This approach to space conditioning creates a more efficient and natural architecture—its liveliness gracefully responding to natural laws.

AUTOMATED SOLAR FACADES

Interior shades, drapes, panels, or louvers may be desirable in many cases. Interior shading devices are not affected by the wind or weather. Further, they can be effective as insulation to heat loss if appropriate materials are used, such as reflective membranes and flexible insulations, and if they are tightly fitted.

The disadvantage of interior shades is that summer sunlight penetrates the glazing surface, changing wavelength upon striking the shade and trapping heat that must be either utilized or evacuated. Normally, high vents, windows, or skylights can be used to exhaust this heated air.

Sunlight is a strong and subtle force; bright colors will fade with ultraviolet exposure and plastics degrade over a period of time. Even interior shades, which are used for solar control, should be made with ultraviolet resistant colors and materials. Sail track of the type used on small sailboats is handy for mounting shades on horizontal or sloping surfaces.

INTERIOR SHADES

Light, flexible *exterior shades* are another way to block excessive sunlight. Many materials that can be rolled or folded, such as canvas, bamboo, wood slats, and snow fencing, can be mounted under roof overhangs on projected beams, outriggers, or freestanding supports. The advantages of exterior shades are their light weight, flexibility, and economy. They can be adjusted to desired shading height and easily removed and stored or neatly closed up against the roof overhang.

The wide variety of colors, textures, and materials available can be used to create many different patterns and effects to complement any building design.

roof

snow fencing

glass

Exterior shades are at the mercy of the elements, and in many areas tie downs and frames may be needed to prevent flapping and tearing loose.

Snow fencing or bamboo shades, a flexible matrix of slats wired or tied together, can roll nicely down sloped glass surfaces to screen and filter sunlight.

EXTERIOR SHADES

side folding

side sliding

Interior panels, which make excellent winter insulation, can also double as summer shading. As with shades, panels used for shading should be resistant to the effects of sunlight, be easy to operate, and allow adequate ventilation above to permit solar-heated air to rise and vent off. If the heated air can be made to accomplish another task while exiting, such as drying fruit, drying laundry, or cooking dinner, the true spirit of passive solar energy is achieved.

overhead hinged

overhead folding

INTERIOR PANELS

Panels on the outside can serve a variety of needs. *Exterior* shading *panels,* adjustable to seasonal sun angle change, can also serve as insulation in the winter or as reflectors to bounce sunlight to a number of places.

Panels should be firmly attached and designed not to rattle, thump, or creak when the wind blows. They should be easy to operate, perhaps from inside, so that inhabitants are encouraged to use them. Sheet metal and plywood make lightweight yet strong panels, capable of enclosing rigid or loose fill insulation. Piano or continuous hinges assure strong, smooth, even swinging. Overhead barn-door hardware is durable and easy to slide.

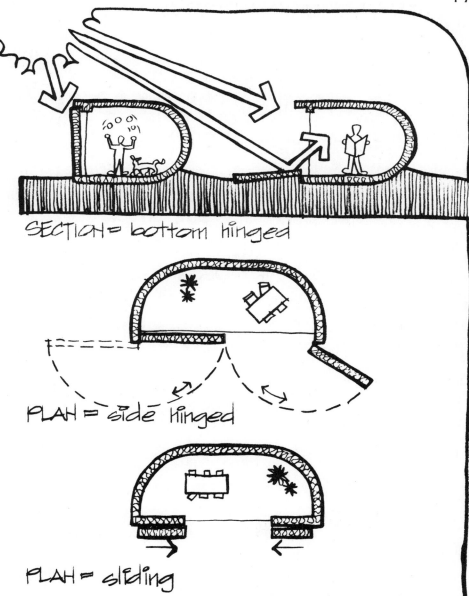

SECTION = bottom hinged

PLAN = side hinged

PLAN = sliding

EXTERIOR PANELS

Reflective solar control *glazing*, with a very thin film of transparent metallic coating on the outside surface, is more effective than tinted glazing for control of solar heat gain.

The majority of solar rays, in the form of short-waves, are bounced off the outside surface before entering the glass material. This reduces the buildup of heat in the body of the glass and, therefore, a single layer can be effective in controlling both light and heat gain to the interior.

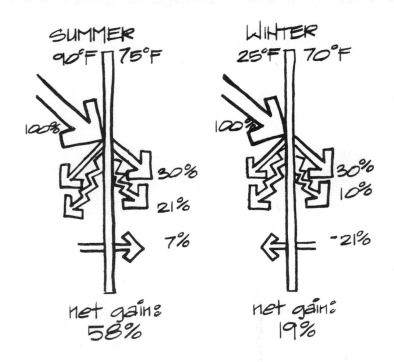

SUMMER
90°F | 75°F
100%
30%
21%
7%
net gain:
58%

WINTER
25°F | 70°F
100%
30%
10%
-21%
net gain:
19%

Various degrees of transparency and reflectivity are available for a wide range of applications. Exterior glare from reflective glazing surfaces can be a problem with large expanses of glass where adjacent buildings, roadways, or pedestrians are affected.

REFLECTIVE GLAZING

A more exotic way of shading by control glazing is the use of glass with *variable* light *transmission* quality. In the same manner as sunglasses that change color and transmission of light on demand, glazing can adapt to the degree of light striking the surface. This can be accomplished by a matrix of polarization, which filters light according to the positioning of linear grids, reducing light transmission when moved from parallel to crossed positions. Chemical color density change, as caused by heat or light intensity, is another method of varying light transmission.

With present technology, these types of control glazings are expensive and are not suitable where heat gain is desirable in certain seasons. However, the concept of variable-transmission glazing is a useful tool for the designer's imagination.

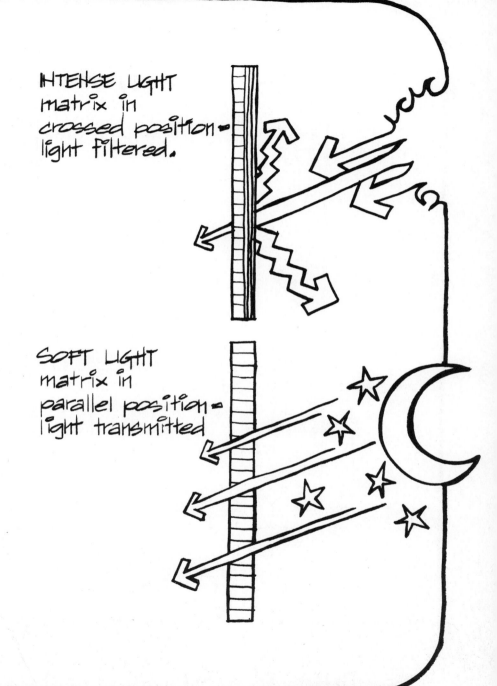

INTENSE LIGHT matrix in crossed position= light filtered.

SOFT LIGHT matrix in parallel position= light transmitted

VARIABLE-TRANSMISSION GLAZING

Solar control glazing, such as *tinted glass,* is useful in reducing solar heat and light gain—a very subtle form of shading. Depending on the degree of tint, the amount of solar gain can be reduced up to seventy-five percent over clear glazing, with some degree of transparency remaining. Of course, this type of control should not be used unless it can be removed when solar gain is desired for winter heating. For example, a storm window of clear glass for winter gain could be replaced by tinted glass for summer shading.

Tinted glass comes in a variety of colors—blue, green, yellow, bronze, silver, and so on. These different colors limit and admit differing wavelengths of light, which we perceive as color. The glass is heated when absorbing the wavelength of light, and this heat should be released to the outside. In most cases double glazing with tinted glass on the exterior and clear glass on the interior is effective. Tinted glass is helpful on west facades for controlling the afternoon sun or where glare from water, snow, sand, parking lots, or adjacent structures is a problem.

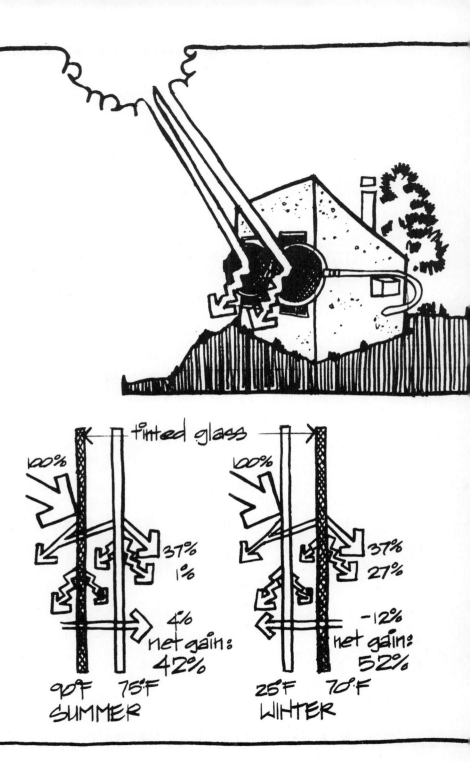

TINTED GLAZING

Double glass or plastic, spaced apart so that it can be filled with insulative *beads* or *bubbles* for nighttime insulation, can also double for summer shading. Partial filling permits adjustable shading from the bottom up. Plastic foam beads that are normally used for insulation are subject to degrading from ultraviolet rays. A more opaque solar-resistant or reflective material might be more desirable for blocking sunlight.

Removable translucent bubbles overhead in a greenhouse can be effective for subduing excessive summer solar gain. Beads or bubbles with various color and transmission qualities can solve a variety of shading needs admitting suitable wavelengths and intensities of sunlight for photosynthesis, lighting, or space heating. Reusable, soaplike bubbles could be dissolved when transparency is desired.

Popcorn—an organic substitute for plastic beads? Be the first on your block to build a solar popcorn heater.

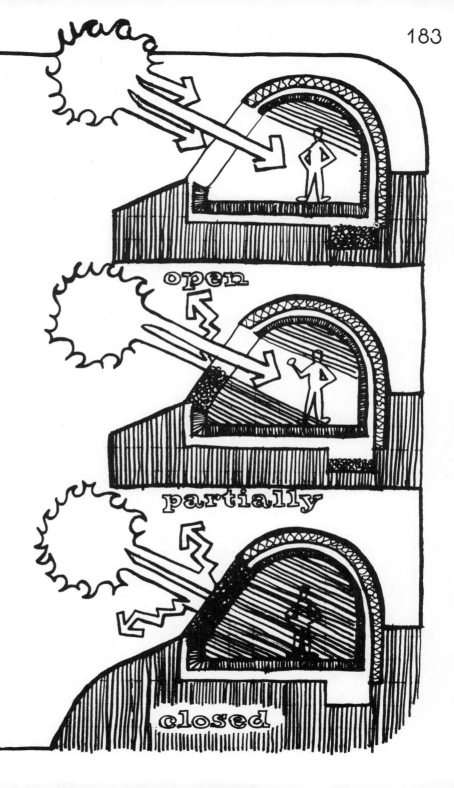

BEAD AND BUBBLE WALLS

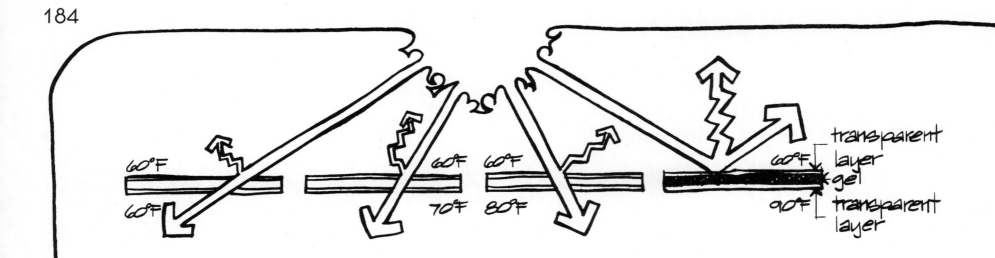

Cloud Gel is a potentially cost-effective device for controlling solar gain. Greenhouses and direct-gain structures, which may tend to overheat and require shading to maintain comfort, usually necessitate either manual or automated shades, blinds, and vents to regulate interior thermal buildup. Cloud Gel is simply a material that is sandwiched between transparent layers of plastic or glass. It has the property of clouding or becoming opaque when heated to a certain tem-

perature, thus blocking further solar gain. By selecting a membrane with an appropriate clouding-point temperature, a control range can be established for various applications, so that when the interior temperature reaches a maximum, preset level, the gel clouds and prevents further heat buildup due to solar gain.

This elegant, useful material is an excellent example of simplicity through technology.

The *Solar Modulator* is an adjustable shading device which monitors sunlight, redirecting it away from the use space and the floor—either onto ceiling-located thermal storage or, when conditions warrant, by rejection to the exterior.

Similar to an inverted venetian blind, the Solar Modulator, with intricate cross-sectional characteristics, accepts a wide range of sun angles throughout each day of a heating season. One side of each louver is metallized for specular reflection and the other side is coated with a light-colored matte finish for glare control. Consequently, with little or no seasonal adjustment, all incident energy can be directed to thermal storage located at the ceiling. Slight adjustment allows all direct sunlight to be rejected to the exterior, while still maintaining views. Further adjustment closes the blades completely. This totally opaque position prevents any sunlight

from entering the interior and could act as an additional insulating device against heat loss or gain.

When combined with various types of insulative transmission surfaces, this device offers great promise in accomplishing the need for shading and direct solar gain on southern, vertical, glazed surfaces.

thermal storage
Solar Modulator

S

W

SOLAR MODULATOR

Ventilation

Air exchange in structures is required for a number of reasons: to replace stuffy, used air; eliminate smoke and odors; evacuate unwanted warm air; and circulate air for comfort. In tightly sealed, solar-heated buildings, where infiltration is minimized, and particularly in subsurface structures, adequate ventilation must be provided.

Ventilation can be used effectively for cooling, but it is also needed during heating periods. Since most passive solar-heating systems utilize radiant thermal mass, some air motion and exchange can occur without adversely affecting the heating process.

Passive ventilation can be achieved several ways. The important thing to remember, in all cases, is to properly size and locate each vent to allow every space within a building to adapt to various seasonal demands. All vents should have adjustable openings and be well insulated and sealed when closed. When air is removed it will be replaced; the incoming air should be tempered, whether cooled or heated, prior to distribution.

Direction and speed of airflow determine the cooling effect of natural ventilation. The dry-bulb, still-air temperature will be effectively lowered 5°F (3°C) if the air is moved at a velocity of 200 feet./minute (61 m/min.). Air speed can be adjusted to suit comfort needs by opening and closing a variety of properly placed windows.

To encourage ventilation there must be an inlet and outlet on opposite or adjacent sides of a space. Airflow into an opening on the windward side of a space is most *effective* when the wind direction is within 30° of normal to the *opening*. Wind scoops, vegetation, and the type of window can be used to channel air into openings from any direction.

On the leeward or downwind side openings should be larger than on the incoming or windward side. This creates a maximum suction effect, facilitating free air movement through a space.

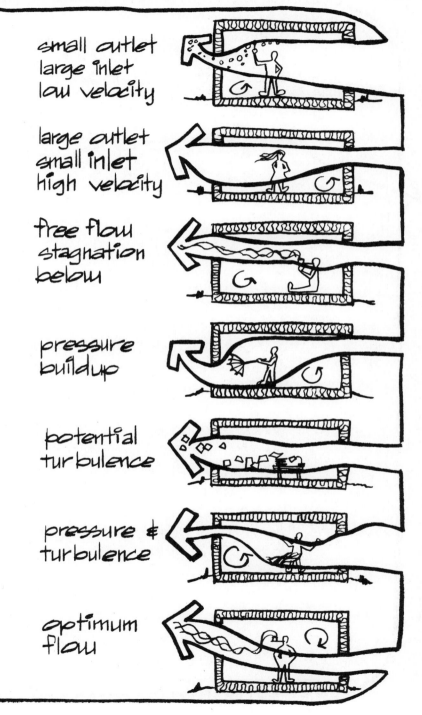

small outlet
large inlet
low velocity

large outlet
small inlet
high velocity

free flow
stagnation
below

pressure
buildup

potential
turbulence

pressure &
turbulence

optimum
flow

EFFECTS OF OPENINGS

Wind acting on a building causes higher pressure on the incident side and a vacuum on the opposite side, drawing air in openings on the windward face and sucking it out downward.

PLAN

SECTION

awning

casement

louver

Door and windows are the natural means of ventilating houses. The placement, size, and type of openings govern the effectiveness of this *fenestration.* By some building codes all habitable rooms of a dwelling must be provided with an operable exterior opening measuring not less than 1/20 of the floor area with a minimum of 5 square feet (.465 sq.m).

Windows can be oriented to catch or slow down prevailing breezes. The type of operating window should be suited to the task. Awning windows allow air to enter but keep out rain. Casement windows can open to catch or buffer wind. Louvered openings permit uninhibited air flow. Hopper windows allow free, upward motion. Since warm air rises and expands, outside air should be brought in low and exited high for ideal cooling.

hopper

FENESTRATION

Operable skylights make effective ventilators and also allow natural illumination. Good commercial units permit opening to the degree desired and seal well when closed, keeping moisture out and minimizing infiltration. Always use double-glazed types for increased insulation. Pressure-spring skylights open upward and restraining chains are used to adjust the opening and for closing. But crank-type skylights are generally superior.

heavy winds

warm air

Operable skylights have the advantage of always being exposed to the wind regardless of where it comes from. In areas of driving rains or heavy winds it is wise to orient the opening away from the storm direction. This type is a good choice for ventilating bathrooms and kitchens.

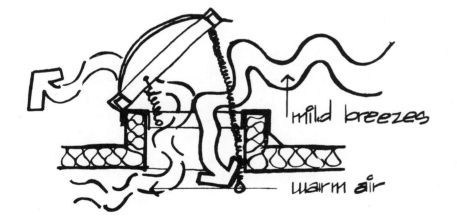

mild breezes

warm air

Airflow through ceiling vents varies with wind direction and speed, inside to outside pressure differential, and temperatures. At times, outside breezes will flow downward into the building; usually, warm air will rise up and out.

OPERABLE SKYLIGHTS

Vents located in joist and beam spaces or between studs under roof overhangs are an economical method of perimeter ventilation. Heated interior air will rise out or cooler outside air will dump down through, as pressure and temperature dictate.

A number of these weatherproofed vents at strategic locations permit zone ventilation at all perimeter walls. It's surprising how effectively these simple devices work.

Insulated wood or metal flaps with weather stripping, piano hinges, and Touch-latch hardware prevent heat loss and infiltration when closed. the *eave* overhang protects the vent in any weather.

Floor vents allow intake of cooler ground air and are a natural complement to eave vents, as they provide the inlet to a ventilation cycle.

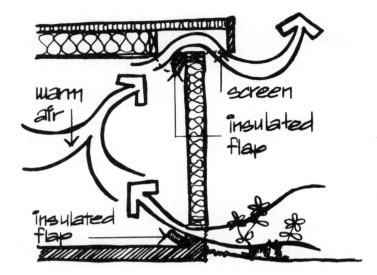

EAVE AND FLOOR VENTS

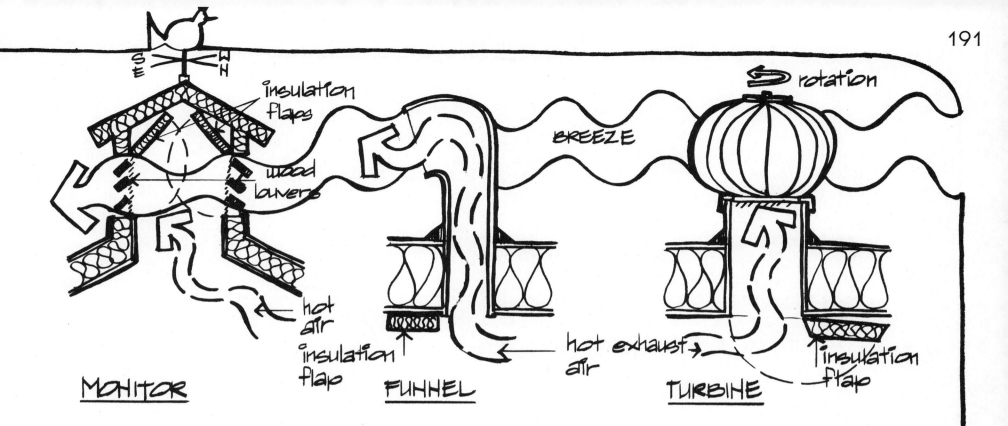

insulation flaps

wood louvers

rotation

BREEZE

hot air insulation flap

MONITOR

hot exhaust air

FUNNEL

insulation flap

TURBINE

Exhausting heated inside air by natural passive means is most easily accomplished at the high point of roofs or attics. This is where the heated interior air gathers and tries to get out. Let it!

The monitor, funnel, and turbine are tried-and-true devices for allowing breezes to aid in exhausting interior air to the outside. When com-

bined with screening and an insulated closure flap on the inside, these roof vent methods are very effective ways to ventilate and keep the weather out.

It may be necessary to extend roof vents to a point above adjacent structures to catch the main wind currents.

ROOF VENTS

Fixed *wind scoops* that reach up and catch faster moving air from prevailing winds are an excellent way of providing air motion through a building in warm climates. Wind currents are generally strongest 20 to 40 feet (6 to 12 m) above the ground. The ventilating air, as it is funneled downward, depends on the velocity of prevailing wind and associated pressure to move through a building. Properly proportioned and located exhaust vents, in combination with ducts, will permit even distribution to various rooms throughout a structure. Remember that the air caught and brought into any space must have a place to exit in order to work well.

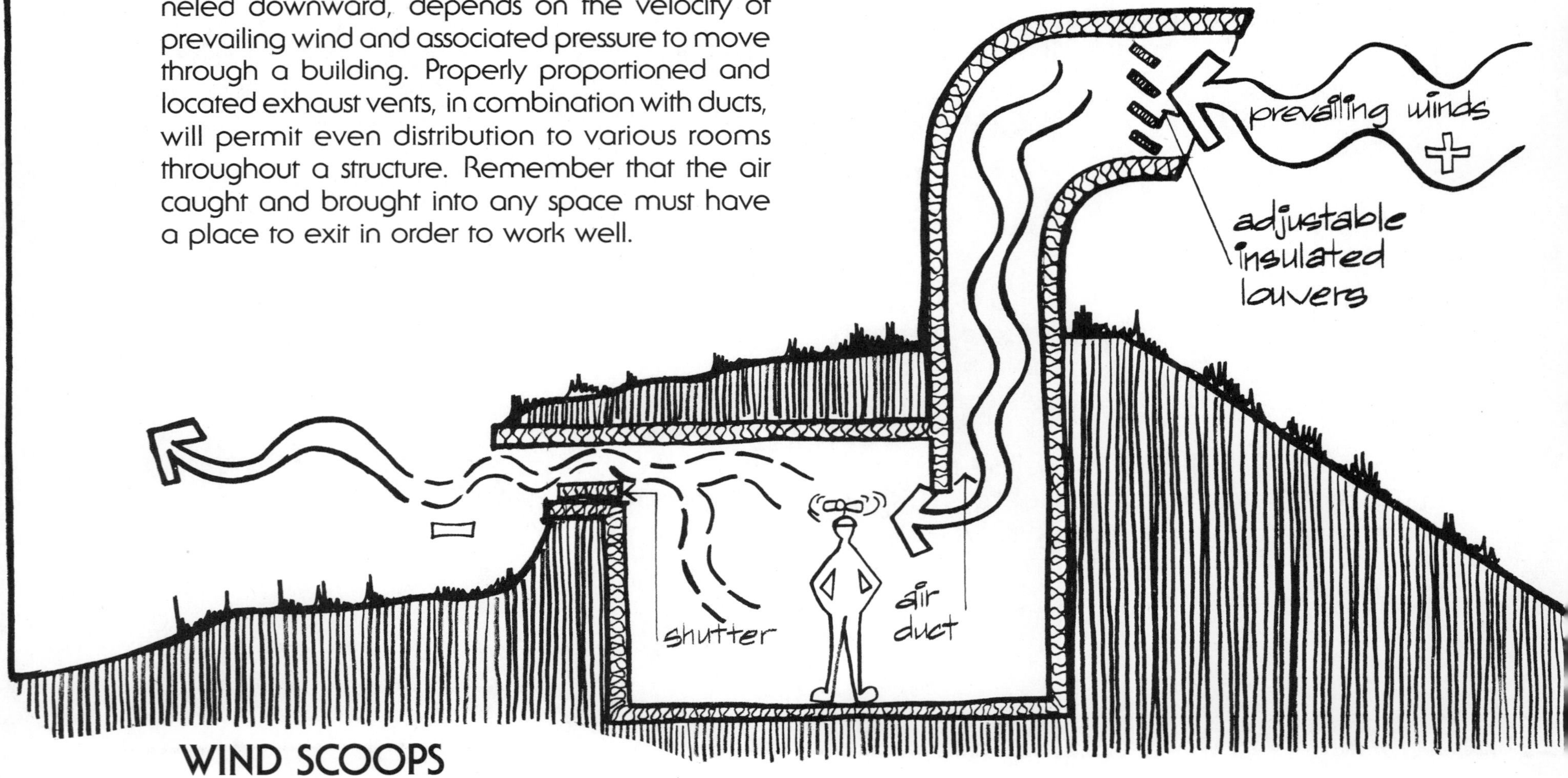

prevailing winds

adjustable insulated louvers

shutter

air duct

WIND SCOOPS

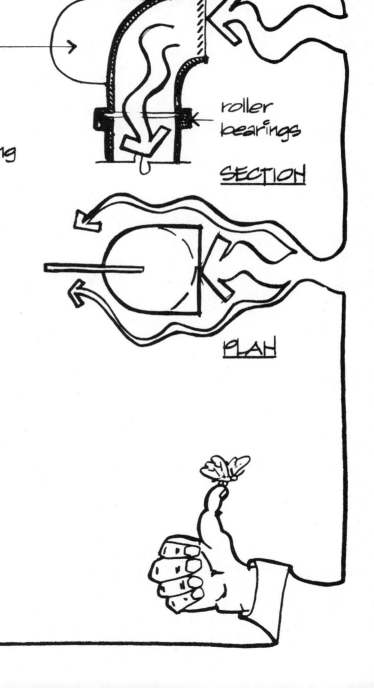

pivot

sail

insulating shutter

MORNING

EVENING

SECTION

roller bearings

PLAN

Multidirectional or *tracking wind scoops* are useful in areas where winds come from varying directions. Many configurations of form are possible.

Where winds blow from one direction in the morning and the opposite in the evening, a two-directional pivot scoop is simple to build and operate. Manually setting the position of the pivot blades allows a rate of flow from fully direct to indirect.

A 360° rotating scoop with a directional sail will react to subtle changes in wind direction, taking maximum advantage of wind force.

It is a good idea to install screens in all vents and to take steps to keep rain or snow out.

TRACKING SCOOPS

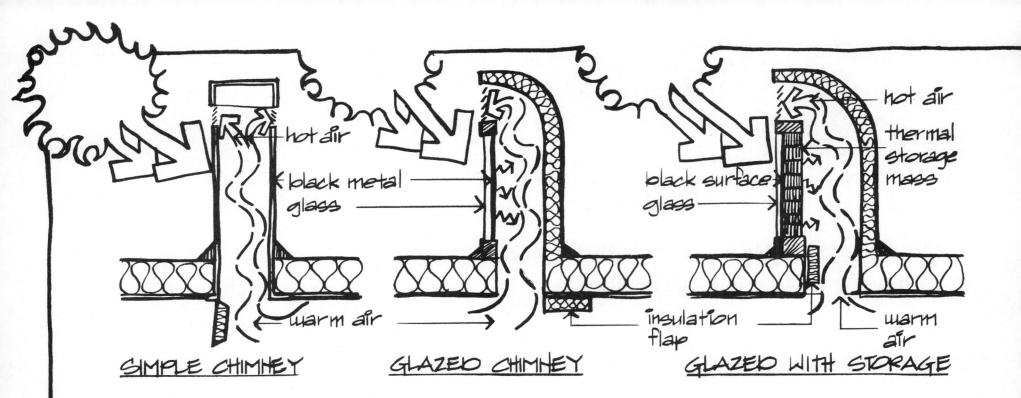

hot air

black metal
glass

warm air

SIMPLE CHIMNEY

black surface
glass

insulation
flap

GLAZED CHIMNEY

hot air

thermal
storage
mass

warm
air

GLAZED WITH STORAGE

Solar chimneys, plenums, or black boxes, located where the sun can warm them, use solar heat to reinforce natural air convection. As a black-metal chimney gets hot during the day, the air inside heats, expands, and rises, in turn pulling interior air up and out. One advantage of the solar chimney is its ability to self-balance; the hotter the day, the hotter the chimney and the faster the air movement.

The shape, area, and height of the chimney should be experimented with to determine the proper airflow for various installations. West-facing, glazed chimney surfaces are suitable for venting during the hot afternoon part of the day. By integrating thermal-storage mass behind the glazing the chimney will actually store daytime heat and continue to exhaust air after the sun has set, thus acting as a night ventilator.

SOLAR CHIMNEY

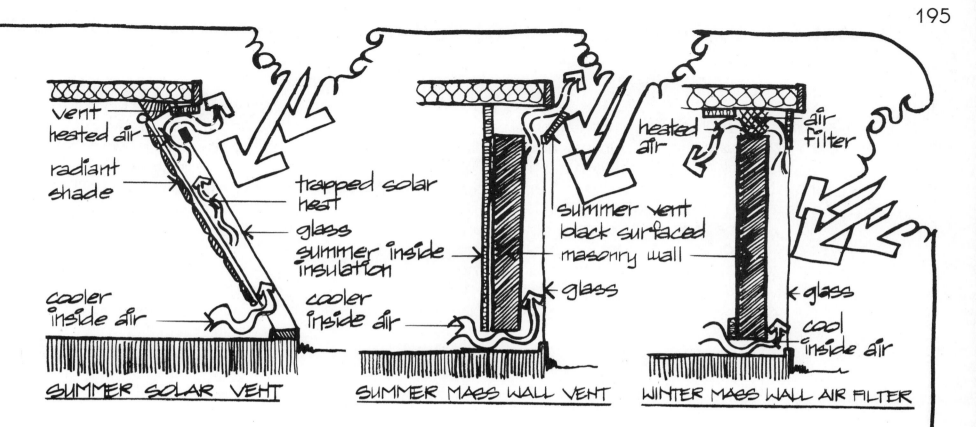

vent
heated air
radiant
shade
cooler
inside air

trapped solar
heat
glass
summer inside
insulation
cooler
inside air

SUMMER SOLAR VENT

summer vent
black surfaced
masonry wall
glass

SUMMER MASS WALL VENT

heated
air
air
filter
glass
cool
inside air

WINTER MASS WALL AIR FILTER

A solar air ramp, windows with radiant barrier curtains, or a solar mass wall can be used for *induction vents*. Where sunlight is trapped behind south or west glazing, air is heated and rises. If the heated air is allowed to vent outside at the top, interior air will be sucked up the solar heated space and exhausted. This exiting air should be replaced by outside air taken from a low, shaded spot, preferably on the north or east side.

During a heating season, an air filter placed in the heated-air return-duct of a solar mass wall will filter out smoke, odors, and particles from reheated interior air. This eliminates much of the need to exhaust and replace used air by cold outside air.

SOLAR INDUCTION VENTS

A *building* can act as a *flue* for ventilating by the chimney effect. In some climates where maximum ventilation is desired to exhaust heated air during the cooling season, or when special rooms require removal of smoke or odors, the building can be shaped to optimize natural convective ventilation. In all cases, steps should be taken to insulate and weatherproof during the heating season. Generally, even tightly sealed buildings will self-ventilate by infiltration at door and window edges and through the weather-skin. During winter months, this unavoidable air exchange can provide adequate air supply, eliminating the need for additional ventilation, except possibly for some smoke or odor removal.

The challenge with ventilation is to provide sufficient fresh air during extreme climate conditions—*effectively* and *comfortably!*

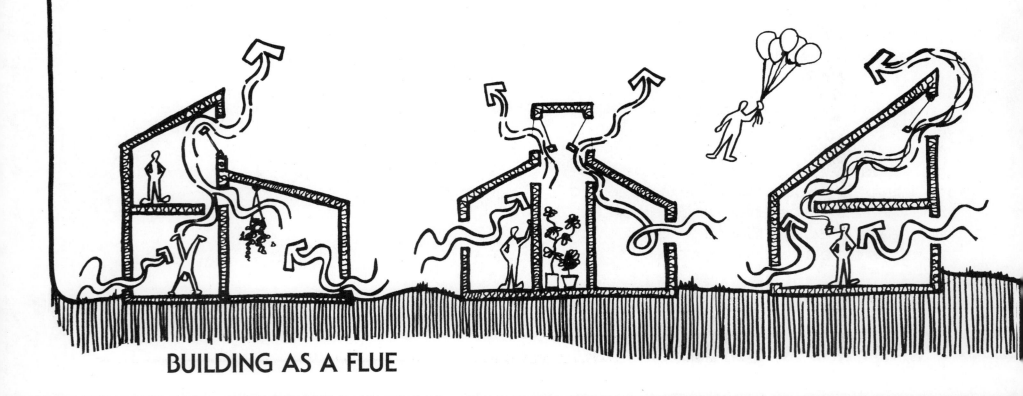

BUILDING AS A FLUE

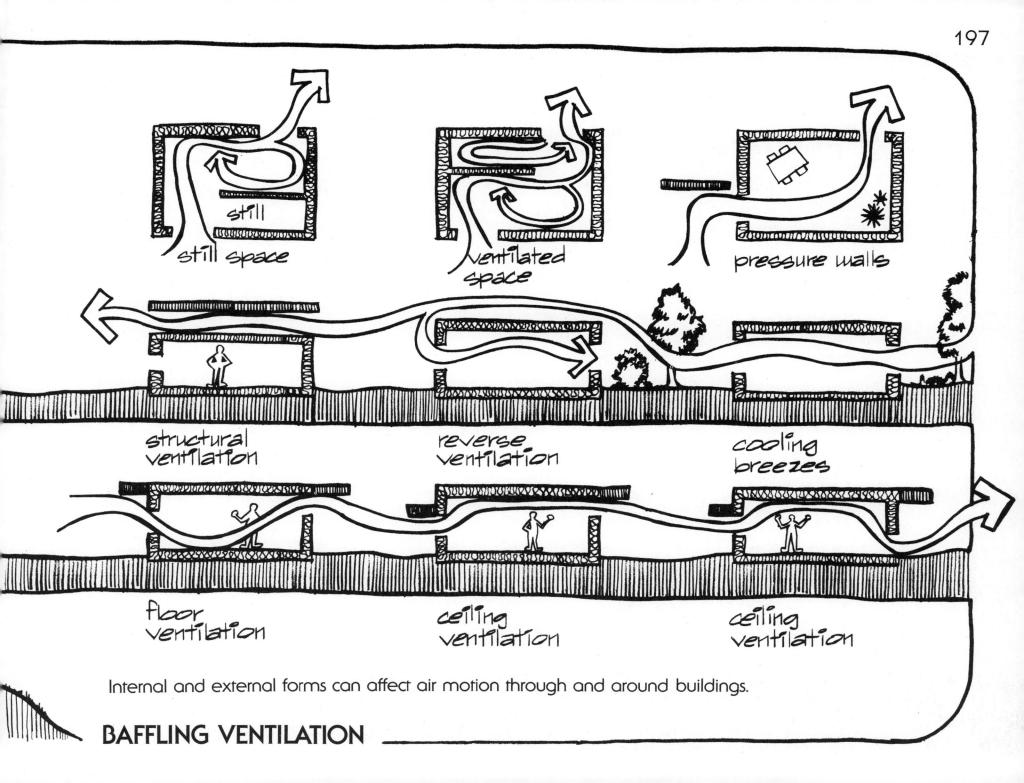

still

still space

ventilated space

pressure walls

structural ventilation

reverse ventilation

cooling breezes

floor ventilation

ceiling ventilation

ceiling ventilation

Internal and external forms can affect air motion through and around buildings.

BAFFLING VENTILATION

Cooling

Usually, the emphasis placed on passive solar use is for heating. Cooling by passive means can be effective for controlling excessive heat in most climates. In some locations, air motion through ventilation may suffice to maintain comfort. In other climates, controlling the heat content of the radiant storage mass may be adequate. The method used may need to be supplemented by adding or removing moisture from the ambient air to achieve a proper humidity/temperature balance.

A heat-storage mass used for heating in winter may be used for *cooling* during summer. Many times control of the mean radiant temperature (MRT) of a structure will do the job of cooling in a simple nonmechanical way. In some climates augmentation by a small amount of conventional cooling may be required, just as some means of auxiliary heating is needed with many solar heating systems. The point is to design

buildings that maximize the natural potential to heat or cool themselves, using as little expensive inefficient fuel energy as possible to make our lives comfortable.

Now that we're so hot for solar heating . . . let's cool it!!

The traditional method used to keep structures of massive construction *cool* is to close them up like a refrigerator during the heat of the day and open them up at *night,* allowing accumulated heat to escape. Thick-walled adobe and stoned structures in the southwestern United States maintain internal comfort during extremely hot weather by this means.

Insulated shutters, used in winter to prevent heat loss, can be utilized in summer to reduce heat gain. Shading all glass, plus south and west walls, helps minimize direct heat gain from the sun. Insulating the outside of walls further prevents heat buildup in the mass of the building. Opening doors, windows, skylights, and vents at night to allow cool breezes to circulate and carry out heat from the interior mass lowers the mean radiant temperature of the space. Internal heat generated by cooking, lights, and motors should be vented outside in summer.

NIGHT-AIR COOLING

Night-sky or deep-space *radiation* is a reversal of the daytime insolation principle. Just as the sun constantly radiates energy through the void of space, heat energy travels, virtually unhindered, from the earth's surface back into this void.

On a clear night when the void of space is our earthly ceiling, the earth and any warm object can cool itself by radiating long-wave heat energy to the infinite cold depth of space. It is possible to cool a body of water or any solid mass to well below the ambient air temperature if its surface is aimed at the night sky and it is insulated from surrounding warm bodies. Glazing and other radiant barriers will inhibit this emission of heat energy.

Structures with movable insulation for preventing solar gain during the day can be designed to open at night, allowing surfaces within to release heat by radiation and convection. It is possible to achieve cooling comfort in many climates by this simple and elegant method.

NIGHT-SKY RADIATION

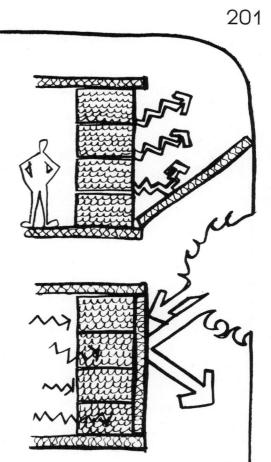

Skytherm systems, using bags or containers of water or other fluids on the *roof,* collect heat during winter days. At night, insulation is placed over the top and heat radiates to the interior. In summer, reversing the process to prevent heat gain during the day and opening the insulation at night, allowing the water mass to iose heat to the night sky, cools buildings. A water depth of 6 to 8 inches (15 to 20 cm) and 1½ to 3 inches (4 to 8 cm) of foam insulation can maintain an interior temperature range of 65 to 70°F (18 to 21°C) over ninety percent of the time in most arid climates. Flooding the top of the bags with water adds to their conductivity of heat; and the evaporative effect further increases the cooling capacity of this elegant water-roof concept.

Exterior *water walls,* drum walls, and mass walls that are insulated during the day and opened at night will function much the same as Skytherm. Glass or transparent membranes used to trap winter sunlight should be removed to allow maximum emission of radiation.

SKYTHERM ROOFS AND WATER WALLS

Shade roofs help a great deal in hot or tropical climates to prevent daytime sun from getting directly to the mass of a structure. The space below an insulated shade roof allows breezes to circulate next to the lower roof, removing heat that may generate from inside.

In tropical climates structural mass should be minimized to avoid storing heat in the fabric of a building. A structure with little heat-retention capacity will cool quickly when rains and breezes are about.

This type of umbrella roof might be adjustable by day or season. In some desert climates, with little or no cooling breezes, roofs which isolate the structure from the sun but open at night to encourage deep space radiation are advantageous.

Sprinkling or flooding the lower roof with water at certain times, such as when breezes prevail, will cool the structure even further.

SHADE ROOF

Many cultures in arid climates have utilized the interior patio or *courtyard* for *cooling*. This open and shaded space can be covered by light-weight shading lattice during the heat of the day to prevent sun intrusion and heat buildup in the interior walls.

Small exterior windows allow prevailing breezes to enter while blocking the sun from the massive room interiors. Vegetation and fountains or ponds add evaporation to the cooling effect of breezes passing in one side and out the other.

At night, by opening all doors and windows and removing the day shade, deep-space radiation, air, and evaporative cooling continually remove heat from the massive walls.

The courtyard environment is a cool, indoor/outdoor private area suitable for many uses.

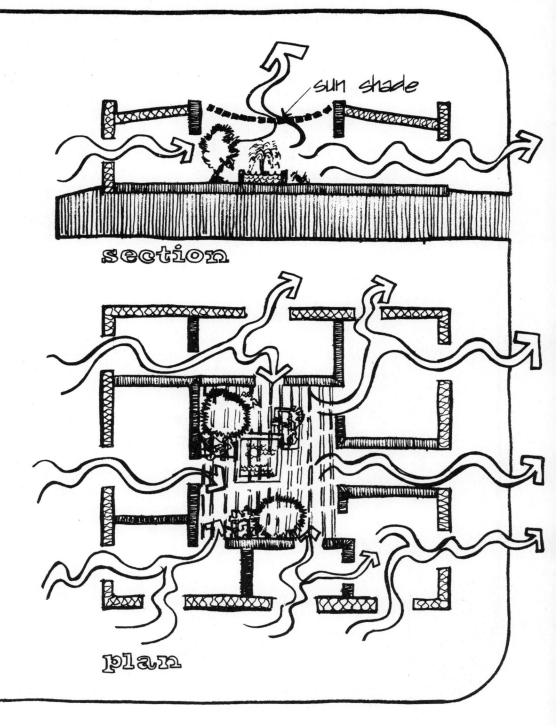

sun shade

section

plan

COOL COURTYARDS

In warmer climates, where subsurface conditions allow, it makes sense to *burrow* into the coolth (area where warmth is absent) of the *earth*. In most locations, the temperature of the earth is stable to within a few degrees of the mean annual temperature at a depth of 5 to 8 feet (1.5 to 2.4 m), if the soil is dry. Thus, at a depth of 5 feet (1.5 m), the earth's temperature will normally not exceed 70°F (21°C) when the air temperature above the ground is near 100°F (38°C).

Subsurface structures are easy to heat in the winter; infiltration and steady-state heat losses are minimal due to the insulation value and impermeability of the enveloping earth.

Adequate vents and light wells must be provided for air change and illumination.

natural light & ventilation

EARTH BURROWING

In southern Tunisia, at the edge of the Sahara Desert, and in other harsh climates, *troglodyte dwellings* provide even-temperature shelter against severe dusty winds, extremely hot summers, and cold winters.

These underground houses, carved out of soft yet stable soil, open off a craterlike central court. Sun penetration is minimal at the bottom, and the rooms maintain a radiant temperature approximating the coolth of the deep earth. Vents to the surface allow air circulation.

Usually, a water cistern below the court captures water runoff in this dry region. The rooms and lower courtyard walls, ceiling, and floors are whitewashed to reflect light. Dining, cooking, and craftwork are done in the courtyard.

These structures are fine examples of native ingenuity in dealing with an extreme environment with minimal material resources.

When the family expands, carve out another room!

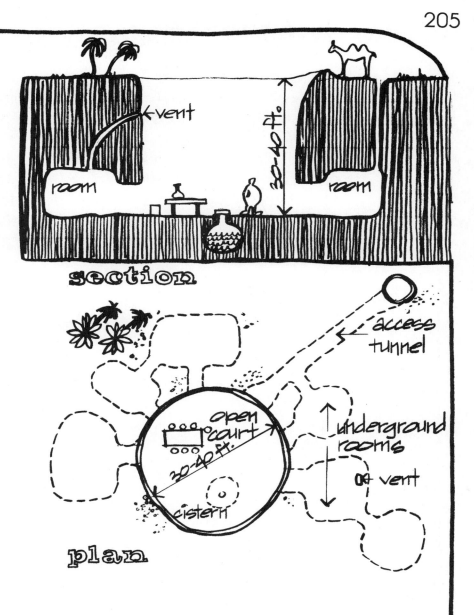

section

plan

TROGLODYTE DWELLINGS

Cooling of a structure can be accomplished by modifying the existing *microclimate*. Carefully located trees and shrubs will shade the structure and surrounding ground, preventing buildup of the sun's heat. Vegetation and structural forms can be placed to channel and concentrate cooling breezes through and around buildings. Ponds of water, fountains, or the sprinkling of vegetation upwind from buildings will cool the ambient air, increasing its heat-carrying capacity before it enters the structure. Sometimes dense vegetation in arid climates can inhibit radiation to the night sky, thus limiting the cooling effect.

However, in most climates a combination of these basic microclimate modifiers, properly selected and located, will maintain temperatures well below that of surrounding areas.

MICROCLIMATE CONTROL

In areas with moderate humidity and an adequate water supply, *evaporation* of water to the air will carry off excess heat. An old-fashioned camp cooler illustrates this principle well. The cooler consists of a series of shelves surrounded by an absorbent fabric, such as burlap or canvas, that acts as a wick. Water drips at a slow rate from above and spreads throughout the wick, keeping it moist. The moistened fabric is porous enough to allow the breeze to blow through the material, picking up moisture by evaporation. The heat-carrying capacity of the air is increased by its water content, and, as it moves through and out of the cooler, more heat is removed than enters. The rate of evaporation is greater as the air motion increases. If you can control the speed of the air, you can vary the temperature in the cooler.

This is the same principle used in "swamp" coolers. Cooling can be regulated by varying the fan speed and water flow.

This idea can be used in several ways for passive cooling of structures.

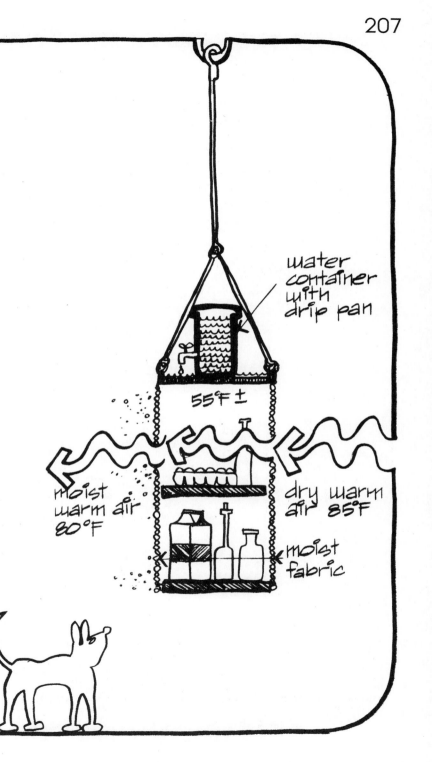

water container with drip pan

55°F ±

moist warm air 80°F

dry warm air 85°F

moist fabric

EVAPORATION

Swamp coolers are *evaporative* air cooling devices that use a large fan to pull or *induce* air through a pad or wick saturated with water. The same result can be accomplished by using a solar vent to move air. A roof vent or solar air ramp that exhausts heated air can, in turn, pull outside air through a cooler pad, or wet burlap sack, or across a pool of water or damp pebble bed. If the air is drawn from a shaded outside area and through the moisture wick, it will be quite cool upon entering the building and will have the thermal capacity for absorbing a significant amount of heat. As the moist air circulates through the building, it will attract heat from all objects before being sucked up and out by the solar-heated convection current. The higher the solar intensity, the greater the potential for pulling cool air through the building.

This method of evaporative cooling is effective in areas where excessive humidity is not a problem.

Dampers should be used to control the volume and velocity of the airflow.

water reservoir

solar heated air

insulation

ambient air

cool, moist air

warmed air

INDUCED EVAPORATION

The nomadic Bedouin people use tents woven of black goat hair as shelter from the hot, dusty, and dry environment of Arab countries.

The *black* insulative surface of the *tents* has little thermal mass. Upon heating in the sun, convection is induced between the fibers and across the inner surface, causing air motion. The low conductivity of the fabric adds little radiative heat to the shaded interior. The hotter the day, the greater the surface rejection of external solar heat. This is due to the low heat capacity of the tent material and the convective current through it.

These portable and flexible tents can easily be adjusted to block hot-blowing, sandy wind and provide shade from the scorching sun. Relatively comfortable interior temperatures can be maintained where daytime temperatures reach 120 to 140°F (49 to 60°C).

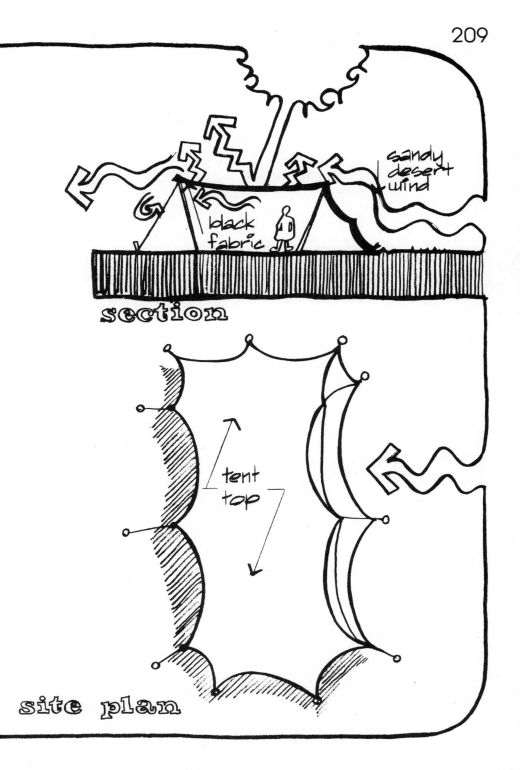

BLACK TENTS

A method for using the earth's thermal mass for cooling is to conduct outside ambient air, induced by vents or solar collectors, through long *tubes* buried underground or in *earth* berms or laid in the bottom of ponds. This method of cooling, using the stable temperature of the earth's mass to absorb heat from air passing through the tubes, also has potential for adding or removing humidity. Gently downward sloping tubes of the proper diameter and length allow cooling air to fall slowly. As the air temperature reaches the dew point of its moisture content,

water will condense. This condensate should be allowed to drain out of the airstream at a point near the bottom end of the tube. A water wick or pan at the same location could add moisture, if humidification is desired.

All tubes should be constructed of clay tile or noncorrosive metal. Inlet vents should be screened and placed on the north side or in a well-shaded area. Insulation may be required above the tubes to keep the earth around them cool.

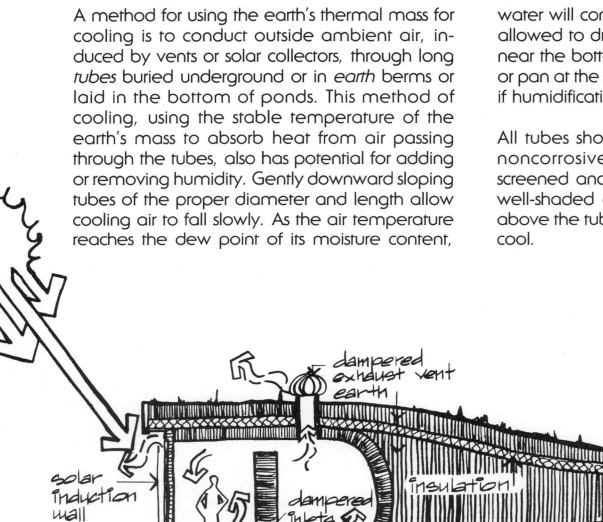

dampered exhaust vent

earth

solar induction wall

dampered inlets

insulation

screened inlet

sloping tubes

condensate drain or humidification pan

EARTH TUBES

In arid regions of the world, some ancient civilizations developed *cooling towers,* which made use of the prevailing breeze and basic thermodynamics. In Persia and Egypt, wind-scoop towers catch above-ground winds and channel the air down masonry shafts. As the air drops through the cool shafts, it circulates past porous clay water vessels. The vessels, which are filled with water daily, gradually sweat moisture, cooling the passing air and increasing its heat-carrying capacity.

In some instances, a pool of water at the bottom further cools the passing air by evaporation. An open mesh with a layer of charcoal is sometimes suspended in the shaft below the clay jars. This charcoal catches and absorbs water dripping from above. As the air passes through this matrix of charcoal, it is cooled and dust particles are filtered out. Finally, the air exits at the opposite, low-pressure end of the building.

With this method it is possible to cool a building well below ambient air temperature in very warm climates.

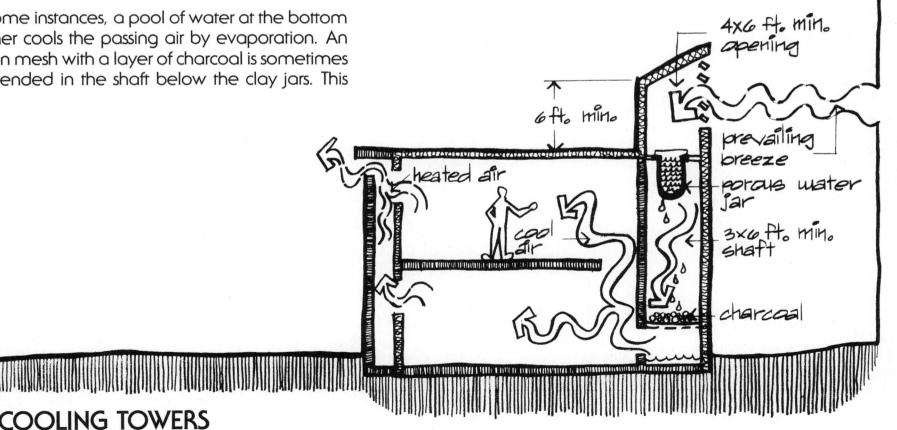

COOLING TOWERS

Ice walls, another ancient method of passive cooling, had been used in the deserts of the Middle East and the East Indies up to the early part of this century to make ice during nonfreezing weather. The long east- and west-oriented earth walls prevent direct solar gain on shallow troughs of water located on the shaded north side. At night, the water radiates long-wave heat energy to deep space. The ice wall allows air stratification in the wind shadow. Insulation of the trough from the earth isolates the water from the ground temperature. Buttresses, perpendicular to the wall, structurally reinforce it, prevent solar

gain from the east and west, and help to still air movement. Two or more parallel ice walls also aid air stratification between them. Temperatures well below ambient air are possible.

Today, structures using a combination of low-energy earth walls, good insulation, and movable covers could take advantage of this ingenious old-fashioned refrigeration system.

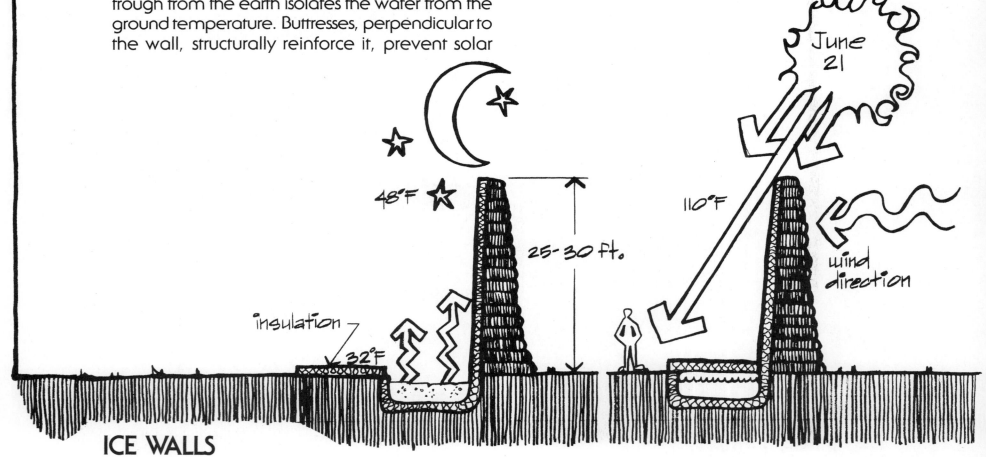

ICE WALLS

A *dew pond* is an ancient device once used in southern England for collecting cool water. These shallow ponds of water, insulated from the earth, radiated heat from their surface to the night sky. The concept of these ponds could be updated, using modern materials instead of the clay, straw, and flint which were traditionally used.

As heat is radiated from the water surface, some evaporation occurs until the temperature drops to the dew point of the night air. Continued cooling causes water to condense out of the immediate atmosphere into the pond. The process continues as long as there is a net radiation heat loss from the pond. Night dew can replace moisture lost by evaporation; this condensing of water into the pond adds some heat to its thermal mass. With an insulated cover, heat gain and evaporation are reduced during summer days.

A dew pond radiating to deep space can lose enough heat energy to drop its temperature to freezing if the moisture content of the surrounding air is low enough. This idea could be adapted to use in structures and provide cooling for buildings in many climates.

night

day

night dew
insulative cover
water
membrane
gravel & sand
insulation

DEW PONDS

4 RULES-OF-THUMB

Introduction

The art of predicting the performance of passive solar buildings has evolved from guesstimation and manual calculation to sophisticated computer analysis. Before any calculations or thermal analyses are performed, rules-of-thumb may be applied. The manual calculation method outlined in this primer is a steady-state, or "static," analysis. This means that average outside design temperature, percentage of possible sunshine, and other solar-design variables are used to predict performance for a particular average time or period. The results of this type of calculation method are very generalized and will roughly indicate the percent of solar heating for a normal season. Many successful buildings have been designed using these manual and "static" analysis methods, which are the basis of all other methods of determining a building's performance. For the person who wishes to know how a passive solar house works, it is very important to perform and understand these simple manual calculation methods.

Once the principles of heat transfer are firmly grasped by the solar designer, there are a number of machine-assisted calculation methods available. These range from small hand-held programmable calculators to mainframe computers with massive data-storage potential. You can purchase a program to run on your own programmable calculator or microcomputer, or you can take your design to a solar engineer for a very complete and accurate computer analysis. These machine calculations can take into account seasonal, daily, and even hourly design variables and hundreds of subtle factors that affect the performance of a solar building. The constantly changing effects and interrelationships of many factors such as wind speed, shading devices, sun angles, and azimuth (to name only a few) are best analyzed with a computer. This type of thermal calculation is called a "dynamic" analysis and is often performed on an hourly variable basis, giving a high degree of accuracy. It can help predict interior temperature at any hour of any day for a building design. Of course, such prediction is based on average climatic data, and actual performance will most likely vary from season to season and year to year from the prediction.

This type of computer simulation is the best performance predictor of a solar design. An analysis of this type can be time consuming and somewhat costly. Shortened versions are often used to help settle on the appropriate solar system and sizing prior to an extensive computer run.

A rule-of-thumb is simply an accepted standard that can be readily applied to a problem at the outset to approximate the proper solution. In the case of solar design, you need to know what kind of system is cost effective and what the general size proportions should be for your climate and needs. Rules-of-thumb are usually used at the outset of any solar-design process to help establish a "ballpark" standard of sizing a system prior to a full-blown analysis. It should be noted that rules-of-thumb vary widely depending on such factors as personal preference and climate suitability.

The following sampling of rules-of-thumb are representative of a wide range of both geographical and climatological areas and are the favorites of a few of the country's leading solar designers. Their rules represent years of trial and error as well as computer analysis and verification. Each architect or engineer was asked to share the rules-of-thumb they most prefer for residential design in their particular city. In most cases these rules are suitable to a larger range of locations. Accordingly, each of these experts was asked to define a general geographical area where his rules should apply.

These rules-of-thumb are offered as a guide to other designers. One or several of these rules may be applicable to your location. The trick is to pick the most suitable for your needs, then to use it effectively as a design tool. You've heard the expression "I'm all thumbs"—use these thumbs well! Good luck.

MISSISSIPPI

Architect: Robert MacDonald Ford, AIA

General Climate Zone:

Inland and coastal areas of Mississippi, Louisiana, and Alabama.

Cooling Methods Preferred:

1. Belvedere (ventilating cupola)
2. Ceiling fans
3. Night ventilation
4. Overhangs
5. Deciduous planting
6. Shade screen

Heating Methods Preferred:

1. Direct gain
2. Greenhouse
3. Solarium
4. Vented (Trombe) wall
5. Clerestories
6. Central atrium
7. Masonry mass wall

Climate (Mississippi State, Mississippi):

Temperate to cool winters; intensive rainfall followed by sunshine; no snow but occasional freezes at night. Summers sunny, hot, and humid with only light breezes.

—Altitude—300 feet
—Heating degree days—2500
—Cooling degree days—2750
—Annual rainfall—55 inches
—Annual percentage of sunshine—65 percent
—January percentage of sunshine—45 percent
—Winter storm direction—south
—January average daily temperature range—36°F to 57°F
—July average daily temperature range—70°F to 92°F

Cooling Rules-Of-Thumb

—Properly located shade trees on south and west very important. Use light-colored roofing to reflect heat. Shade roof with tree cover if possible. Ventilate roof spaces very well.

—Maximize ventilation through entire building by use of open planning and high ceilings. Vertical organization of three or four floors enhances stack effect. Rooftop belvedere or operable clerestory windows will vent warmer air out of high spaces. Large awning windows on all sides of spaces maximize cross ventilation and allows ventilation during rainfall. Pocket doors and transoms between rooms encourage airflow. Louver doors in closets and cupboards allow ventilation and prevent mildew.

—Overhead ceiling fans with reversible blades and speed control supplement natural ventilation.

—Air velocity in breezeway ("dog-trot") between building elements is greater than prevailing breezes.

Heating Rules-Of-Thumb

—Extensive use of deciduous trees on south and west allows direct winter sun. Heavy evergreen cover on north to minimize cold northern breezes.

—Use well-sealed double-glazed wood windows throughout. Optimize glass exposure to east, for early morning heat gain, and south (under properly calculated overhangs) for gain throughout day.

—Movable window insulation not economically feasible. Consider exterior louvers or shutters to both shade in summer and reduce heat loss in winter.

—Open planning allows easy movement of warm air through spaces. Use overhead ceiling fans to bring heat down from high ceilings.

—Wood stoves and fireplaces provide inexpensive auxiliary heating due to plentiful wood supply. Consider central location.

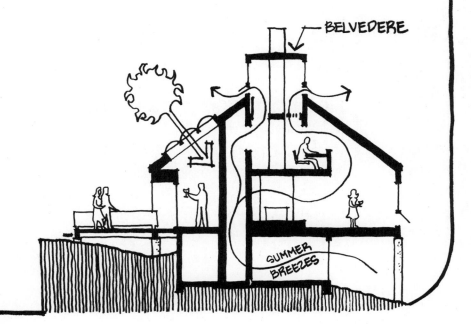

VIRGINIA

Architects: One Design, Inc.

General Climate Zone:

General south and southeastern states.

Heating Methods Preferred:

1. Water mass wall**
2. Direct gain combined with interior water walls**
3. Clerestories
4. Greenhouses/sunspaces

Cooling Methods Preferred:

1. Overhangs
2. Deciduous planting
3. Exterior shades
4. Night ventilation
5. Attic whole-house ventilation

Climate (Winchester, Virginia):

Cool, rainy winters with moderate sunshine. Hot, humid, sticky summers with warm nights and breezes.

—Altitude—950 feet
—Heating degree days—5010
—Cooling degree days—940
—Annual rainfall—40 inches
—Annual percentage of sunshine—58 percent
—January percentage of sunshine—48 percent
—Winter storm direction—northwest
—January average daily temperature range—23°F to 41°F
—July average daily temperature range—64°F to 86°F

Heating Rules-Of-Thumb:

—Orient house within 30° of south (easterly preferred). Place living spaces on south with bed-

room/buffer spaces on north.
—Insulate walls to R-19 minimum (R-23 preferred), roof to R-30 minimum (R-38 preferred), and perimeter to R-10 (R-19 preferred). Tighten weatherskin to minimize air infiltration.
—Size south glazing equal to 15 to 25 percent of the floor area. Minimize north, east, and west glazing. Spread solar glazing equally across the facade to prevent overheating in any one room. Design half of solar glazing for direct gain windows or clerestories and half for water mass wall.** Use 30 to 45 pounds of water fully exposed to sun (30 to 45 BTUs of storage) per square foot of glazing when mass is directly swept by the sun. When mass is not directly swept by the sun, use twice that amount.
—Double glazing is adequate in most southern climates. Triple glazing, using highly solar transparent film or glass,

is cost effective in lieu of movable insulation in most cases. Movable insulation is cost effective in colder locations.
—In greenhouses, use water mass wall** with a total surface area equal to 60 to 80 percent of the glass area.

Cooling Rules-Of-Thumb
—Shade east and west windows. To help prevent summer overheating, avoid any sloped glazing on winter solar heating system. Shade south glazing with deciduous trees or vine arbors. Do not create fixed southern overhangs that shade south glazing in winter.
—Place windows properly to encourage cross ventilation. Ventilate attics with continuous ridge and soffit vents (oversized preferred).
—Water mass walls** help keep inside temperatures cool. Ventilate house and

mass at night by opening doors and windows.
—Design any greenhouse to be fully ventable by opening doors, windows, and so on, equal to 50 percent or more of the glazing. Shade greenhouse as much as possible.

**Denotes One Design Waterwall or Waterwindow.

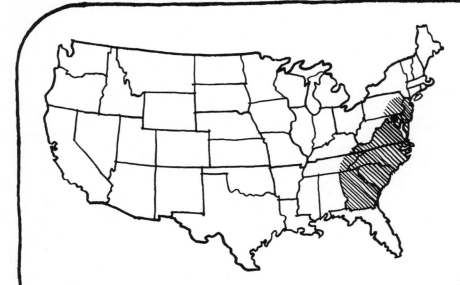

MARYLAND

Architects: Price & Partners

General Climate Zone:
Atlantic Coast: generally Georgia to New Jersey.

Heating Methods Preferred:
1. Direct gain
2. Solarium
3. Greenhouse
4. Central atrium
5. Water tube storage
6. Clerestories

Cooling Methods Preferred:
1. Overhangs
2. Deciduous plantings
3. Shade screen
4. Night ventilation
5. Semi-earth integration
6. Coolth field
7. Evaporative cooler

Climate (Takoma Park, Maryland):
Pleasant spring and fall. Summers humid and hot, winters sometimes cold. Heavy, frequent rainfall. Reliable land and sea breeze.

—Altitude—64 feet
—Heating degree days—4333
—Cooling degree days—1800
—Annual rainfall—27 inches
—Annual percentage of sunshine—58 percent
—January percentage of sunshine—40 percent
—Winter storm direction—northwest
—January average daily temperature range—28°F to 43°F
—July average daily temperature range—73°F to 93°F

Heating Rules-Of-Thumb
—Double south glazing *with operable insulation* not to exceed 40 to 45 percent of

the floor area on single family detached homes and 30 to 35 percent of the floor area on commonwall structures.

—Thermal floor storage mass is very important with direct-gain systems. Extreme cold spells are infrequent and overheating in winter will occur if thermal mass is sized inaccurately low. Size 2 to 3 square feet of dense floor mass for each square foot of south glazing. Color of mass not critical (5 percent difference); aesthetics govern.

—Insulate walls to R-19-25 and roof to R-35 minimum. Perimeter-slab foam insulation of at least 2-inch thickness. Movable window insulation is necessary but counterproductive if greater than R-4 value.

Cooling Rules-Of-Thumb

—Windows should be operable for maximum ventilation. Casement type pro-vides wide breeze-catching opening and is preferred to double hung. Seal all windows and doors well.

—Abundant thermal mass, earth integration, and shade vegetation do wonders for summer cooling. Though underground structures cool well, condensation and seepage can be problems if structures not properly designed.

—Shade overhangs are a must. Overhangs at one foot above window head should be equal to one-half the vertical glass height.

—Reflective louvers on the east, west, and south windows help cooling tremendously.

—Porches, awnings, trees, lattice arbors, and interior shades on the east and west facades are critical for cooling.

—In high-humidity areas, large ceiling fans and, to some extent, night cooling are effective.

—When temperatures reach mid to high nineties and humidity is above 80 percent, only dehumidifiers and air conditioning will maintain comfort. Use them only when you must and only in single rooms, i.e. window air conditioner in bedrooms at night.

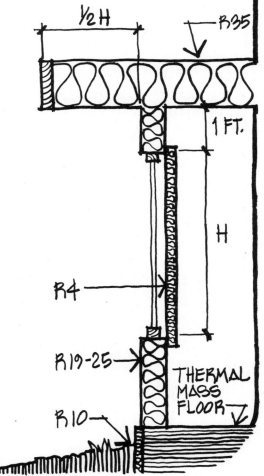

CONNECTICUT

Architect: Donald Watson, FAIA

General Climate Zone:
Southern New England states.

Heating Methods Preferred:
1. Solarium
2. Greenhouse
3. Clerestories
4. Direct gain
5. Central atrium
6. Masonry mass wall

Cooling Methods Preferred:
1. Night ventilation
2. Overhangs
3. Shade screens
4. Deciduous planting
5. Coolth tubes or fields

Climate (Guilford, Connecticut):
Cool to cold winters with an average of 50 percent clear days during winter months. New England coastal climate milder than inland but having greater daily variation. Summers generally pleasant with overheating typically limited to "hot spells" in July lasting two to three weeks.

—Altitude—169 feet
—Heating degree days—6350
—Cooling degree days—584
—Annual rainfall—45 inches
—Annual percentage of sunshine—58 percent
—January percentage of sunshine—58 percent
—Winter storm direction—northwest
—January average daily temperature range— 16°F to 34°F
—July average daily temperature range—57°F to 74°F

Heating Rules-Of-Thumb

—South glazing at 20 to 25 percent of floor area is optimal for a house design if all glazing is insulated at night. Limit south glazing to approximately 10 to 12 percent of floor area if night insulation cannot be used.

—Solar mass storage exposed directly to sunlight should be about 3 square feet of area for every square foot of south glazing, if masonry or tile on slab is used.

—Insulate walls to R-25 or greater and roof to R-40 or greater.

—Insulation strategies are equal to solar strategies in southern New England. Insulation strategies should predominate in northern New England, where cloudiness predominates. Winter days are typically cloudy; therefore, mass not in direct sun does not get fully "charged."

—Design for human comfort, create beautiful settings for interior spaces that focus on the solar-oriented (solarium, greenhouse, atrium) space.

Cooling Rules-Of-Thumb:

—Place doors and operable windows to allow free cross and night ventilation.

—Earth contact through concrete slab on grade is beneficial for summer cooling effect if shaded. Expose slab to air movement for condensation prevention.

—Shade glazing with overhangs, shade screens, and deciduous planting.

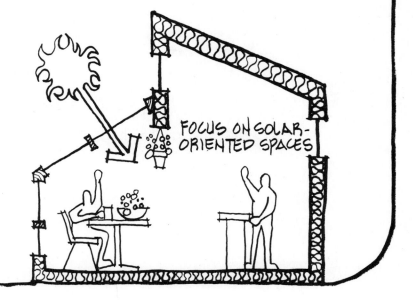

FOCUS ON SOLAR-ORIENTED SPACES

MINNESOTA

Architect: Architectural Alliance

General Climate Zone:
The upper Midwestern and upper New England States.

Heating Methods Preferred:
1. Direct gain with mass floors and/or mass walls
2. Greenhouse
3. Solarium
4. Clerestories
5. Central atrium

Cooling Methods Preferred:
1. Natural ventilation (day and night)
2. Overhangs
3. Deciduous plantings
4. Awnings

Climate (Minneapolis, Minnesota):
Severely cold climate with moderate to low winter sunshine and a small summer cooling load due to temperature and humidity.

—Altitude—822 feet
—Heating degree days—8300
—Cooling degree days—585
—Annual rainfall—26 inches
—Annual percentage of sunshine—58 percent
—January percentage of sunshine—50 percent
—Winter storm direction—northwest
—January average daily temperature range—4°F to 21°F
—July average daily temperature range—63°F to 83°F

Heating Rules-Of-Thumb:
—Reduce heating load by designing an efficient weatherskin. Insulate walls to minimum R-25 (optimum R-40) and ceilings to minimum R-40 (optimum R-70).
—Minimize infiltration to a natural level of one-tenth to one-half air change per hour. Always

use air-lock entries on all commonly used entrances. With low infiltration construction, an air-to-air heat exchanger is necessary to introduce fresh air efficiently.

—For economy of construction, size south glazing in the range of 10 percent to 15 percent of the floor area. Glazing must be double or triple glazed with night insulation. Quad glazing can be used in lieu of night insulation.

—With moderate solar glazing, most of the solar gain goes to offset daytime losses. Therefore, a small amount of thermal mass will be sufficient to stabilize temperatures. For economy use a direct gain system with 2 to 3 inches of concrete over a wood-joist floor, or north-south interior mass walls.

—Select auxiliary heating systems carefully for size and efficiency. Pulse furnaces and boilers, induced draft furnaces, and electrical-resistance heaters all deal with combustion air and flue waste effectively.

—Sunspaces such as solaria and greenhouses act as good thermal buffers that are enjoyable during long, cold winters.

—Aesthetics are important. Good architecture means good energy design; the two are synergistic, not exclusive.

Cooling Rules-Of-Thumb:

—Provide good cross ventilation. Size relief openings on the north side up to twice as large as south openings. Design openings with security and weather protection in mind so that vents can be left open at night or during rainfall. Pay attention to the design of interior openings between rooms to assist summer ventilation.

—Shade south glazing with overhangs, louvers, screens, or vegetative planting.

—Minimize east and west glass as it receives two to three times more summer solar radiation than unshaded south glass.

—In temperate climates, earth sheltering is an important cooling strategy. Some form of mechanical cooling or dehumidification may be required for a limited part of the summer.

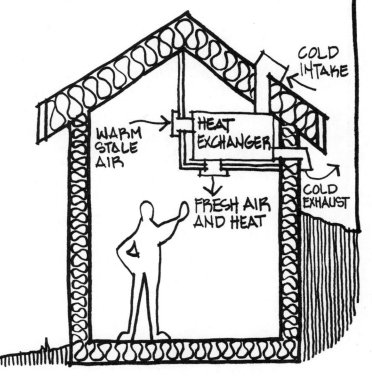

WISCONSIN

Architect: The Hawkweed Group, Ltd.

General Climate Zone:
General Midwestern states: north Minnesota to south Illinois.

Heating Methods Preferred:
1. Direct gain
2. Masonry mass wall
3. Vented Trombe wall
4. Solarium
5. Greenhouse
6. Clerestories
7. Solar attic

Cooling Methods Preferred:
1. Night ventilation
2. Overhangs
3. Shade screens
4. Deciduous plants
5. Coolth tubes or field

Climate (Osseo, Wisconsin):
Long, cold, snowy winters. Warm and sometimes humid summers.

—Altitude—900 feet
—Heating degree days—8388
—Cooling degree days—459
—Annual rainfall—30 inches
—Annual percentage of sunshine—55 percent
—January percentage of sunshine—45 percent
—Winter storm direction—northwest
—January average temperature range—6°F to 25°F
—July average temperature range—60°F to 86°F

Heating Rules-Of-Thumb:
—Winter climatic control is dominant need. Maximize thermal efficiency of building. Insulate walls to R-42, ceiling or roof to R-78, crawlspace to R-42, perimeter to R-8. Reduce glazing at all walls; if possible use only south-facing glass. Use nighttime insulative cover-

ings on all windows. Careful attention should be paid to caulking and weatherstripping to ensure a tight building.

—Earth integrate where possible to reduce infiltration.

—Use 16 to 20 percent of floor area in south glazing, balanced with the super insulation values above, to achieve approximately 90 percent solar contribution and minimal auxiliary heating.

—Provide adequate mass to absorb and store heat. Two hundred pounds of masonry or concrete for each square foot of south glazing, if in direct sun most of the day. All internal materials thoroughly isolated from direct solar gain can be considered at one-quarter value of direct mass (floor slabs, quarry tile, drywall, furniture, and so on).

Cooling Rules-Of-Thumb:

—Super insulation and thermal efficiency will greatly reduce heat gain.

—In many Midwest locations natural cooling will suffice. Use approximately 5 percent of the floor area in openings to admit southwest breezes. Night cool building and close up during the day to retain coolth.

—Overhangs should be designed to block direct sun in summer.

—Insulative shutters inside or out eliminate glare and reduce heat gain.

—Low planting outside below low windows will reduce humidity, exhaust high at north to increase efficiency of airflow. Do not plant deciduous trees or tall shrubs too close to south of building as the branching pattern will block winter solar gain.

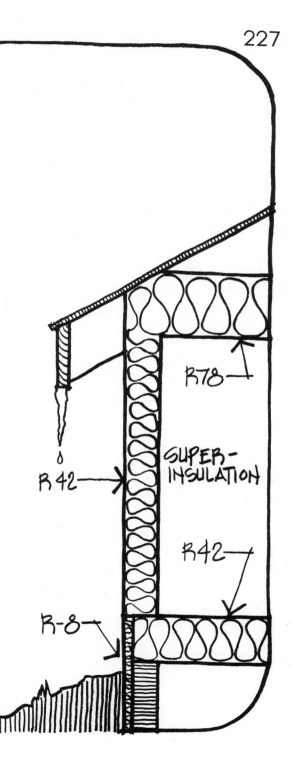

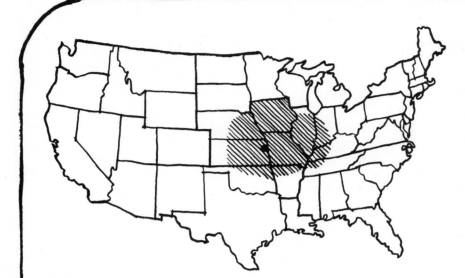

KANSAS

Solar Engineer: Ron H. Wantoch, P.E.

General Climate Zone:
South-central Midwestern states.

Heating Methods Preferred:
1. Clerestories
2. Direct gain
3. Masonry mass wall
4. Greenhouse
5. Central atrium
6. Solarium

Cooling Methods Preferred:
1. Night ventilation
2. Overhang and deciduous planting to south
3. Shade screens and planting to east and west
4. Mechanical air conditioning
5. Coolth fields
6. Evaporative cooler

Climate (Overland Park, Kansas):
Cold, snowy winters with reasonable sunshine; hot, humid summer days with warm nights; short fall and spring.

—Altitude—791 feet
—Heating degree days—4711
—Cooling degree days—1609
—Annual rainfall—34 inches
—Annual percentage of sunshine—60 percent
—January percentage of sunshine—53 percent
—Winter storm direction—northwest
—January average daily temperature range—23°F to 40°F
—July average daily temperature range—71°F to 92°F

Heating Rules-Of-Thumb:
—Orientation within 30° of south.

—Continuous vapor barrier. Seal greenhouse airtight during winter. For very tight houses, provide fresh air to control odor and humidity. Consider air-to-air heat exchanger or earth coolth tube.

—For solar fraction between 60 and 80 percent, use ratio of south glazing to heat load coefficient (sq. ft. to BTU/hr/°F) of one to one. Use double or triple glazing. Triple preferred. Night insulation for solar fractions over 70 percent. No east or west glazing on greenhouse.

—No added mass required for solar fractions below 30 percent. Ceiling and interior wall mass locations preferred to floor. If mass is in direct sunlight, use one cubic foot of mass per square foot of glazing. If mass not in direct sunlight, use two cubic feet of mass per square foot of glazing.

Cooling Rules-Of-Thumb:

—Shade trees on east, southeast, west, and southwest. Ground planting to minimize summer ground reflectance.

—Minimize or eliminate sloped glass or skylights. Minimize east/west glass. No tinted or reflective glass; use smaller windows instead.

—Exterior or between glazing shades preferred. Thermally isolate and ventilate greenhouse and/or use exterior shade screen.

—Overhang length: one-third of window height for solar fraction less than 50 percent; two-thirds of window height for solar fraction greater than 70 percent.

—Provide cross ventilation windows (southwest to northeast). Screened porches on east or northeast for ventilation. Ventilate attic spaces, provide 1 to 2 square inches of vent per square foot of roof.

—To prevent condensation and mildew, avoid buffer spaces between living space and earth contact spaces. Two-inch extruded polystyrene insulation on earth contact walls from grade to footing.

2 FT. ABOVE LARGEST DOG

FRESH AIR

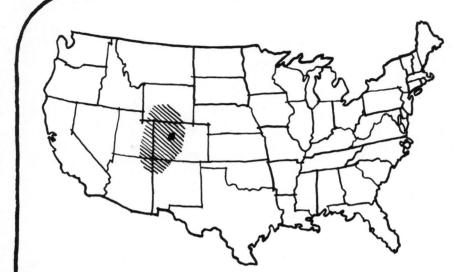

COLORADO

Architect: Sunup Ltd., Architects

General Climate Zone:
Central Rocky Mountains.

Heating Methods Preferred:
1. Direct gain
2. Vented (Trombe) mass wall
3. Clerestories
4. Greenhouse
5. Masonry mass wall
6. Water mass wall
7. Solarium and central atrium

Cooling Methods Preferred:
1. Earth contact
2. Overhangs
3. Night ventilation
4. Shade screen
5. Deciduous planting
6. Evaporative cooler

Climate (Snowmass, Colorado):
Cold, snowy, and sunny winters. Moderate summers with cold nights.

—Altitude—7400 feet
—Heating degree days—8426
—Cooling degree days—0
—Annual rainfall—30 inches
—Annual percentage of sunshine—60 percent
—January percentage of sunshine—50 percent
—Winter storm direction—northwest
—January average temperature range—8°F to 36°F
—July average temperature range—44°F to 79°F

Heating Rules-Of-Thumb:
—Attain a solar savings fraction of 80 percent or greater by achieving a building load coefficient of 3 to 4 BTU/DD/sf.
—Area of south glazing equal to 25 to 30 percent of the floor area and is generally half direct gain and half thermal-storage wall. Limit

nonsouth glazing to 5 to 8 percent of floor area. Clerestories and high interior (single glazed) windows are used liberally to light and heat interior rooms. Minimum double glazing with night insulation of R-4 to R-10. Consider use of new multiple glazings (Heatmirror and Weather Shield Quad Pane) to reduce expense of nighttime insulation and selective surfaces on thermal storage. Thermal shutters and shades are used on all nonsouth glazing.

—Earth integration works well here. Retaining walls and 6-inch thick concrete floor slabs usually provide sufficient thermal storage mass. Double drywall ceilings and stone or other masonry interior walls provide additional mass as needed for distribution and fine tuning.

—Interior spaces open as possible for thermal convection and architectural effect.

Cooling Rules-Of-Thumb:

—Cooling not a problem at higher elevations but of significant concern at lower elevations.

—Design roof overhangs to provide full shading at noon summer solstice, yet allow full penetration at winter solstice with about 40 percent shading at spring and fall equinoxes. Light-colored roof surfaces are used to reflect unwanted summer gain and to enhance winter reflective gain. Shading screens (manual and interior) having about 85 percent gain reduction are used between summer solstice until autumnal equinox and beyond as necessary.

—Natural night ventilation is dependable and relied on. Provide operable north windows of 3 to 5 percent of the floor area for cross ventilation. Greater area on the south.

—Partial earth integration and berming provide good earth contact cooling.

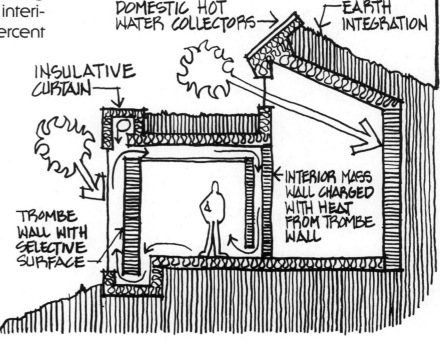

DOMESTIC HOT WATER COLLECTORS

EARTH INTEGRATION

INSULATIVE CURTAIN

INTERIOR MASS WALL CHARGED WITH HEAT FROM TROMBE WALL

TROMBE WALL WITH SELECTIVE SURFACE

NEW MEXICO

Architects: Mazria/Schiff & Associates

General Climate Zone:

Central and Rio Grande high desert area of New Mexico.

Heating Methods Preferred:

1. Direct gain
2. Greenhouse
3. Solarium
4. Trombe wall

Cooling Methods Preferred:

1. Night ventilation
2. Evaporative cooler
3. Overhangs
4. Deciduous plants
5. Shade screen

Climate (Albuquerque, New Mexico):

Cold, dry, sunny winters. Hot summer days with cool nights.

—Altitude—5312 feet
—Heating degree days—4292
—Cooling degree days—1310
—Annual rainfall—8 inches
—Annual percentage of sunshine—77 percent
—January percentage of sunshine—73 percent
—Winter storm direction—north
—January average daily temperature range— 22°F to 46°F
—July average daily temperature range—66°F to 92°F

Heating Rules-Of-Thumb:

—Appropriateness: each of the preferred systems has special characteristics just as each building has unique architectural requirements. It is most important to match the appropriate passive system to the architectural requirements.
—Conservation: insulation of roof and walls should range R-20 to -30. Glass areas and in-filtration are the biggest sources of heat loss. Glass should be insulated at night. For super-tight houses, an air-to-air heat exchanger should be used.
—Glazing, direct gain ratio: 20 to 25 percent south glass-to-floor area; sunspace: 30 to 35 percent south glass-to-floor area; Trombe wall: 30 to 35 percent south glass-to-floor area. A

combination of systems is recommended highly for architectural "fine tuning."

—Thermal mass: should be spread around to be most effective; 2 to 8 inches thick walls, 4 to 6 inches thick on floors. Rockbeds discouraged (due to high expense) in favor of "thermal engine" warm-air loops from greenhouses, which work especially well in two-story applications.

—Avoid huge concentrated areas of direct-gain glass as this will cause overheating and glare. Glass should be distributed in a space-specific manner; architectural considerations should be carefully integrated with passive solar solutions. Sunlight should be bounced around and reflected to minimize temperature swings; avoid direct sun on dark surfaces (except in Trombe wall and greenhouses).

—Passive solar buildings do not represent much improvement if they are thermally uncomfortable and full of glare. Careful calculation and modeling of each design and system choice are musts!

Cooling Rules-Of-Thumb:

—Siting, orientation: prevailing winds are from west to northwest. Use of low vents on wind side and high clerestory openings and/or east door opening allow good night cooling. Day ventilation not recommended.

—Conservation: color of roof very important, as flat roofs are popular. Use white or silver coating to enhance reflectivity. Shading is a must for south glass. Shading is also recommended for east and west walls with vegetation or architectural screen devices. Greenhouses *must* be shaded on both horizontal and vertical exposures. Shade greenhouse on *outside* of glass, with venting at upper part of greenhouse volume. Isolate greenhouse from living areas with *shaded* mass wall.

—Thermal mass: mass to south glazing area: 9:1 surface area ratio is ideal. Nighttime temperatures are quite low; therefore, night cooling of building mass is the most effective method of cooling.

—Thermostatically controlled evaporative cooling is economical and a pleasant cooling supplement. Well-distributed building mass is critical to success of this very stable and economical system.

DISTRIBUTE MASS EVENLY

"THERMAL ENGINE"

Heating Methods Preferred:

1. Direct gain
2. Thermosyphon air collector
3. Greenhouse (isolated)

Climate (Phoenix, Arizona):

Pleasant dry winters with sunny days and cool nights. Two summers (five months): six weeks of humid and hot; three and one-half months of very hot and dry.

—Altitude—1400 feet
—Heating degree days—1500
—Cooling degree days—4000
—Annual rainfall—7 inches
—Annual percentage sunshine—86 percent
—January percentage sunshine—77 percent
—Winter storm direction—west
—January average daily temperature range—
37°F to 63°F
—July average daily temperature range—74°F
to 98°F

ARIZONA

Architect: Jeffrey Cook, AIA

General Climate Zone:

Lowest southwest desert—Phoenix to Yuma, Blythe, and Death Valley.

Cooling Methods Preferred:

1. Orientation/shading/planting
2. Insulation and high mass
3. Night ventilation/ceiling fans
4. Refrigerated air conditioning
5. Two-stage (indirect) evaporative cooling
6. Single-stage evaporative cooling
7. Earth contact/semi-underground

Cooling Rules-Of-Thumb:

—Cooling is primary, needs strong defense tactics. Glass must be completely shaded for six months. Double glazing cost effective. Maximum ventilation capability for night ventilation during swing (i.e., spring and fall) seasons (screened for insects).

—Insulation: wall R-20, roof R-40.

—Use reflective exterior colors, especially on roof.

—Small window areas limited to 12 percent of floor area. North or south preferred, never west. Dark adjacent exterior areas (landscaping) to reduce reflective gain. Exterior shades to provide 50 percent reduction of light for glare control.

—Maximum cost-effective thermal storage.

—Weatherstrip for infiltration, dust, and insect control.

—Shaded outdoor use spaces; patios especially on north side for nighttime use.

Heating Rules-Of-Thumb:

—Direct gain with double glazing 7 to 9 percent of the floor area south and 3 to 5 percent north. Twelve percent maximum total glazing.

—Movable insulation not cost effective. Double glazing preferred.

—Two-story sunspace with large overhang and vertical glazing only. Used from October through April. Thermally isolated from house during summer, open to interior during winter days. Orient 0 to 25° east of south, 15° east of south preferred.

—Thermosyphon air collector installed outside of weatherskin. Couple with interior thermal storage if possible. Optimizes winter gain without compromising summer overheating. Area up to one-third of total south glazing, 2 percent total.

—Open fireplaces preferred for auxiliary heating system. Radiant effect nice, not needed all night.

—Sunny outdoor-use spaces.

—Secret solution: ponded roof (Skytherm) 100 percent summer and winter passive comfort possible with careful attention to humidity control and microclimate fine tuning.

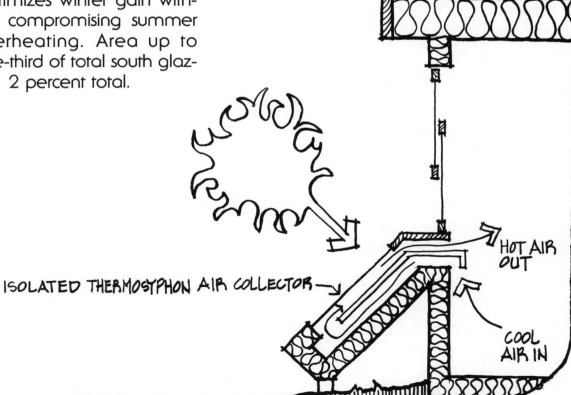

ISOLATED THERMOSYPHON AIR COLLECTOR

HOT AIR OUT

COOL AIR IN

CALIFORNIA

Architect: David Wright Associates, AIA

General Climate Zone:

Central to northern California mountain foothills.

Heating Methods Preferred:

1. Direct gain
2. Clerestories
3. Greenhouse
4. Masonry mass wall
5. Solarium
6. Central atrium

Cooling Methods Preferred:

1. Shade screen
2. Overhangs
3. Deciduous planting
4. Night ventilation
5. Earth contact
6. Evaporative cooler
7. Coolth field

Climate (Nevada City, California):

Cold, wet winters with dependable sunshine. Warm, dry summers with cool nights.

—Altitude—2500 feet
—Heating degree days—4687
—Cooling degree days—253
—Annual rainfall—53 inches
—Annual percentage of sunshine—70 percent
—January percentage of sunshine—45 percent
—Winter storm direction—southwest
—January average daily temperature range— 28°F to 51°F
—July average daily temperature range—49°F to 91°F

Heating Rules-Of-Thumb:

—Try to achieve a building heat-load coefficient of 4 to 10 BTU/dd/sq. ft.(floor area). Insulate walls R-19 to -25, roof R-30 to -40; use perimeter insulation.

—Use double glazing. Orient solar glazing within 30° of south, easterly preferred. Solar glazing equal in area to 25 percent of floor area. Distribute glass in proportion to individual room area and function; cool (buffer) rooms have little to no glazing.

—Size thermal mass area to be four to eight times glass area. Use lower mass area if mass is in sunlight most of the day; higher mass area if *not* directly sunlit for most of the day (except Trombe walls). Slab floors need be only 4 inches thick. Interior mass walls sunlit on two sides may be up to 8 inches thick. Distribute mass evenly throughout space on floors, walls and ceilings when possible (improves cooling performance). Masonry partition walls running north-south provide many thermal, acoustical and structural benefits.

—Insulating curtains or shutters,

having a thermal resistance of 4 to 6, are cost effective for reducing nighttime heat loss out windows.

—Light-colored furniture will help reflect solar gain to darker colored mass surfaces and reduce the likelihood of fading. Arrange furniture to allow the best possible exposure of the mass to the sun.

Cooling Rules-Of-Thumb:

—Night ventilation used in conjunction with daytime exterior shading of glass area works well for cooling buildings in the Sierra foothills. Close up during warm days.

—Low operable windows or vents to the south and high exhaust vents to the north take advantage of prevailing daytime breezes. Night breezes generally flow from east to west in west sloping foothill locations. Place low openings on the east and

high openings on the west for night ventilation. A minimum vent area equal to 10 to 15 percent of the floor area is adequate to cool the internal fabric of the building at night.

—Roof overhangs, sized to block all direct sunlight from entering south-facing windows on the summer solstice, may actually block only half of the total sunlight striking the window due to the potentially high quantity of diffuse and reflected sunlight. For this reason, shade screen or deciduous vegetation is necessary for south, east, and west glass. Operable shade screen with a shading coefficient of 0.5 to 0.8 is the most flexible shading option as it can be used at any time of the year. Light-colored insulating curtains may be used in the summer to help control daytime heat gain.

238

OREGON

Architects: Church/Davis Architects

General Climate Zone:

Pacific northwestern states. Generally from Portland, Oregon, to the coast and the region south to Eugene, Oregon.

Heating Methods Preferred:

1. Direct gain
2. Masonry mass wall
3. Solarium
4. Clerestories

Cooling Methods Preferred:

1. Movable shading
2. Night ventilation
3. Deciduous shading

Climate (Portland, Oregon):

Moderate winters with extended cloudy periods and rainfall; warm summers with cool nights.

—Altitude—21 feet
—Heating degree days—4792
—Cooling degree days—300
—Annual rainfall—48 inches
—Annual percentage sunshine—54.8 percent
—January percentage of sunshine—39.1 percent
—Average number of days with snow cover—2 days
—Winter storm direction—southwest/rain; east-northeast/snow
—January average daily temperature range—33°F to 44°F
—July average daily temperature range—55°F to 79°F

Heating Rules-Of-Thumb:

—Orientation: Orient the building with the solar aperture (solar wall or solar glazing) close to the south. Up to 30° east or west of south is acceptable.

- Building conservation: Insulate walls to R-25 and ceilings to R-38. Detail the building to achieve a one-quarter air change per hour (caulk sill plates, seal pipe and electrical holes, and seal door and window jambs). Install a continuous vapor barrier, an air-to-air heat exchanger may be required to control air quality.
- Building shape: Minimize exterior walls as client and site needs allow.
- Solar aperture: Place most of the available glass on the south side. As a starting point, begin with 12 percent of the gross floor area as south windows. A smaller percentage will result in a dark room with significant window glare, and will require super insulation to maintain low energy demands; larger percentages will result in greater nighttime losses and the potential for

spring and fall overheating unless additional corrective steps are taken, including exterior shadings, night insulation, and additional storage mass.

- Thermal mass: Provide 35 BTU/°F of thermal-storage capacity for every square foot of south-facing glass. Distribute solar mass over as large an area as possible in sunlit spaces.
- Heat distribution: Use small, low-volume fans to move heat where needed.
- Auxiliary heating system: Control is the key. Multiple small gas or electric heaters allow room-to-room zoning and are preferable to a central system. In this climate, heat pumps are not cost effective and, in many cases, their efficiency is the same as electric resistance heating.

Cooling Rules-Of-Thumb:

- Thermal mass: Spread it out over as large an area as

possible. If mass is used on exterior walls, insulation must be on the outside surface.

- Shading: Use movable exterior shades.
- Ventilation: Design for nighttime ventilation air-change rates of 2 per hour. When house designs do not lend themselves to natural ventilation, use fans. Make certain that fans are sealable for winter and can be insulated.

MINIMIZE EXTERIOR WALLS BY STRIVING FOR A CUBIC SHAPE. REDUCES EXPOSURE TO COLD.

ROLL-DOWN SHADES

ORIENT WITHIN 30° OF SOUTH

5 APPLYING THE TOOLS

In order to facilitate the design process for passive solar conditioned structures, a checklist for planning is useful. To develop the idea of a solar project from little more than a gleam in one's eye to a well-conceived and -engineered reality is an involved process, requiring an amazing number of decisions. Each step along the way should be taken carefully and in proper sequence. This simplifies the process of developing a holistic concept embracing all of the important environmental considerations.

The following checklist is a procedural outline used by architects and designers, which is helpful in the design process. Each person will have his own variation. There are many other considerations that may be important to you, but the basics are here.

A. SELECT AND ANALYZE THE SITE:

Consider all past, present, and future microclimate factors—

Landscape

—man's influence
—land type
—soil conditions
—vegetation
—profile
—materials
—water supply
—latitude
—pollution
—view
—noise

Climate

—temperatures
—weather cycles
—sunlight
—precipitation
—humidity
—air motion

Other

—acts of God
—regional "style"
—land cost
—sewage treatment
—utilities
—land title
—access
—zoning
—adjacent uses
—future neighbors
—community facilities

When investigating a particular site, cost of land, zoning, neighboring influences, and the like are not usually all in accord with an ideal situation. Certain value judgments are required—either the problems with the site can be dealt with effectively or the site should be rejected.

Don't chew your pencil too much!

PLANNING CHECKLIST

B. STUDY THE SITE:

—land use patterns
—utilities
—sewage
—solar exposure
—views
—access
—shelter
—slope
—soil conditions

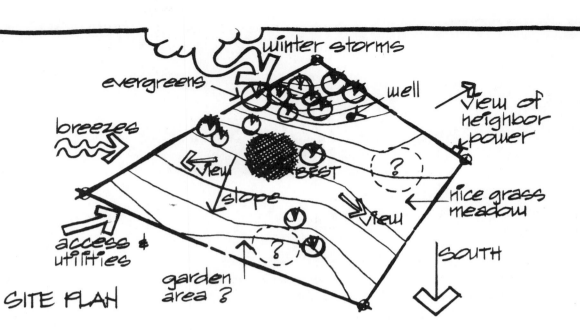

SITE PLAN

Select the obvious and most preferred site to test for a design. You should retain some alternative locations in case your mind is changed during the design process. There may be a dozen locations, one of which should be the best—find it!

C. DEVELOP PLAN AND FORM:

Sketch a bubble diagram or schematic of how you think the structure should work with the site influences, your lifestyle, and the functional needs in mind. The bubbles should be scaled approximately. Keep it loose!

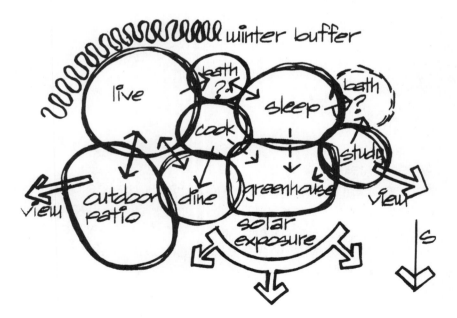

—Investigate a passive solar system that best suits the microclimate characteristics and schematic floor diagram.

—Develop an external form or envelope (profile section) that works with the external influences, solar function, materials, and plan ideas.

—Overlay sections with schematic floor diagram to see if they are compatible in three dimensions.

—Rearrange schematic floor diagram if necessary to suit the solar system, structure, and your needs. Refine the plan—show wall thicknesses, hallways, utility rooms, closets, water heater collectors, and so on. Do it to scale!

—Examine the structure and determine the best marriage of the plan, solar system, beams, walls, foundation, windows, doors . . . Keep it simple!

—Now apply your rules-of-thumb for proportioning the solar system. Adjust solar glazing, thermal mass, overhangs, and all the passive solar elements as necessary.

—Repeat all the previous steps from a different point of view. This will allow thorough evaluation of all possibilities.

keep an open mind.

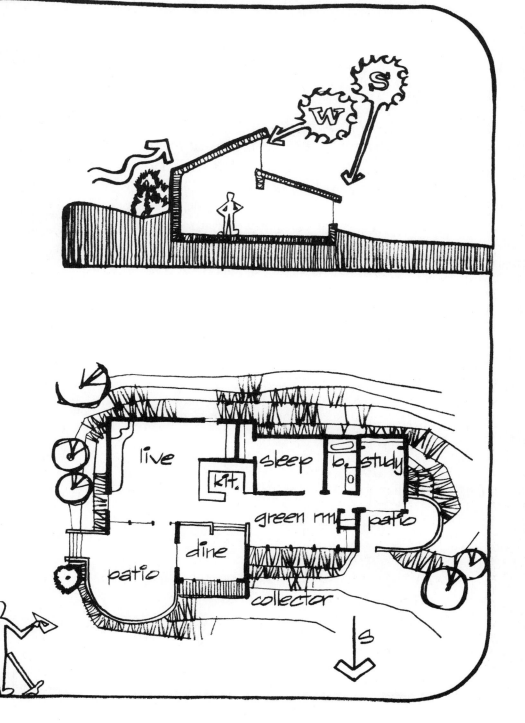

D. CALCULATE THE THERMAL PERFORMANCE:

Now that you have a decent design solution and have applied your rules-of-thumb to be sure that you are in the ballpark, and before developing the drawings completely, try your hand at determining how it will work.

—Select all weatherskin materials, including windows, doors, roofing, insulation, and siding.

—Determine insulation values for each of the exterior surfaces.

—Total various areas of weatherskin—windows, doors, walls, roofs, and perimeter floor edges.

—Find exterior and interior design temperatures for each month of the heating season.

—Calculate steady-state heat loss through each exterior surface area, room-by-room or by zone. Don't forget the sol-air effect.

—Total the steady-state heat loss for entire structure for the heating period.

—Size room or zone volumes and determine infiltration heat loss. Then total the infiltration heat loss for structure.

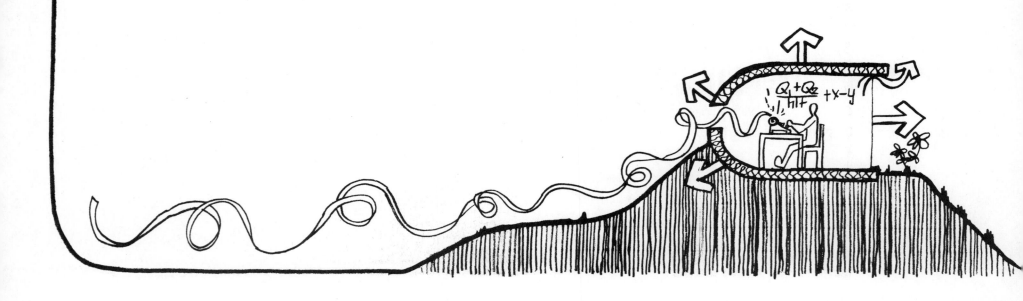

—Add totals of steady-state, slab-edge, and infiltration heat losses. Now you have an idea of how much heating is required. Don't forget that in a residence, internally generated gains are a bonus—what energy rating is your dog?

—If your total heat loss is greater than 10 to 12 BTU/hour/sq. ft. of floor area, you should tighten your thermal envelope by adding insulation, reducing window area, and following other, similar guidelines.

—Determine the solar energy available and collected for use on a typical day each month based upon your total collection area; remember to account for all mitigating factors (percent of possible, occlusion, and so on).

—Calculate the percent of solar heating for a normal season; if you believe this value is too low, you should enlarge the collection area or tighten the weatherskin even more, or live with it.

—By knowing the probable duration of winter cloud cover in number of days, (overcast periods between clear solar days), you can determine a period of probable need for solar storage.

—Calculate the volume and heat capacity of the storage mass between the highest and lowest comfort temperatures, (65 to 85°F) (18 to 29°C). If the total storage capacity is less than the total heat loss for the number of days the storage might be relied on, more storage mass should be added or your dependence on auxiliary heating will increase.

E. CHECK IT OVER:

When you are happy with tightness of the weatherskin, comfort range, and solar collection and storage, check the natural lighting, ventilation, and air circulation possibilities. Be sure that enough windows, doors, and vents are strategically located, allowing for natural circulation of air, lighting for daytime tasks, and removal of smoke, odors, and excess heat.

F. REVIEW THE WHOLE PROCESS:

See what can be done throughout the year, under all use and weather conditions, to improve on the design. Modify the design accordingly.

G. NOW BUILD A SCALE MODEL:

This process helps to see how the structure will go together and will solve some problems and details prior to construction. Do not make it too detailed, but sufficient enough to understand connections, joints, materials, and so on. The model will give you a good idea of what the building will look like in three dimensions.

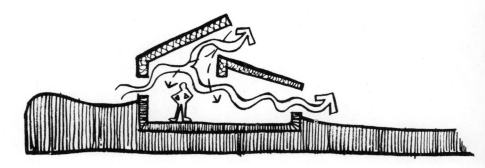

H. DRAW IT UP:

Complete the drawings needed to obtain a building permit and to build the structure. Always understand what you draw and look at it from the point of view that "you might have to build it."

I. PLAN OF ATTACK:

After all the successful designing you've done, you're ready for logistics. Do a materials list and cost estimate, get bids, figure units of time and steps involved. This planning is fun, and you are getting close to the real thing. If your planning is neat and orderly, chances are the building will be also.

J. BUILD IT!:

Building is hard work whether you do it yourself or contract it, but it will be very rewarding if you have accomplished all of the preceding tasks. You will make mistakes—some are unavoidable; minimize and understand them. Don't try and live in the middle of construction. Take your time and build carefully. Try to maintain a relaxed attitude. The strain on your muscles, marriage, and pocketbook is probably temporary.

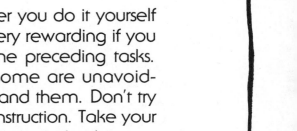

K. MOVE IN AND LIVE WITH IT!:

Monitor temperatures and operate controls faithfully for the first year. This is the shakedown period. If the weather is what you consider normal, you can, by reviewing the temperature records in various rooms, operational data, and amount of auxiliary needed, determine what, if anything, needs to be done to improve your building's performance.

In all likelihood, if you have planned carefully, the building will perform at least as well as expected.

No passive solar design should fail completely. The performance and amount of solar heating is relative to your design expectations. The proof of the pudding is in the livability of your design.

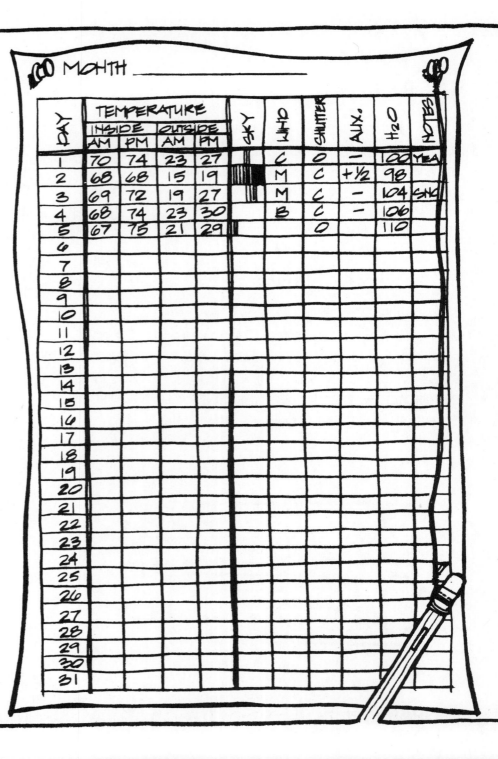

MONTH _____

DAY	TEMPERATURE				SKY	WIND	SHUTTER	AUX.	H₂O	NOTES
	INSIDE		OUTSIDE							
	AM	PM	AM	PM						
1	70	74	23	27		C	O	–	100	YEA
2	68	68	15	19	▮	M	C	+½	98	
3	69	72	19	27		M	C	–	104	SNO
4	68	74	23	30		B	C	–	106	
5	67	75	21	29			O		110	
6										
7										
8										
9										
10										
11										
12										
13										
14										
15										
16										
17										
18										
19										
20										
21										
22										
23										
24										
25										
26										
27										
28										
29										
30										
31										

6

LOOKING AHEAD

Things change. Today's dreams and visions may be tomorrow's reality. As our civilization evolves, we should be able to simplify our use of technology. Architecture and space-conditioning systems must change as we modify our concepts of energy use.

The potential for using nature's passive energies to directly power all of our basic life-support systems is immense. If we approach the design, construction, operation, and maintenance of our structures with an eye to low-temperature thermal conversion and life-cycle energy economics, we will become aware of different ways of coping with our physical world and the universe.

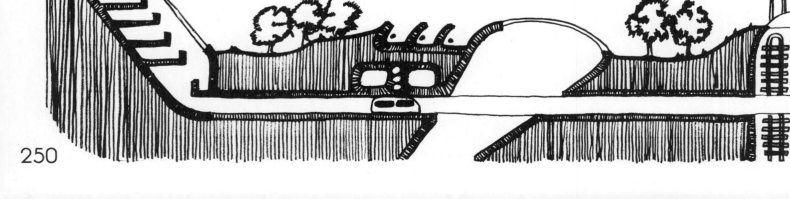

The following examples—perhaps visionary, maybe illusionary, probably realistic—are extrapolations of many of the principles and ideas discussed, placed into the form of usable, yet unusual, habitats. If the *solar age* is to catch the imagination of architects, bankers, builders, and people of all walks of life, then let's not stop short of the goal either aesthetically or technically. We know that each structure, whether a single-family dwelling or a complex megastructure, has more than enough solar, electrostatic, wind, and cosmic energy acting on it to provide all of the basic power needs. Let's learn how to use these!

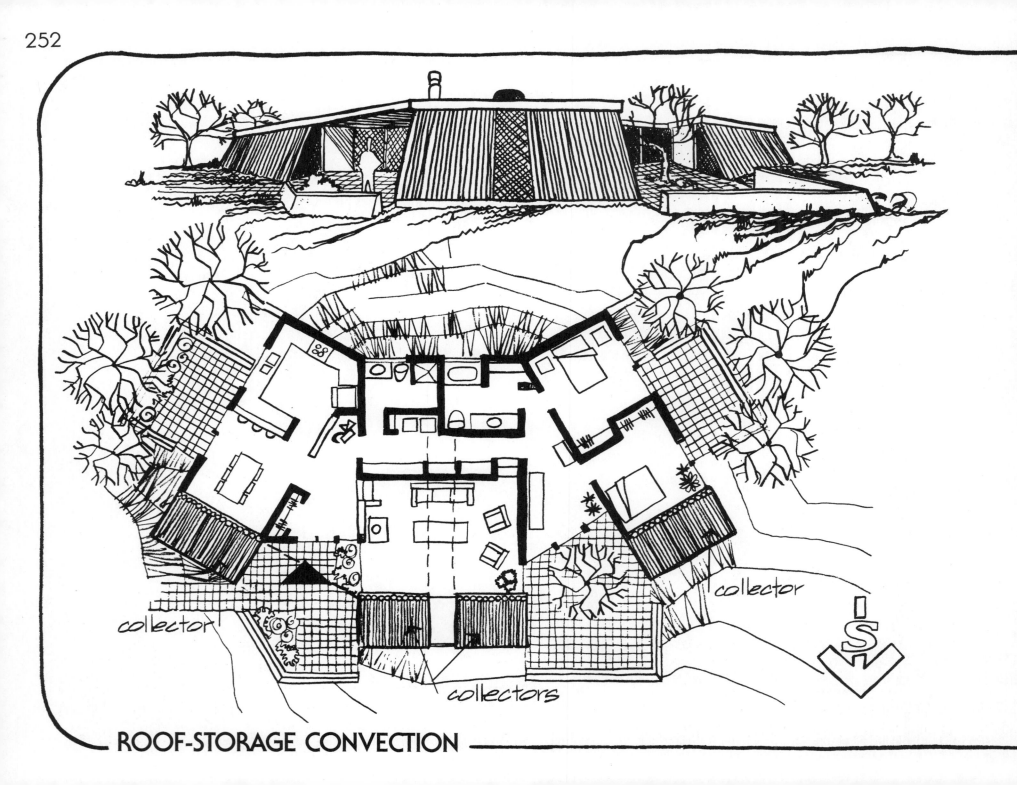

collector

collector

collectors

ROOF-STORAGE CONVECTION

This system, suited for cold climates where some cooling may be needed, includes the following:

—structural steel roof and water tubes with thermosyphoned flat-plate collectors; collectors drain automatically during freezing weather
—roof storage insulated on top
—photovoltaic cells on roof surface
—reverse pumping of collector at night for space cooling.

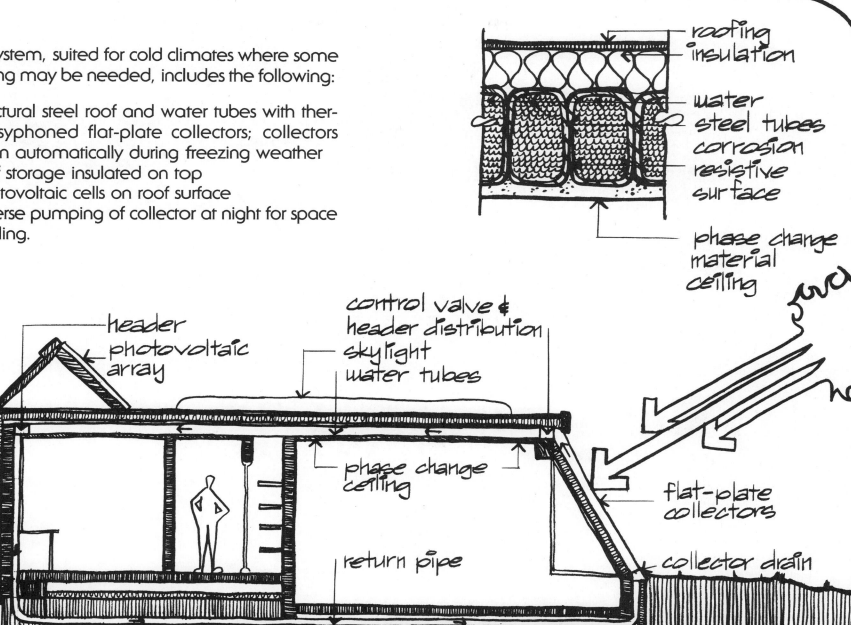

roofing
insulation
water
steel tubes
corrosion resistive surface
phase change material ceiling

header
photovoltaic array

control valve & header distribution
skylight
water tubes

phase change ceiling

flat-plate collectors

return pipe

collector drain

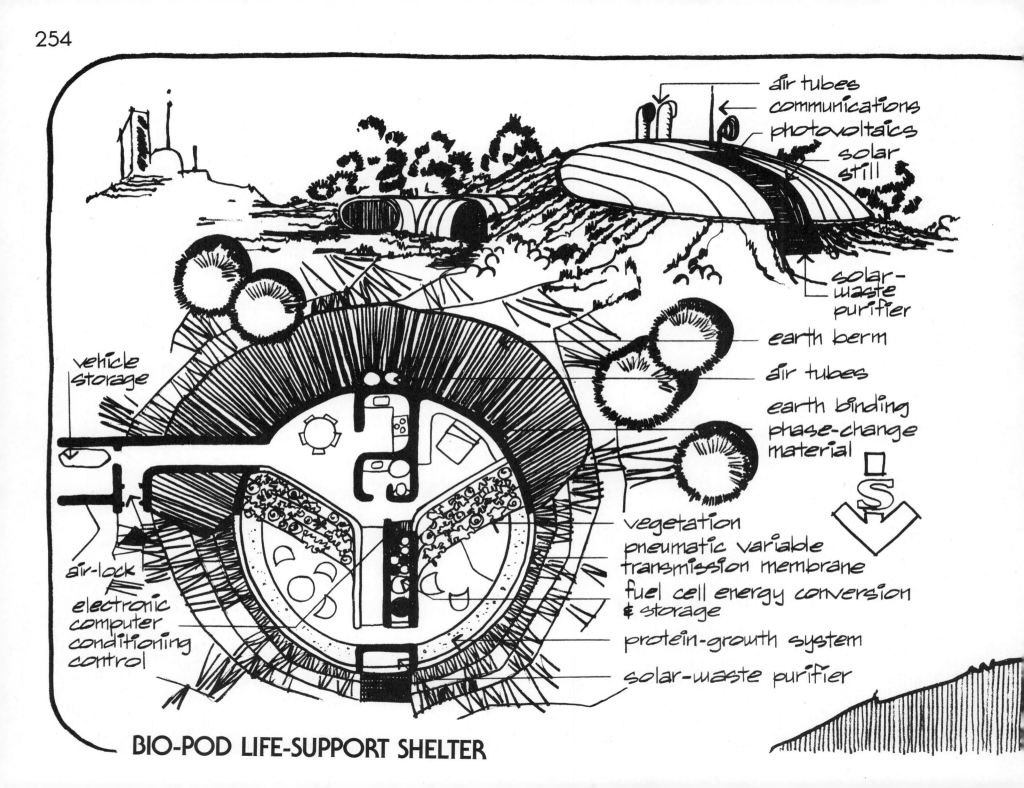

air tubes
communications
photovoltaics
solar still
solar-waste purifier
earth berm
air tubes
earth binding
phase-change material

vehicle storage

air-lock

electronic computer conditioning control

vegetation
pneumatic variable transmission membrane
fuel cell energy conversion & storage
protein-growth system
solar-waste purifier

BIO-POD LIFE-SUPPORT SHELTER

A life-support pod, suitable for any climate:

—variable transmission/insulative membrane is electronically activated by computer to control, by zone, all required heat and light functions
—photovoltaic cells and atmospheric static precipitator provide electrical energy with fuel-cell storage
—all wastes purified or converted by solar oven
—all water and moisture recycled via solar still, holding tanks, and humidity-control system

—flat-plate collector for water heating and cooling
—internal growth of vegetable and protein food supply by growth pods and hydroponic tanks
—all life-sustaining requirements met by integrally generated systems.

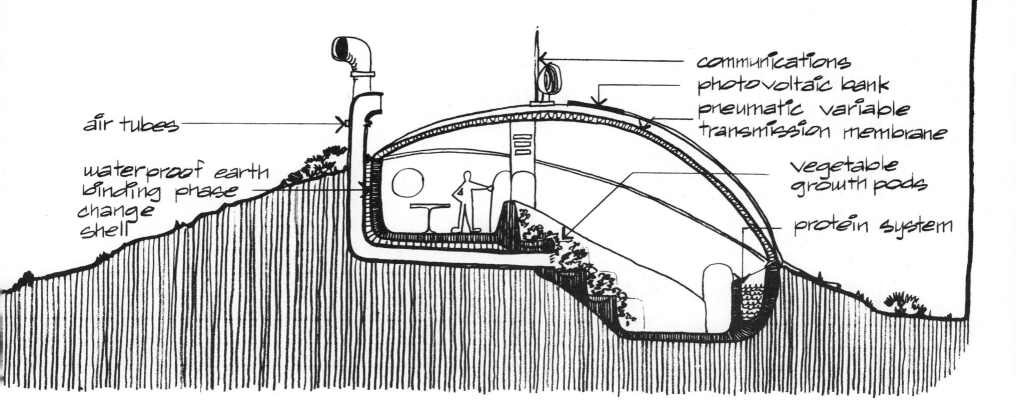

air tubes

waterproof earth binding phase change shell

communications
photovoltaic bank
pneumatic variable transmission membrane

vegetable growth pods

protein system

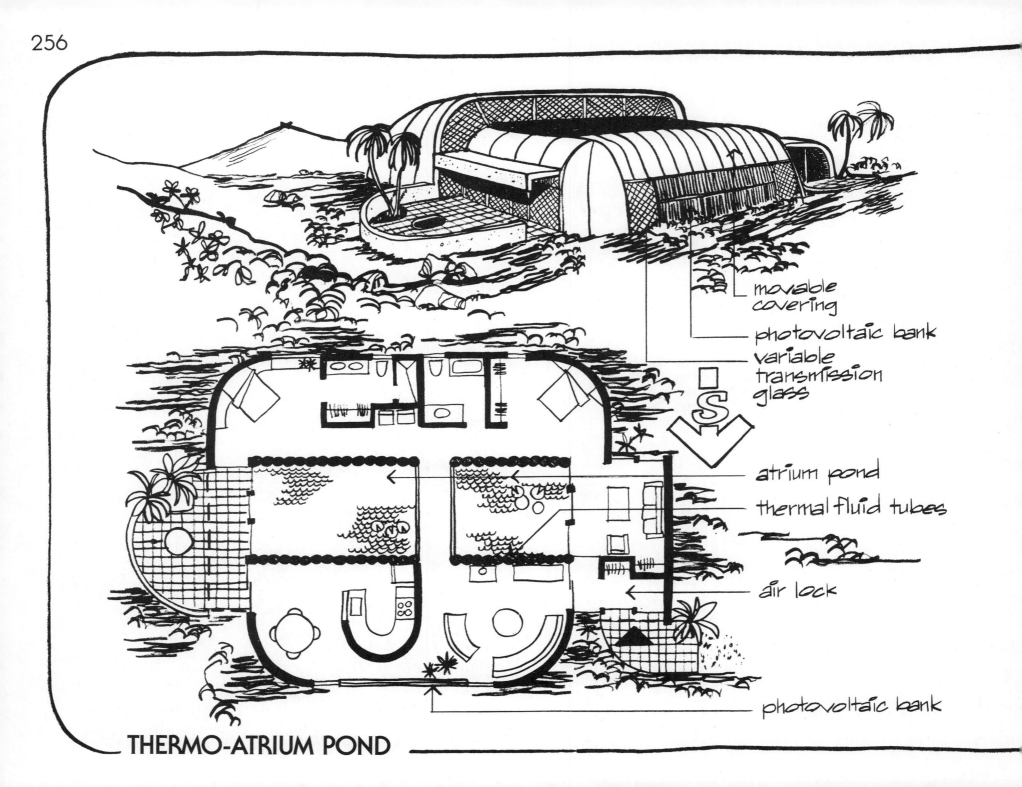

movable covering

photovoltaic bank

variable transmission glass

atrium pond

thermal fluid tubes

air lock

photovoltaic bank

THERMO-ATRIUM POND

This dwelling type, suitable for prefabrication, is a Thermos-like structure, ideal for hot, dry areas where high cooling and low heating demands predominate. Included are:

—solar water heater
—insulated, heat-reflecting metallic skin
—internal thermal fluid tubes capable of collecting, rejecting, and storing heat
—movable insulative and glazing shells automated by internal and external sensors
—photovoltaic cell skin with integral electrical storage
—water flooding of atrium to increase summer coolth storage by evaporative cooling and deep-space radiation
—variable-transmission glazing electronically controlled
—lightweight shell structure requiring no foundations.

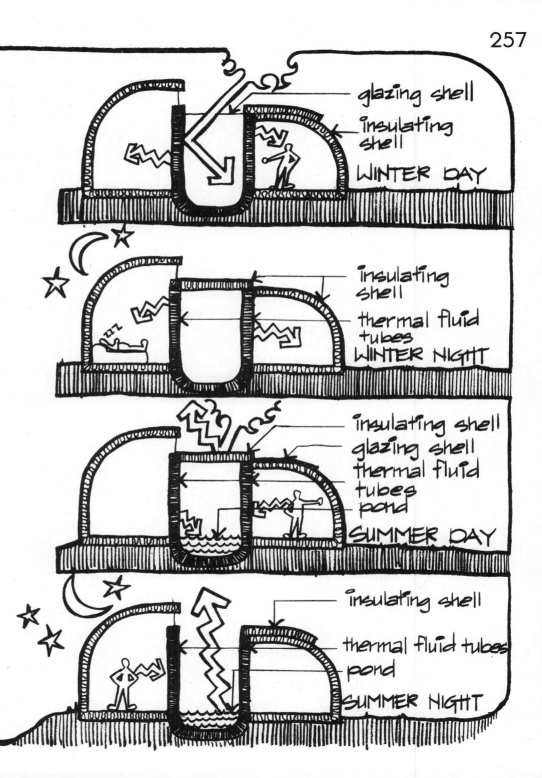

glazing shell
insulating shell
WINTER DAY

insulating shell
thermal fluid tubes
WINTER NIGHT

insulating shell
glazing shell
thermal fluid tubes
pond
SUMMER DAY

insulating shell
thermal fluid tubes
pond
SUMMER NIGHT

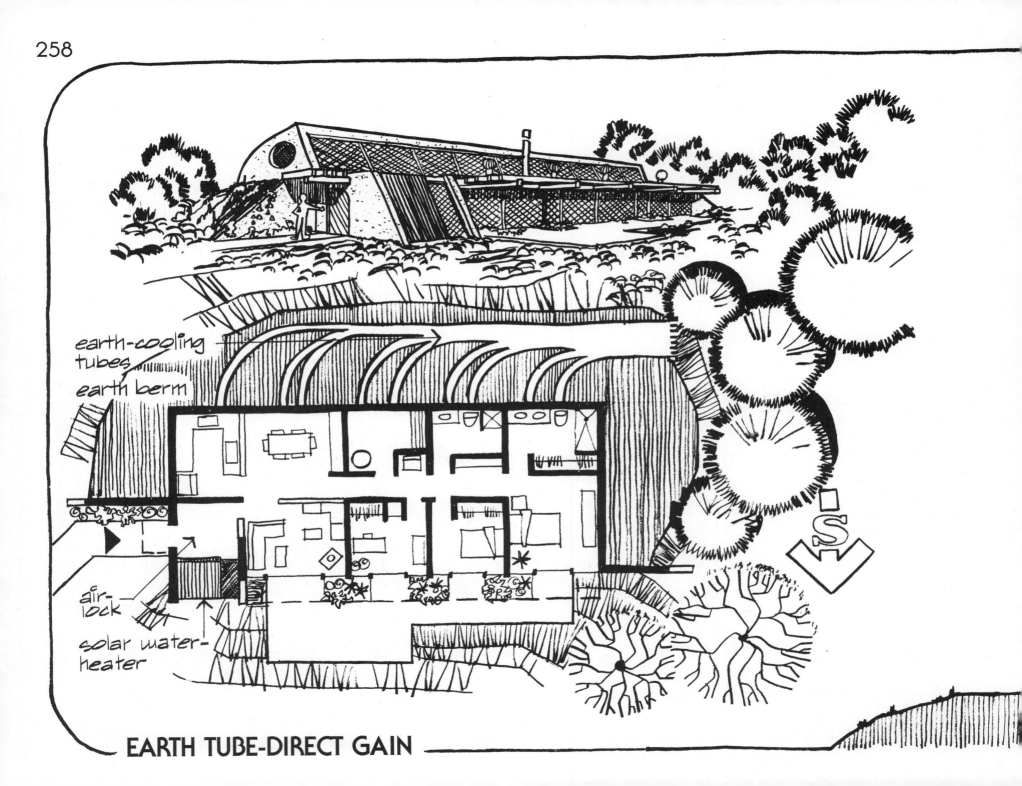

earth-cooling tubes

earth berm

air-lock

solar water-heater

EARTH TUBE-DIRECT GAIN

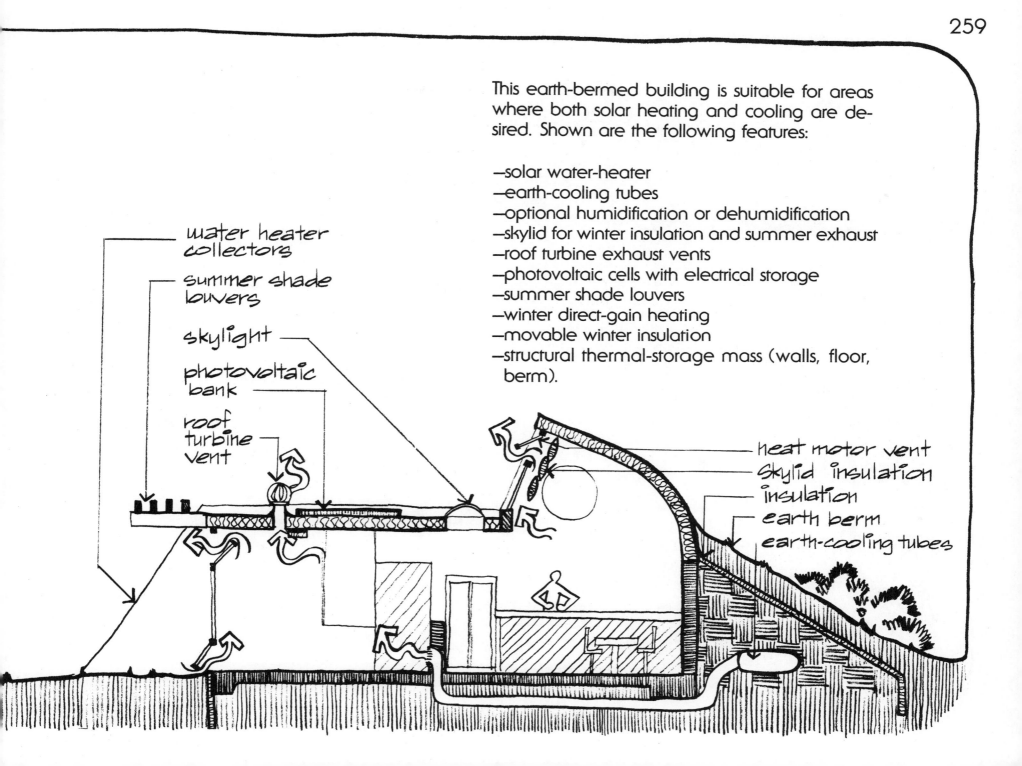

This earth-bermed building is suitable for areas where both solar heating and cooling are desired. Shown are the following features:

—solar water-heater
—earth-cooling tubes
—optional humidification or dehumidification
—skylid for winter insulation and summer exhaust
—roof turbine exhaust vents
—photovoltaic cells with electrical storage
—summer shade louvers
—winter direct-gain heating
—movable winter insulation
—structural thermal-storage mass (walls, floor, berm).

water heater collectors

summer shade louvers

skylight

photovoltaic bank

roof turbine vent

heat motor vent
skylid insulation
insulation
earth berm
earth-cooling tubes

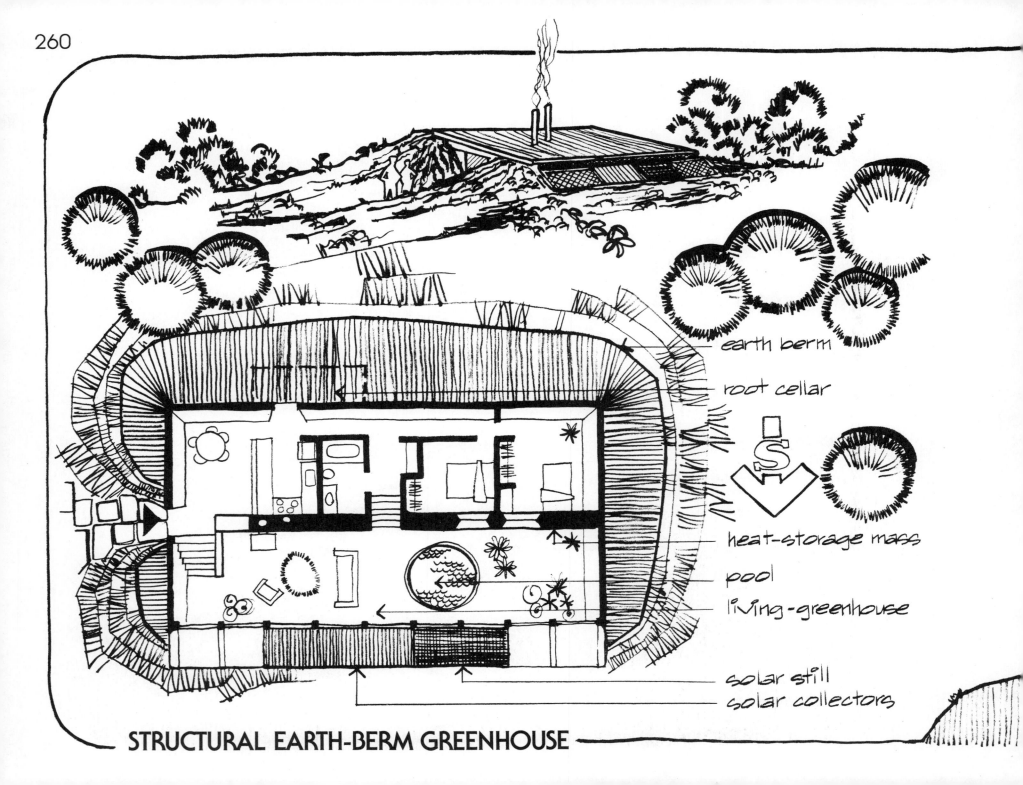

earth berm

root cellar

heat-storage mass

pool

living-greenhouse

solar still
solar collectors

STRUCTURAL EARTH-BERM GREENHOUSE

This dwelling, maximizing the use of local materials, is energy efficient in terms of structure and operation. Many variations on this scheme are possible for a variety of climates. Illustrated are:

—machine-placed and -compacted, thick, earth-bearing walls, which avoid masonry or form work and act as insulation and heat-storage mass
—nonconventional structural foundation, walls, and floor
—greenhouse-living area heat loss and gain controlled by Skylids or manual-insulative ceiling louvers
—natural convection air circulation and venting

—interior berm surfaces stabilized by stone rip rap, wire-mesh gabions, ferroconcrete plaster, sandbags, stabilized earth plaster, and the like
—rooftop water collection, cistern, and solar still for gray water
—passive (thermosyphoned) solar water heating.
(*Note*: Not suitable in locations with subsurface water problems, too much rock, or unstable soil).

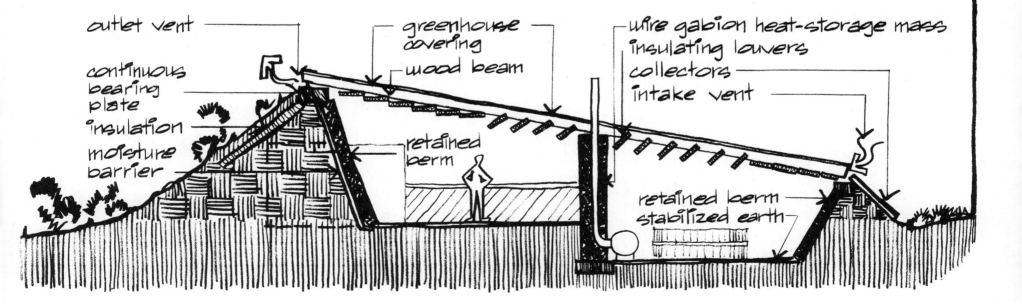

APPENDIX

Nomenclature

A = area, sq. ft.

Ac = collector area, sq. ft.

anc = air heat capacity, $BTU/ft.^3/°F$

c = specific heat constant, $BTU/lb./°F$

d = density, $lbs./ft.^3$

D = days of storage

DD = degree days

e = system efficiency

gf = ground-reflectance factor

h = number of hours

hf = sky haze factor

k = thermal conductivity, $BTU\ in./hr./sq.ft./°F$

m = mass, lbs.

mo = number of months

n = number of air changes per hour

$\%p$ = percent of possible sunshine, %

q = thermal capacity, $BTU/ft.^3/°F$

Q = heat content, BTU

Qc = conducted heat, BTU/hr.

Qhl = heat loss, BTU

$Qhlt$ = total heat loss, BTU

Qi = infiltration heat loss, BTU

Qin = heat input, BTU

Qit = total infiltration heat loss, BTU

Ql = latent heat energy, BTU

Qs = incident solar radiation, BTU/sq. ft.

Qss = total solar energy collected, BTU

Qst = total heat storage, BTU

r = thermal resistance per inch of thickness, $hr.sq.ft.°F/BTU$

R = thermal resistance for thickness given, $hr.sq.ft.°F/BTU$

Rf = radiation factor

$Rtotal$ = total thermal resistance, $hr.sq.ft.°F/BTU$

$\%Sa$ = percent annual solar heated, %

$\%Smo$ = percent solar heated for month, %

Δt = temperature differential, °F

ti = interior temperature, °F

to = outside design temperature, °F

tf = glazing transmission factor

T = thickness, inches

U = coefficient of heat transfer, BTU/hr./sq.ft./°F

V = volume, $ft.^3$

Metric Conversion

Length

meter (m)
kilometer = 1,000 m (km)
hectometer = 100 m (hm)
dekameter = 10 m (dkm)
meter = 1m (m)
decimeter = 1/10 m (dm)
centimeter = 1/100 m (cm)
millimeter = 1/1,000 m (mm)
miles × 1.609 = km
yards × 0.914 = m
feet × 0.305 = m
inches × 0.025 = m
inches × 2.540 = cm
inches × 25.40 = mm

Area

square meter (m²)
sq. kilometer = 1,000,000 m² (km²)
hectare = 10,000 m² (ha)
are = 100 m² (a)
sq. meter = 1m² (m²)
sq. centimeter = 1/10,000 m² (cm²)
sq. millimeter = 1/1,000,000 m² (mm²)
sq. miles × 2.59 = km²
acres × 0.004 = km²
sq. yards × 0.836 = m²
sq. feet × 0.093 = m²
sq. inches × 6.452 = cm²
sq. inches × 645.163 = mm²

Volume

liter (L)/cubic meter (m³)
kiloliter = 1,000 L (kL)
hectoliter = 100 L (hL)
dekaliter = 10 L (dkL)
liter = 1L (L)
deciliter = 1/10 L (dL)
centiliter = 1/100 L (cL)
milliliter = 1/1,000 L (mL)
cu. feet × 0.028 = m³
cu. inches × 0.0016 = cm³
gallons × 3.785 = L
quarts × 0.946 = L
pints × 0.473 = L
fl. ounces × 29.573 = mL

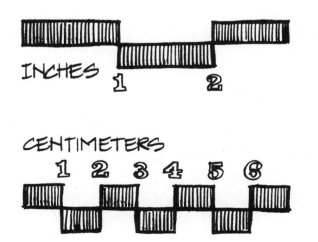

INCHES 1 2

CENTIMETERS 1 2 3 4 5 6

SQUARE INCH

SQUARE CENTIMETER

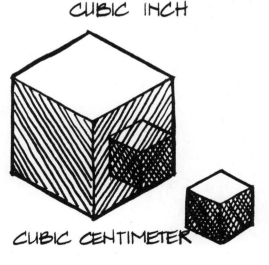

CUBIC INCH

CUBIC CENTIMETER

SYSTEM INTERNATIONAL (SI)

Mass/Weight

gram (g)
kilogram = 1,000 g (kg)
hectogram = 100 g (hg)
dekagram = 10 g (dkg)
gram = 1g (g)
decigram = 1/10 g (dg)
centigram = 1/100 g (cg)
milligram = 1/1,000 g (mg)
ounces × 28.35 = g
ounces × 0.028 = kg
ounces × 28,349.53 = mg
pounds × 453.59 = g
pounds × 0.454 = kg
tons × 907.180 = kg

1 POUND

1 KILOGRAM

Temperature

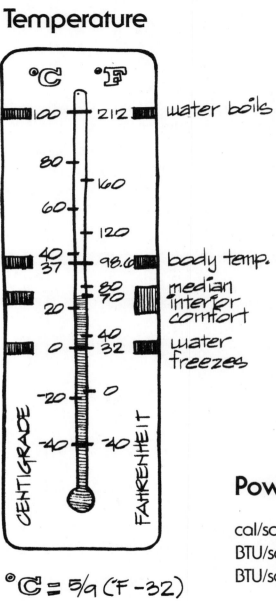

°C = 5/9 (°F −32)

°F = 9/5 (°C +32)

Energy

calorie (cal)/joules (J)
BTU × 251.99 = cal
BTU × 1,055.06 = J

Energy Density

calories/sq.cm. (cal/cm²)
BTU/sq.ft. × 0.271 = cal/cm²
langley × 1.0 = cal/cm²

Power

calories/minute (cal/min.)
BTU/hr. × 0.238 = cal/min.
BTU/hr. × 3.414 = watts
watt × 1.0 = J/sec.

Power Density

cal/sq.cm./min. (cal/cm²/min.)
BTU/sq.ft./hr. × .00452 = cal/cm²/min.
BTU/sq.ft./hr. × .000315 = watt/cm²

REFERENCES

Author's Note: Many of these interesting reference books are out of print but available used online:

Anderson, Bruce and Michael Riordon. *The Solar Home Book.* Andover, Massachusetts. Brick House Publishing Company, 1976.

Andrews, A. *Nomad Tent Types in the Middle East,* Part 1, Vol. 2. Beihefte Zum Tubinger. Atlas Des Vorderen Orients. 1997.

Anlnk, D., Chiel Boonstra, C. and Mak, J. *Handbook of Sustainable Building: An Environmental Preference Method for Selection of Materials for use in Construction and Refurbishment.* James and James, London, 1996.

Aronin, Jeffrey Ellis. *Climate and Architecture.* New York: Reinhold Publishing Corporation, 1953.

ASHRAE Handbook of Fundamentals. New York: American Society of Heating, Refrigerating, and Air Conditioning Engineers, 1981.

Auliciems, A. and Szokolay, S. Thermal Comfort. University of Queensland Printery, 1997.

Balcomb, Douglas, et al. *Passive Solar Design Handbook. Volume Two: Passive Solar Design Analysis.* Springfield, Virginia: US DOE/NTIS (#DOE/CS-0127/2), 1980.

Balcomb, J. D. *Heat Storage and Distribution Inside Passive Solar Buildings.* Los Alamos National Laboratory, Report No. LA-9684-MS, USA, 1983.

Beamon, S. and Roaf, S. *The Ice-houses of Britain.* Routledge, London. 1990.

Berge, B. *Ecology of building materials.* Architectural Press, Oxford, 2000.

Butti, Ken and J. Perlin. *A Golden Thread: 2500 Years of Solar Architecture and Technology.* New York: Van Nostrand Reinhold Company, 1980.

Carpenter, P. *Sod It.* Coventry University Press, 1992.

Caudill, William, et al. *A Bucket of Oil.* Boston: Cahners Books, 1974.

Chambers, N. Simmons, C. and Wackernagel, M. *Sharing Nature's Interest: Ecological Footprints as an Indicator of Sustainability.* Earthscan Publications, London, 2000.

Chiras, Daniel D. *The Natural House: A Complete Guide to Healthy, Energy-Efficient, Environmental Homes.* Chelsea Green, 2000.

Clegg, P. and D. Watkins. *The Complete Greenhouse Book.* Charlotte, Vermont: Garden *Way* Publishing, 1978.

Climatic Atlas of the United States. Washington, D.C: U.S. Department of Commerce, 1968.

Cook, J. *Extreme Climates and Indigenous Architecture.* Proceedings of the PLEA

Conference, Dead Sea, published by Desert Architecture Unit, Ben-Gurion University of the Negev, Israel, 1994.

Conklin, Groff and S. Blackwell Duncan. *The Weather Conditioned House.* New York: Van Nostrand Reinhold Company, 1982.

Crowther, Richard and Solar Group Architects. *Sun/Earth: Sustainable Design.* Denver, Colorado: A.D. Hirshfeld Press, Inc., 1976. Updated and revised edition by Van Nostrand Reinhold Company, 1983.

Davis, A.J. and R. P. Schubert. *Alternative Natural Energy Sources in Building Design.* New York: Van Nostrand Reinhold Company, 1977.

Diamond, Jared. *Collapse - How Societies Choose to Fall or Succeed.* Viking Press, 2005.

Duffie, J. A. and Beckman, W. A. *Solar Engineering of Thermal Processes.* Wiley Interscience, New York and London, 1977.

Egan, David. *Concepts in Thermal Comfort.* Englewood Cliffs, New Jersey: Prentice-Hall, Inc., 1975.

Energy Research Group. A Green Vitruvius: Principals and Practice of Sustainable Architecture. James and James, London, 1999.

Fanger, P.O. *Thermal Comfort: Analysis & Applications in Environmental Engineering*, McGraw-Hill, 1972.

Fisher, Rick and W. Yanda. *The Food and Heat Providing Solar Greenhouse: Design, Construction, Operation.* Santa Fe, New Mexico: John Muir Publications, 1976.

Fisk, Marian Jacobs and H. C William Anderson. *Introduction to Solar Technology.* Reading, Massachusetts: Addison-Wesley Publishing Co., Inc., 1982.

Givani, B. (1994) *Passive and Low Energy Cooling of Buildings, Van Nostrand, New York*

Gore, Al. *An Inconvenient Truth – The Planetary Emergency of Global Warming and What We Can Do About It.* Rodale Books, 2006.

Haggard, Ken, and Polly Cooper. *Fractile Architecture: Design for Sustainability.* North Charleston, S.C., Book Surge Publishing, 2006.

Haggard, Ken, Polly Cooper and Jennifer Rennick, *Natural Air Conditioning of Buildings In Alternative Construction: Contemporary Natural Building Methods.* Lynne Elizabeth and Cassanera Adams, eds. Hoboken, N.J.; John Willey & Sons, 2000.

Haggard, Ken and Phil Niles. *The Passive Solar Handbook For California.* The California Energy Commission, 1975.

Hall. K. (ed.). *The Green Building Bible,* 3rd edition. Green Building Press, 2006.

Herschong, L. *Thermal delight in Architecture.* The MIT Press, Cambridge, Mass, 1979.

Hollis, Murray. *Practical Straw Bale Building.* CSIRO Publishing, 2005.

Hyde, R. *Bioclimatic Housing: Innovative Designs for Warm Climates,* Earthscan Publications Ltd., 2007.

Johnson, Tim. *Solar Architecture: The Direct Gain Approach.* New York: McGraw-Hill, 1981.

Kachadorian, J. *The Passive Solar House.* Chelsea Green Publishers, 1997.

King, Bruce. Design of Straw Bale Buildings: The State of the Art. Green Building Press, 2006.

Krishan, A. *Climatically Responsive Energy Efficient Architecture - a Design Handbook.* 1. Department of Planning at Delhi University, Delhi, 1995.

Krishan, A., Yannas, S., Baker, N. and Szokolay, S. *Climate Responsive Architecture,* McGraw-Hill Publishing Co., Delhi, 2001.

Lawson, B. *Building Materials, Energy and the Environment.* Royal Australian Institute of Architects, Canberra, Australia, 1996.

Lebens, R. *Passive Solar Heating Design.* Applied Science Publishers, 1980.

Libbey-Owens-Ford. *Sun Angle Calculator.* Toledo: Libbey-Owens-Ford Company, 1974.

Lippsmeier, G. *Tropenbau Building in the Tropics.* Verlag Callwey, Munich, 1980.

Louvins, Amory. *Soft Energy Paths: Towards a Durable Peace.* New York, Harper Collins, 1979.

Lyle, John Tillman. *Regenerative Design For Sustainable Development,* Wiley Publishers, 1996.

Malin, Nadav. *Life Cycle Assessment for Buildings, Seeking the Holy Grail.* Environmental Building News II, #3, March 2002.

Mazria, Edward. *The Passive Solar Energy Book.* Emmaus, Pennsylvania: Rodale Press, 1979.

McCann, J. *Clay and Cob Building.* Shire Publications, 2004.

McClend, Charles, ed. *Landscape Planning for Energy Conservation.* Reston, Virginia: Environmental Design Press, 1977.

McCullagh, J. C. *The Solar Greenhouse Book.* Emmaus, Pennsylvania: Rodale Press, 1978.

McDonough, William & Michael Braungart. *Cradle to Cradle.* New York: North Point Press, 2002.

McFarland, R. D. and Stromberg, P. *Passive Solar Design Handbook.* Editors Balcomb, J. D. and Anderson, B., Department of Energy, Washington, DC., 1980.

McHarg, I. *Design with Nature.* Doubleday & Company Inc., 1971.

Morley, Michael. *Building with Structural Insulated Panels (SIPS),* The Taunton Press, 2000.

Niles, Philip and K. Haggard. *Passive Solar Handbook for California.* Sacramento, California: California Energy Commission, 1980.

Olgyay, Aladan and V. Olgyay. *Solar Control and Shading Devices.* Princeton, New Jersey: Princeton University Press, 1967.

Olgyay, Victor. *Design with Climate.* Princeton, New Jersey: Princeton University Press, 1963.

Oliver, P. *Encyclopedia of Vernacular Architecture of the World.* Cambridge University Press, Cambridge, 1997.

Rapoport, A. *House Form and Culture.* Englewood Cliffs, New *Jersey:* Prentice-Hall, Inc., 1969.

Rawlings, R.H.D. *Ground Source Heat Pumps* (TN 18/99). BSRIA, 1999.

Regional Guidelines for Building Passive Energy Conserving Homes. Washington, D.C: AIA Research Corporation, 1978.

Roaf, S., Horsley, A. and Guptal, R. *Closing the Loop: Benchmarking for Sustainable Buildings,* London, RIBA Publications, 2004

Roaf, S., Manuel Fuentes, Stephani Thomas, *Ecohouses* (third Edition), Oxford, U.K., Architectural Press, 2007.

Robinette, G. O. *Plants, People and Environmental Quality.* Washington, D.C: U.S. Department of the Interior, National Park Service, 1972.

Rudofsky, Bernard. *Architecture without Architects: A Short Introduction to Non-Pedigreed Architecture.* University of New Mexico Press, 1980.

Santamouris, M. and Asimakopoulos, D. (eds) *Passive Cooling of Buildings*. London, 1996.

Shurcliff, William. *Solar Heated Buildings of North America: 120 Outstanding Examples.* Andover, Massachusetts: Brick House Publishing Company, 1978.

Shurcliff, William A. *Thermal Shutters and Shades.* Andover, Massachusetts: Brick House Publishing Company, 1980.

Snell, C. and Callahan, T. *Building Green*. Lame Books, 2006.

Stein, Reynolds, Gromdziky, Kwok. *Mechanical and Electrical Equipment for Buildings, Tenth Edition.* New York: John Wiley and Sons, 1980.

Strong, S, and Scheller, W. *The Solar Electric House.* Sustainability Press, 1993.

Swan, Christopher C. *Electric Water: The Emerging Revolution in Water & Energy.* New Society Publishers, 2007.

Thomas, H. R. and Rees, S.W. "The Thermal Performance of Ground Floor Slabs – A Full-Scale In-Situ Experiment," *Building and Environment* 34(2), 139-164, 1999.

Underground Space Center, University of Minnesota. *Earth Sheltered Housing Design,* New York: Van Nostrand Reinhold Company, 1979.

Wackenagel, Mathis & William Rees, *Our Ecological Footprint: Reducing Human Impact on the Earth*, Gabriola Island, B.C., New Society Publishers, 1996.

Watson, Donald, ed. *Energy Conservation through Building Design.* New York: McGraw-Hill Book Company, 1979.

Watson, Donald and K. Labs. *Climatic Design for Home Building.* Guilford, Connecticut: Donald *Watson, 1980.*

Wells, M. *Gentle Architecture*. McGraw-Hill, New York, 1982.

GLOSSARY

Absorptance: The ratio of radiation absorbed by a surface to the total energy falling on it; expressed as a decimal fraction or a percentage.

Absorber: The blackened surface in a solar collector that absorbs solar radiation and converts it to heat.

Active solar energy system: A system that requires outside energy sources (for example, electricity) in conjunction with solar sources and techniques.

Adobe: A sun-dried, unburned brick of clay (earth), sand, and straw used in construction; sometimes stabilized with oil based additives. Within the United States, adobe is used primarily in the Southwest.

Air changes: A measure of the exchange in a building. One air change is an exchange of a volume of air equal to the interior volume of a building.

Altitude angle: The angular distance from the horizon to the sun.

Ambient temperature: Dry-bulb temperature of the air in the immediate microclimate, as in the average air temperature outside a building.

Angle of incidence: The angle that the sun's rays make with a line perpendicular to a surface.

Array: An assembly of several photovoltaic (PV) modules connected in series and/or parallel.

ASES: Abbreviation for the American Solar Energy Society

ASHRAE: Abbreviation for the American Society of Heating, Refrigerating and Air Conditioning Engineers, Inc.

Auxiliary system: A supplementary unit to provide heating or cooling when the solar unit cannot do so. This is usually necessary during periods of cloudiness or intense cold.

Azimuth: The angular distance, measured in degrees, between true south and the point on the horizon directly below the sun's position.

Back flow: The unintentional reversal of fluid flow in a distribution system. Also referred to as back syphoning.

Backup system: See *Auxiliary system.*

Barrel wall: See *Drum wall.*

Beam radiation: See "direct radiation."

Berm: A man-made mound or small hill of earth.

British thermal unit (BTU): A measure of heat, specifically, the amount of heat required to raise the temperature of one pound of water 1°F. One BTU is approximately equal to the amount of heat given off by burning one kitchen match.

Building load factor: An indication of heat loss through the building skin. As a rule of thumb, 3-6 is considered excellent, 6-9 is very good, and 9-12 average. Units are BTU/sq. ft./day.

Calorie: A unit of heat; the amount of energy needed to raise the temperature of one gram of water 1°C. One hundred calories is approximately equal to four BTUs.

Carbon footprint: The effect of a person, object, material, or system with regard to its energy impact/pollution factor on global warming.

Celsius (°0): A temperature scale in which the freezing point of water is set at 0°C and the boiling point of water is set at 100°e. Celsius temperatures can be derived from Fahrenheit temperatures by the equation C = 5/9(OF - 32).

Chimney effect: The tendency of air to rise when heated, because of its lowered density. This principle is used to help cool a building by allowing hot air to rise and flow out through upper-level windows. This creates a sub-atmosphere, which draws cooler outdoor air in through windows at a lower level.

Clerestory: A window placed vertically (or nearly vertical) in a wall above one's line of vision to provide natural light or ventilation.

Climate: The meteorological conditions, including sunlight, temperature, precipitation, humidity, wind, and weather patterns, that characteristically prevail in a particular region.

Coefficient of heat transfer: See *U value.*

Collection surface: The part of the solar collector where solar energy is collected, generally darkened to increase absorption. It is often called an absorber.

Collector; flat-plate: An assembly containing a panel of metal or other suitable material, usually with a dark color on the sun side, that absorbs solar radiation and converts it into heat. The panel is generally contained in an insulated box, covered with glass or plastic on the sun side to retard heat loss. Heat in the collector transfers to a circulating fluid, such as air, water, oil or antifreeze, and then flows to where it is used immediately or stored for later use.

Collector; focusing: Also called concentrating collectors, these collectors use one or more reflecting surfaces to concentrate sunlight onto a small absorber surface.

Collector, solar: A device used to collect solar energy and convert it to heat.

Collector tilt: The angle between the inclined surface of a solar collector and the horizontal plane. A collector surface receives the greatest possible amount of direct sunshine when its tilt is perpendicular to the sun's rays.

Condensation: Process by which water is released from the air.

Conductance (C): The amount of heat that flows through one square foot of material in one hour at a 1°F temperature difference between its surfaces. Conductance values are given for a specific thickness of material. For homogeneous materials such as concrete, dividing it conductivity (k) by its thickness (X) gives the conductance (C).

Conduction: The process by which heat energy is transferred through materials (solids, liquids, or gases) by molecular excitation of adjacent molecules.

Conductivity (k): The amount of heat that flows through one square foot of material one inch thick, in one hour, at a temperature difference of 1°F between its surfaces.

Convection: The transfer of heat within or by a moving fluid medium (liquid or gas).

Convective loop: A system for the transfer of heat from one point to another by convection. After losing or transferring the heat, the transfer medium returns to the source of heat to complete the cycle or loop.

Cooling pond: A body of liquid that dissipates heat by evaporation, convection, and radiation. Usually a fluid such as water.

Coolth tubes: Conduits used to cool a transfer fluid such as water or air by dissipating heat contained in the fluid to a heat sink surrounding the tubes.

Cross ventilation: The flow of air through a building by virtue of openings located on opposite walls.

Dead air space: An air space that is sealed to prevent convective heat transfer into or out of the space.

Degree day (DD), cooling: See *Degree day (DD) heating:* the base temperature is generally established at 65°F by the National Weather Service. Cooling degree days are often measured above that base. For the thermal performance simulations in this book, 65°F was used.

Degree day (DD), heating: An expression of a climatic heating requirement expressed by the daily difference in degrees F below the average outdoor temperature for each day and an established indoor temperature base of 6SOF. The total number of degree days over the heating season indicates the relative severity of the winter.

Demand limiter: A device that selectively switches off electrical equipment whenever total electrical demand rises beyond a predetermined level.

Density: The mass-per-unit volume of a substance, expressed in pounds per cubic foot.

Desiccant: A material which has the property of absorbing moisture from the air.

Differential thermostat: A control thermostat with two temperature sensors, typically one at the heat source and one at the storage site, to automatically control all or a part of a system.

Diffuse radiation: Radiation that has traveled an indirect path from the sun because it has been scattered by the particles in the atmosphere, such as air molecules, dust, and water vapor.

Direct (beam) radiation: Light that has traveled a straight path from the sun, as opposed to diffuse sky radiation.

Direct-gain system: Solar energy collected as heat and stored directly within a building.

Drum wall: A type of water wall in which drums are stacked for solar heat collection and storage.

Dry-bulb temperature: A measure of air temperature when it is independent of radiation effects from surroundings, and when air motion relative to the measuring devices is not significant.

Earth tempering: The heating or cooling of a fluid or space by association with the ambient temperature of the adjacent earth.

Emissivity: The ratio of the radiant energy emitted from a surface at a given temperature to the energy emitted by a black body at the same temperature.

Energy: The capacity for doing work; it may take a number of forms, all of which can be transformed from one into another: thermal (heat), mechanical (work), electrical, and chemical; in customary units, measured in kilowatt hours (kWh) or British thermal units CBTU).

Environmentalism: The human movement to protect the earth's environment, hence the term environmental architect or environmentalist.

Equinox: Either of the two times during a year when the sun crosses the celestial equator and the length of the day and night are approximately equal: the autumnal equinox, on or about September 22, and the vernal equinox, on or about March 22.

Eutectic salts: Salts used for storing heat. At a given temperature, such salts melt, absorbing large amounts of heat; this will be released when the salts freeze. See *Phase-change thermal storage.*

Fahrenheit degrees (°F): A temperature scale in which the freezing point of water is set at 32°F and its boiling point at 212°F. Fahrenheit temperatures can be derived from centigrade temperatures by the equation of $= 1.8 \times °C + 32$.

Fenestration: A term used to signify an opening in a building to admit light and/or air; windows.

Glazing: A covering of transparent or translucent material (glass or plastic) used for admitting light. Glazing retards heat losses from re-radiation and convection. Examples: windows, skylights, greenhouses, collector coverings.

Glazing, double: A sandwich of two separated layers of glass or plastic enclosing air to create an insulating barrier. Sometimes the space is evacuated or filled with an inert gas to increase insulation value.

Global warming: The effect of polluting the earth's upper atmosphere with carbon dioxide and other gaseous elements, thus increasing the "green house affect" causing the earth's oceans and mass to heat up over time.

Green: Having to do with energy conservation or the environment in a beneficial way.

Greenhouse: See *Sunspace.*

Greenhouse effect: The characteristic tendency of some transparent materials, such as glass, to transmit shorter wavelength solar radiation (light) and absorb thermal radiation of longer wavelengths (heat), thus reducing heat loss and increasing heat gain.

Ground source heat pumps: Heat pumps using the sub surface earth heat sink for achieving heating and cooling of structures.

Heat capacity: The amount of heat that a cubic foot of material can store with a one-degree increase in its temperature.

Heat exchanger: A device usually consisting of a coiled arrangement of metal tubing used to transfer heat through the tube walls from one fluid to another.

Heat gain: An increase in the amount of heat contained in a space, resulting from absorbed solar radiation of internal gain.

Heat load: The total energy required for space heating.

Heat loss: A decrease in the amount of heat contained in a space, resulting from heat flow through walls, windows, roof, and· other building-envelope components.

Heat pump: A thermodynamic device that transfers heat from one medium to another. The first medium (the source) cools while the second (the heat sink) warms up.

Heat sink: A substance capable of accepting and storing heat.

Hybrid solar energy systems: Systems that use passive design concepts in combination
with active components (fan, pumps, etc.) for collection, storage, or distribution of energy.

Heat-transfer medium: A medium, either liquid or gas, used to transport thermal energy.

Heating season: The period of the year during which heating the building is required to maintain comfort conditions.

Incident angle: The angle between incoming direct solar radiation falling on a surface and a line perpendicular (normal) to that surface.

Indirect-gain system: A solar heating system in which sunlight first strikes a thermal mass located between the sun and a living space. The sunlight absorbed by the mass is converted to heat and then transferred to the space.

Infiltration: The uncontrolled movement of outdoor air into the interior of a building through cracks around windows and doors or in walls, roofs, and floors.

Insolation: The total amount of solar radiation – direct, diffuse, and reflected – striking a surface exposed to the sky.

Insulating shade: Window or door shades with insulative properties to prevent heat *loss* or gain when closed.

Insulation: Materials or systems used to prevent heat loss or gain, usually employing very small dead-air spaces to limit conduction and/or convection, or reflective surfaces to minimize radiation.

Internal heat gain: An increase in the amount of heat contained within a space resulting from the energy given off by people, lights, equipment, machinery, pets, or other elements.

Isolated-gain system: A system in which solar collection and heat storage are isolated from the living spaces.

Latent heat: A change in heat content of a material that occurs without a corresponding change in temperature, accompanied by a change of state (for example, ice changing to water or water to steam). *See Phase-change thermal storage.*

Latitude: The angular distance north or south of the equator, measured in degrees of arc.

Longitude: The arc of the equator between the meridian of a place and the Greenwich meridian measured in degrees east or west.

Low-E glass: Has coatings that are microscopically thin, virtually invisible layers deposited on a window surface primarily to reduce the U-factor by suppressing radiative heat flow. Coating a glass surface with a low-emittance material reflects a significant amount of this radiant heat, thus lowering the total heat flow through the window. Low-E coatings are transparent to visible light, and opaque to infrared radiation. Different types of Low-E coatings have been designed to allow for high solar gain, moderate solar gain, or low solar gain. These coatings reflect radiant infrared energy. Heat originating from indoors is reflected back inside, keeping heat inside in the winter, and infrared radiation from the sun is reflected away, keeping it cooler inside in the summer.

Mass wall: A wall composed of material with a relatively high thermal storage capability and conductance, such as concrete, masonry, or adobe. Usually placed inside of exterior glazing.

Mean radiant temperature: The weighted average surface temperature of walls, floors, ceilings.

MMBTU/yr.: Million British thermal units per year.

Night cooling: The cooling of a building or heat storage device by the radiation of *excess* heat into the night sky.

Night ventilation: The cooling of a building by night ventilation. Night ventilation can be achieved by forced means, such as a fan, or by natural means, such as the chimney effect or turbine vents.

Night ventilation cooling fraction: The percentage of the cooling load supplied by night ventilation in a solar house.

Opaque: Impenetrable by light.

Orientation: The orientation of a surface is in degrees of variation away from solar south, towards either the east or west. Solar or true south should not be confused with magnetic south, which can vary owing to magnetic declination.

Parasitic energy: The amount of energy derived from a depletable fuel source (coal, gas, oil etc.) to run a solar system. For example, fans and pumps require parasitic energy.

Passive solar energy systems: Systems that *rely* upon the building's design and construction for collection, storage, and distribution of the sun's energy for heating and cooling. In a strict sense, such a system would use no energy other than the natural sources of sun and wind.

Peak oil: The point of reaching the maximum peak of world petroleum production followed by decline, leading to the ultimate eventual depletion as a usable energy resource.

Percent of possible sunshine: The amount of time between sunrise and sunset that the sun is shining (not obscured by clouds), usually represented as a monthly or annual average.

Phase-change thermal storage: Materials which release or take in a quantity of heat when changing from solid to liquid or liquid to solid.

Photovoltaic cells: Devices for converting solar energy to electricity.

Radiant heating systems: Using in-the-floor hydronic or other radiant surfaces for space conditioning.

Radiant heat transfer: The transfer of heat by heat radiation. Heat radiation is a form of electromagnetic radiation. Radiant heating resulting from infrared radiation is very prevalent in passive systems.

Radiation: The direct transfer of energy through space by means of electromagnetic waves.

Radiation, infrared: Electromagnetic radiation, whether from the sun or from a warm body, with wavelengths longer than the red end of the visible spectrum (greater than 0.75 microns). We experience infrared radiation as heat; 53 percent of the radiation emitted by the sun is in the infrared band.

Radiation, solar: Electromagnetic radiation emitted by the sun. *Reflectance:* The ratio of the amount of light reflected by a surface to the amount incident. What is not reflected is either absorbed by the material or transmitted through it. Good light reflectors are not necessarily good heat reflectors.

Regionalism: Having to do with the inherent characteristics of a region – environmentally, architecturally, culturally, or historically considered by some to be the basic unit of sustainability.

Relative humidity: The water content of moist air with respect to saturated air, expressed as a percentage.

Resistance (R): The opposite of conductivity. *See also R value. Retrofit:* Installation of solar water heating and/or solar heating or cooling systems in existing buildings not originally designed for that purpose.

R value: A unit of thermal resistance used for comparing insulating values of different materials; the higher the R value of a material, the greater its insulating properties.

Rock bed: See Rock bin.

Rock bin: Rocks placed in bins to store heat or coolth for later use.

Roof monitors: Skylights or glazing on the roof to admit solar energy and light to the interior of a building.

Roof-pond system: An indirect-gain heating and cooling system where the mass-water in plastic bags is located on the roof of the espace to be heated or cooled. As solar radiation heats the water, the heat is transferred into the space, usually through a metal support ceiling.

Selective surface: A surface or coating that has a high absorptance of incoming solar radiation but low emittance of longer wavelengths (heat).

Skylight: A clear or translucent panel set into a roof to admit sunlight into a building. Usually fixed, sometimes operable for venting.

Solar altitude: The angle of the sun above the horizon, measured in a vertical plane.

Solar aperture: An opening designed or placed primarily to admit solar energy into a space.

Solar chimney (also called a solar inducer): A type of solar collector with a dark absorption surface used to heat and move air. Usually located to receive summer sunlight. The heated air moves up and out the top of the chimney, causing an induction of outside or pre-tempered air into the building.

Solar collector: See Collector, solar.

Solar constant: The quantity of radiant solar heat received at the outer layer of the earth's atmosphere. Equal to 429 BTU/ ft^2 hr (± 1.5%).

Solar electric: Electricity made from solar radiation; such as using photovoltaic cells.

Solar fraction (or percentage solar): The percentage of the total heat load supplied by the solar heating system, including useful losses from the storage.

Solar heating fraction: The percentage of the heating load supplied by solar energy.

Solar radiation: The energy-carrying electromagnetic radiation emitted by the sun. This radiation comprises many frequencies, each relating to a particular class of radiation: high-frequency/short-wavelength ultraviolet; medium-frequency/medium-wavelength visible light, and low-frequency/high-wavelength infrared

Solar thermal: Heat produced from solar radiation such as is captured on solar hot water collectors.

Space ship earth: The concept that our planet is a space craft, in orbit around the sun, with passengers, which is self contained and sustainable.

Specific heat (Cp): The amount of heat required to raise the temperature of one pound of a substance 1°F in temperature Units of BTU/lb. °F.

Stack effect: See Chimney effect. Usually associated with hot air escaping from a building, increasing ventilation potential.

Stratification: In solar-heating context, the formation of layers in a substance (fluid or gas) where the top layer is warmer than the bottom. Also called thermal stratification.

Sunspace: A glazed space attached to a building in which solar heat and light are collected for growing plants and/or space heating.

Sustainability: The concept of achieving a sustainable balance of human habitation and impact on the earth. This applies on global, national, and regional levels.

Thermal conductance: The thermal transmittance through 1m^2 of material of a given thickness for each 1 K temperature difference between its surfaces (W m^{-2}K).

Thermal admittance (q): The amount of heat a square foot of surface will admit in one hour.

Thermal break (thermal barrier); An element of low heat conductivity placed to reduce or prevent heat flow.

Thermal conductivity: The thermal transmission through a material 1-m-thick for each

1 K temperature difference between its surfaces (W m^{-2}K).

Thermal flywheel (also called thermal inertia): The tendency of a building with large quantities of heavy materials to remain at the same temperature or to fluctuate only *very* slowly.

Thermal mass: The potential heat-storage capacity available in a given building. Mass walls, adobe, stone, brick, concrete, and water are examples of thermal mass.

Thermosyphon: The hydraulic *system* in which fluid circulation is caused by temperature

differences. Warmer fluids expand and rise, cooler fluids contract and fall.

Tilt: The angle of a plane relative to a horizontal plane.

Tracking: The process of altering the tilt of a module throughout the day in order to face the sun and thus maximize the power output.

Translucent: Having the quality of transmitting light but causing sufficient diffusion to eliminate perception of distinct images.

Transmittance: The ratio of the radiant energy transmitted through a substance to the total radiant energy incident on its surface.

Transparent: Having the quality of transmitting light so that objects or images can be seen as if there were no intervening material.

Trombe wall: A masonry exterior wall (south facing) that collects and releases stored solar energy into a building by both radiant and convective means. This wall is insulated from the exterior by glass or other transparent material. Developed by Dr. Felix Trombe.

Two-stage evaporative cooling: An evaporative cooling system that does not introduce water into the cooling air stream.

U value (overall coefficient of heat transfer): The amount of heat in BTU that flows through one square foot of roof, wall, or floor, in one hour, when there is a 1°F difference in temperature between the inside and outside air, under steady-state conditions. The U value is the reciprocal of the total R value. Units are BTU/hr. ft.^{2}°F

Ultraviolet radiation: Electromagnetic radiation having wavelengths shorter than visible light. This invisible form of radiation is found in solar radiation and plays a part in the deterioration of plastic glazings, paint, and furnishing fabrics.

Vapor barrier: A building material which inhibits the flow of moisture and air as well as minimizing condensation in walls, floors, and roofs.

Ventilation losses: The heat losses associated with the continuous replacement of warm, stale air by fresh cold air.

Volumetric heat loss coefficient (G –value): The total heat loss of a dwelling (through the fabric and ventilation), divided by the heated volume and the temperature differential at which the loss occurs (W m^{-1}K).

Watershed: The land area that drains to a common outlet, such as the outflow of a lake, the mouth of a river, or any point along a stream channel.

Water wall: An interior wall of water-filled containers constituting a thermal storage mass. See *Drum wall*

Weather: The state of the atmosphere at a given time and place, described by such variables as temperature, moisture, wind velocity, and barometric pressure.

Weatherizing: The process of improving the properties of the weatherskin: increasing insulation, double-glazing, caulking, weatherstripping, *etc.*

Weatherskin: The exterior of a building, separating the conditioned interior from the exterior.

Weatherstripping: Narrow or jamb-width sections of thin metal or other material to prevent infiltration of air and moisture around windows and doors.

Wet-bulb temperature: The lowest temperature attainable by evaporating water into the air without altering its energy content.

Wing wall: Vertical projection on one side of a window or wall used to increase or decrease the wind pressure or solar incidence on the wall or window.

Zenith angle: The angular distance from the sun to the zenith, the point directly above the observer (at noon = latitude solar declination).

INDEX